Cybercrime and Digital De

Cybercrime and Digital Deviance is a work that combines insights from sociology, criminology, and computer science to explore cybercrimes such as hacking and romance scams, along with forms of cyberdeviance such as pornography addiction, trolling, and flaming. Other issues are explored including cybercrime investigations, organized cybercrime, the use of algorithms in policing, cybervictimization, and the theories used to explain cybercrime.

Graham and Smith make a conceptual distinction between a terrestrial, physical environment and a single digital environment produced through networked computers. Conceptualizing the online space as a distinct environment for social interaction links this text with assumptions made in the fields of urban sociology or rural criminology. Students in sociology and criminology will have a familiar entry point for understanding what may appear to be a technologically complex course of study. The authors organize all forms of cybercrime and cyberdeviance by applying a typology developed by David Wall: cybertrespass, cyberdeception, cyberviolence, and cyberpornography. This typology is simple enough for students just beginning their inquiry into cybercrime. Because it is based on legal categories of trespassing, fraud, violent crimes against persons, and moral transgressions it provides a solid foundation for deeper study.

Taken together, Graham and Smith's application of a digital environment and Wall's cybercrime typology makes this an ideal upper level text for students in sociology and criminal justice. It is also an ideal introductory text for students within the emerging disciplines of cybercrime and cybersecurity.

Roderick S. Graham is an Assistant Professor of Sociology in the Sociology and Criminal Justice Department at Old Dominion University. He teaches courses on cybercrime, research methods, and racial inequality. He is the coordinator of the interdisciplinary Cybercrime bachelor's degree at Old Dominion University. He has published research in *Deviant Behavior, First Monday*, and *Youth and Society.*

'Shawn K. Smith is a Criminologist and Assistant Professor of Criminal Justice in the Department of Criminal Justice at Radford University. His areas of research and pedagogy include social networking theories in crime, public policy in criminal justice, and advanced research procedures. He has published research in *Sociological Focus, Journal of Race and Ethnicity, Criminal Justice Studies: A Critical Journal of Crime, Law, and Society*, and *African Journal of Criminology and Justice Studies.*

Cybercrime and Digital Deviance

Roderick S. Graham and 'Shawn K. Smith

Routledge
Taylor & Francis Group

NEW YORK AND LONDON

First published 2020
by Routledge
52 Vanderbilt Avenue, New York, NY 10017

and by Routledge
2 Park Square, Milton Park, Abingdon, Oxon, OX14 4RN

Routledge is an imprint of the Taylor & Francis Group, an informa business

© 2020 Taylor & Francis

The right of Roderick S. Graham & 'Shawn K. Smith to be identified as authors of this work has been asserted by them in accordance with sections 77 and 78 of the Copyright, Designs and Patents Act 1988.

Library of Congress Cataloging-in-Publication Data
A catalog record for this title has been requested

ISBN: 978-0-8153-7630-9 (hbk)
ISBN: 978-0-8153-7631-6 (pbk)
ISBN: 978-1-351-23809-0 (ebk)

Typeset in Times New Roman
by Deanta Global Publishing Services, Chennai, India

Visit the eResources: www.routledge.com/9780815376316

This book is dedicated to my wife, Eun Kyoung Kim. She put up with me spending many a weekend in my office pecking away at this manuscript.

Rod Graham

I dedicate this book to McKenzie and Aunt 'Nita.

'Shawn Smith

Contents

Figures

Tables

Acknowledgments

I thank my colleagues at Old Dominion University for providing intellectual support. As a sociologist dabbling in criminology, I leaned heavily on their insight and comments.

I also thank the students in my cybercrime classes who suffered through countless revisions of muddled chapters, sat through lectures that can at best be described as "organic," and gamely took quiz after quiz filled with unclear questions. Their feedback made the contents of this book more readable and the supplements more meaningful.

I thank my dear friend Dr. 'Shawn Smith for agreeing to coauthor this work with me. I looked forward to our monthly textbook meetings where we drank overpriced coffee, talked about politics, culture, and our profession. On occasion, we even managed to talk about the progression and direction of the textbook.

Rod Graham

First and foremost, I wish to acknowledge my writing partner, colleague, and friend, Dr. Roderick Graham, for initiating the journey that resulted in this book, and especially for his gracious entertaining of countless random ponderings throughout the process.

I further wish to recognize a number of longtime research mentors, colleagues, and friends embodying the intellectual standard I endeavored to offer in this work: Dr. Kurt Schimmel, Dr. Andrew P. Tuck, Mr. Christopher Bumcrot, Dr. Ben Kim-Gervey, Ms. Jay Jolliffe, Mr. Bill Jon, Dr. Ruth Triplett, Dr. Randy Gainey, Dr. Garland White, and Dr. Gwen Lee-Thomas.

An additional note of gratitude is extended to my Radford University colleagues from whom I received an endless supply of energy and encouragement to fuel this project.

Finally, a special thanks to our extremely supportive family and friends without whom this labor of love would not have been possible. You are appreciated.

'Shawn K. Smith

Introduction: The Challenges of Studying and Investigating Cybercrime

Nick Sauer, a Republican state representative from Illinois, resigned from his office in August of 2018 after his ex-girlfriend Kate Kelly filed a "revenge porn" complaint against him. Kelly alleged that Sauer created a fake Instagram account using photos of her. The account, she claimed, used nude pictures of her to bait men into online sexual conversations. The Huffington Post[1] reported on August 2, 2018:

> Kelly's complaint reportedly says a man she did not know reached out to her on July 12 via her personal Instagram account to say he'd "been communicating for 4 months with some-one pretending" to be her. After that, Kelly says, she wrote to Instagram, who disabled the account, and talked to Sauer about it. Sauer allegedly admitted to everything.

On January 9, 2019, Sauer was charged with 12 felonies.

Sauer was a rising star in Illinois politics. Ironically, Sauer had served on a legislative task force on sexual harassment and had cosponsored legislation that would require sexual harassment training for lawmakers.

The Nick Sauer case is a relatively small story about a congressman who may not be known outside of the state of Illinois. However, the story can be used to illustrate many of the challenges faced by people who study, investigate, and write about cybercrime. We discuss five of these challenges below (see Figure 0.1).

Defining Cybercrimes

Kelly filed a complaint with the local police under Illinois' revenge porn laws.[2] **Revenge porn** describes the public displaying or sharing of sexually explicit photographs of a current or former intimate partner. Images between two adults that are knowingly shared—for example, between two people in an intimate relationship—are legal. It becomes unlawful when those images are shared publicly or with a third party.

Figure o.1 The challenges in studying and investigating cybercrime.

The naming of the violation as "revenge porn" derives from the practice of someone sharing previously confidential photos of an intimate partner publicly in order to humiliate or shame because they have been rejected or jilted. But revenge porn does not need to be about revenge *per se*. One could share private photos to deceive another person, as Sauer allegedly did.

One of the authors conducted a web search of the media attention placed on the case in 2018. Web results showed that revenge porn was *not* the phenomenon the media had focused on the most, although it is the crime Sauer was alleged to have done. Instead, media attention had been placed more on the **catfishing** done by Sauer—using a false online identity to lure people into relationships. One of the authors of this text was even asked to write his opinion for a London newspaper about *catfishing* … not revenge porn. Catfishing is a form of cyberdeviance that is worthy of study, however it is not illegal and is not the violation attached to Sauer.

This illustrates one of the challenges in studying and investigating cybercrime. The public does not have an adequate vocabulary and set of definitions to employ when trying to talk about and understand cybercrime-related phenomena. As we move through this text we will pay close attention to definitional matters. To begin we start with a broad definition of **cybercrime**, from criminologist MajidYar:

> cybercrime refers not so much to a single, distinctive kind of criminal activity, but more to a diverse *range* [emphasis in original] of illegal and illicit activities that share in common the unique electronic environment ("cyberspace") in which they take place.

> (Yar, 2013, 5)

This definition implies that the activity itself matters less than in what environment it takes place. Any criminal or deviant activity that is mediated with computer technology or the Internet is cybercrime or cyberdeviance. An example of this is stalking. Stalking someone is a traditional crime. Depending upon the state, this crime encompasses the perpetrator generating fear in the victim and presenting him- or herself as a credible threat to the victim. When this stalking is done via social media—in cyberspace—stalking becomes cyberstalking, and thus a cybercrime. Similarly, theft is a crime. When that theft encompasses the stealing of data on a computer, this becomes a cybercrime—usually falling under the broad heading of hacking.

We can apply this understanding of cybercrime to deviance. If deviance is a behavior, value, or belief that violates cultural norms, then cyberdeviance is deviant behavior done in cyberspace. Cyberdeviance is somewhat harder than cybercrime to identify. While cybercrimes are violations of formal law, **cyberdeviance**, by contrast, is fluid and depends upon the context in which one operates. One example is communication practices in online spaces. One of the authors of this textbook was in attendance at a small conference, and took photos of one of the presenters. He posted these photos to Twitter with the conference hashtag. This, he realized from the comments he received from his colleagues, was against the norms of the group. Although the presenter was in a public space and the photos were for a public conference, he was not an acquaintance of the presenter. Because he was not familiar with the presenter, it was seen as "bad taste" to take photos of the presenter and place them on social media. Thus, the posting of photos to Twitter was an instance of cyberdeviance for that group of conference goers.

Another example would be speech. The same word or phrase can be considered the norm, slightly unusual, or deviant depending upon the context. Consider someone making a statement on a public forum such as: "I enjoyed the hunting trip with my friends. We bagged several deer, and made a barbeque." On some forums this may be considered extremely deviant if the majority of the users are vegetarian. On the other hand, it may be entirely acceptable in online spaces where users hunt, eat meat, or enjoy venison. Importantly, for both the posting of photos and the hunting example, the deviance occurs in the digital environment (or cyberspace, as it is commonly called).

Rapidly Changing Laws

The legal system has been scrambling to keep up with changes in technology. Kelly's complaints to law enforcement would have been interpreted differently had they been made in 2013. In 2013 Illinois did not have specific legislation prohibiting the unauthorized sharing of adult photos. The state did not pass a revenge porn law until 2014. Under the current law, someone convicted of revenge porn is subject to 1 to 3 years in prison and up to a $25,000 fine.

While changes in laws are necessary to keep pace with changes in technology and social patterns, problems arise as lawmakers scramble to enact laws to address cybercrimes. One problem is that new laws may be misplaced because of a lack of understanding about the phenomena. By misplaced, we mean that they may not address the actual phenomenon they are intended to. As mentioned earlier, much media attention has been placed on the catfishing aspect of the story. Some have called for the possession of a false identity online to be made illegal to curtail catfishing.[3] But being anonymous online is an important aspect of the digital environment. Consider a person who may be thinking about a change of identity—gender, religious, political. They may wish to explore aspects of this identity away from their current social networks. They may want to connect with and interact in online forums with people who share that identity. They will need the freedom to create a new persona and interact with others without obligating themselves. Or, consider a whistle-blower who wants to share sensitive information about government misconduct without revealing their identity. Speaking truth to power may require creating a fake Facebook or Twitter account. Thus, uninformed laws that are misplaced, such as banning of false identities, may end up doing more harm than good.

A second problem is the appropriateness of penalties. On the one hand, a revenge porn law is meant to protect people who have been justly victimized. On the other hand, some may question the harshness of the punishment. In the example of Sauer, is prison time a just punishment for Sauer's actions? In other words, does the punishment for violating a law fit the crime? The answer to that question is always debatable. Unfortunately, the rapidity in which new questionable behaviors arise and the relative lack of understanding by the public makes it more possible that overly harsh penalties can be attached to legislation.

Changes in Law Enforcement Practices

Research suggests that the perpetrators of most cybercrime come from different backgrounds and social contexts than perpetrators of the crimes that have traditionally dominated media narratives. The Federal Bureau of Investigation releases a yearly report entitled the Uniform Crime Report (UCR). The UCR is a compilation of what is commonly called "street crimes." The UCR records four types of violent crime—murder, rape, robbery, aggravated assault, and four types of property crime—burglary, larceny, motor vehicle theft, arson. Individuals who are more likely to commit street crimes are young, in poverty, and male. In the United States, they are disproportionately people of color who live in segregated and impoverished neighborhoods. They are likely to come from challenging home environments where there may be addiction or domestic violence.

Cybercrime scholars are still coalescing on the profiles of cybercriminals. This is a challenge that must be addressed, but we can be confident that profiles of cybercriminals will be different than the profiles of people who commit street crime. This is especially so for the more technologically based cybercrimes such as hacking and phishing. Cybercriminals are more likely to be educated. They are more likely to be white and come from less challenging social and family circumstances.

In order to combat rises in cybercrimes, law enforcement will have to reorient themselves to this new criminal. Law enforcement infrastructure and cultural patterns are oriented towards street crimes and the types of individuals who are more likely to commit them. For example, in Chapter 8, we will talk about the use of algorithms in **predictive policing**. These algorithms are designed to predict street crime. There is not yet an equal effort to predict cybercrime.

As cybercrime increases, efforts will be needed to reorient law enforcement agencies, especially local police, toward cybercriminals.

Another change in law enforcement has been the learning and institutionalizing of investigative techniques unique to cyberspace. In this regard, law enforcement has responded accordingly in at least three ways:

1. Law enforcement has had to learn how and when to request evidence from **intermediaries** (through court order, subpoena, and warrant). In the Sauer case, Instagram is a third party that potentially holds **inculpatory** or **exculpatory** evidence and at the minimum a subpoena will likely be needed to obtain relevant evidence.
2. Law enforcement has developed strategies for following the bread crumbs of a person online—their digital trail. People are fairly loose about what they put on their social media. This public information—the posts, tweets, and images—are often enough to place a suspect at a scene or connect the suspect to the victim.
3. Specially trained professionals can identify and extract digital evidence at the binary level on a hard drive—**digital forensics**. With a warrant they can acquire Sauer's computing hardware and examine it for potential evidence (my guess is that this case is, as they say, "open and shut"and does not require this level of investigation).

Despite the new techniques developed, cybercrimes can be much more difficult to investigate and solve than street crimes. This is because of the unique properties of cyberspace, one of which is the ability of computer users to form connections across time and space. This property creates new opportunities for criminals. Kelly was in some ways fortunate that she could contact the local police in which the alleged perpetrator, Sauer, lived. In many cases, local police struggle to investigate cybercrimes because the perpetrator lives in a state or country different from the victim. For many cybercrimes such as hacking, ransomware, or denial of service attacks, this means that federal agencies conduct the investigations. However, even federal agencies can run into difficulties when a suspect is in another country. Agencies in other countries may not wish to share information or the laws in the perpetrator's country are different than the laws in the victim's country.

Understanding the Context

In 2017 film producer Harvey Weinstein was charged with several counts of sexual misconduct. Weinstein's case was high-profile, with many well-known actresses alleging they were sexually assaulted by Weinstein. In October of that year, the hashtag #MeToo spread via social media. The "#MeToo Movement" has been instrumental in publicizing sexual misconduct. By February of 2018, 71 men holding positions of power had been fired or forced to resign because of sexual misconduct.[4] These include Jerry Richardson, former owner of the Carolina Panthers National Football League team, Matt Lauer, former cohost of the *Today Show*, and Russell Simmons, cofounder of Def Jam records.

Sauer's reactions to the allegations cannot be understood without taking into account the current cultural climate towards power imbalances and sexual misconduct. Sauer's resignation is as much about informal norms of sexual behavior in cyberspace—**cyberdeviance**, as it is about formal violations of law—cybercrime. In decades past, Sauer may have been able to withstand the negative press associated with Kelly's complaint. In times past, many male authority figures have been able to mistreat women with few negative sanctions. Today, however, these allegations are impossible to dodge.

Cybercrime scholars cannot ignore the cultural context in which cybercrime occurs. Indeed, the argument can be made that because so much of cybercrime is symbolic in nature, how the crimes and the victimizations are socially constructed matter more than for other types of crimes. In other words, a physical assault on one's person is less subject to interpretation than the effects of cyberbullying or the theft of someone's identity online. Consider a negative post on social media. It can be understood lightly as "just words," or taken with more gravity as "potentially causing psychological trauma" depending upon the context.

A prime example of the importance of context is hate speech. In most European countries, it is illegal to deny the Holocaust occurred. Germany will impose a fine of up to $58 million on social media sites if they do not remove messages denying the Holocaust within a reasonable time frame. In the United States, however, Holocaust denial is deviant behavior, but is not considered criminal. Social media sites may still remove this type of content, but in many cases *this removal will be seen as deviant* by free-speech advocates such as the ACLU. These variations in how to address Holocaust denial and other forms of speech are grounded in historical and cultural differences between the US—with traditionally strong individual liberty norms and a relative distance from Nazi aggression, and European countries—with stronger state bureaucracies and direct experiences with Nazism.

Understanding the "How"s and "Why"s of Cybercrime

Theory can be a rather dull subject for those interested in studying or investigating cybercrime. However, if we are to understand how and why cybercrimes occur, theoretically informed scholarly research must be conducted. The "how"s and "why"s form the foundation for almost all insights into cybercrime phenomena:

- Effective laws and social policies come from rigorous, nonpartisan scholarship that accurately defines and describes cybercrime phenomena
- Knowing root social causes of cybercrime offending and developing accurate profiles of cybercriminals can aid law enforcement in anticipating and investigating cybercrime
- Scholarship on victimization can help social workers and other victim assistance professionals treat those who have been hurt by cybercrimes

Cybercrime scholarship is growing but is in its infancy. To date, social scientists have been able to use traditional criminological and sociological theories to explain cybercrime patterns.

After all, whether a crime is committed in the digital environment or not, it is still human behavior.

For example, many forms of cyberbullying are functionally the same as revenge porn. People can post nude images of a former intimate partner in order to humiliate them—cyberbullying through revenge porn. Research on cyberbullying has used strain theory to predict why someone would cyberbully. The rationale behind **strain theory** is that people who are facing challenging or stressful circumstances—"strains," may respond to those strains by lashing out at others. Young people are especially subject to strains, the theory goes, because they face so many new challenges in their lives, from dating to fitting into new peer groups, finishing high school or college, or witnessing family breakups. Studies have shown that strain increases the likelihood of a young person bullying another. Strain may be, then, a predictor of many instances of revenge porn. However, the scholarship is scant in this area, illustrating the newness of the phenomenon and the need for more research.

In the chapters that follow we will further explore the challenges already examined. We do so by addressing cybercrime and cyberdeviance from a social science perspective. We incorporate research from a wide range of disciplines including psychology, economics, communications, sociology, and criminology.

The coauthors are trained in sociology and criminology, respectively, and therefore the bulk of the research informing this text is drawn from these two disciplines. Although sociology and criminology research is used, previous sociological and criminological knowledge is not assumed, and entry-level college students from all disciplines will be able to grasp the material.

We attempt to make the text as current and engaging as possible. One way is by clear, everyday language. We decided to avoid jargon whenever possible. We aim to be informative, but not confusing. Another way is by using contemporary examples drawn from national headlines. Our use of the Nick Sauer case is emblematic of our approach throughout this text. We are fortunate in that our topic is interesting enough that the media has supplied us with a never-ending series of stories about cybercrime-related phenomena. We incorporated these stories liberally throughout the text.

We have listed several challenges for the field of cybercriminology. We believe that one way of meeting these challenges is by training the next generation of law enforcement, lawyers, scholars, and writers. This textbook is our contribution to that training.

NOTES

1 "Illinois Lawmaker Resigns After Ex Says He Catfished Men with Her Nudes," August 2, 2018, *The Huffington Post* www.huffingtonpost.com/entry/illinois-lawmaker-resigns-catfish-nudes_us_5b631767e4b0de86f49ec7ec

2 "Quinn Signs 'Revenge Porn' Ban Into Law," December 30, 2014, *The Chicago Tribune*, www.chicagotribune.com/news/local/politics/ct-quinn-signs-illinois-revenge-porn-law-met-1230-20141229-story.html

3 "Should 'Catfishing' be Made Illegal?" February 24, 2017, *BBC News*, www.bbc.com/news/uk-39078201

4 "After Weinstein: 71 Men Accused of Sexual Misconduct and Their Fall From Power," February 8, 2018, *The New York Times*, www.nytimes.com/interactive/2017/11/10/us/men-accused-sexual-misconduct-weinstein.html

REFERENCE

Yar, M. (2013). *Cybercrime and society* (2nd ed.). Los Angeles: Sage.

Chapter 1

Understanding Cybercrime in the Digital Environment

Introduction: A Brief History[1]

The origins of the Internet began as a military project funded by the Defense Advanced Research Projects Agency (DARPA). It was through this project that computer scientists developed the protocols (computer language) used to transfer information between computers. In 1969 the first computer to computer links—or network—was established between four university computers. The network was called ARPAnet.[2] The first message was sent from a computer at the University of California, Los Angeles to Stanford University. The first message sent was "lo." The intended message was "login," but the system crashed before the entire message could be sent. From these humble beginnings grew the Internet of today.

In those early years of government-funded research and development, computer networks were in universities, military installations, and some financial institutions. The National Science Foundation (NSF) funded the construction of several lines that connected these several computer networks, *inter*connecting separate *net*works, forming what can be considered the original Internet backbone. This investment by the NSF led to DARPA ceding control over the administration of the Internet to the NSF.

From the beginning of the Internet's development in the 1960s through its NSF years, there was no need for Internet security as we know it today. The users of the network were few in number, and those that could use a computer network were generally highly skilled academics or military personnel. Advances in usability and the existence of **Graphical User Interfaces** (GUIs) were not common. Moreover, there was no **e-commerce** of any kind. There wasn't a need for the users who operated a computer to prove it was truly them.

The modern Internet began in 1993, with the NSF granting licenses to several commercial service providers who could then sell Internet service to citizens. Most of these providers were phone companies, as it was through a phone line that a person could connect their computer to the network. This commercialization could be said to have created the Internet as we know it.

Economic incentives compelled companies providing internet service to gain subscribers. This included building new telecommunication lines out to new areas of the country and finding cheaper ways of connecting people.

Economic incentives were also the foundation for the many innovations that occurred, as companies developed services and products to sell through the technology. E-commerce, pornography, search engines, and more were all developed shortly after the commercialization of the Internet. The convergence of people and commerce made the Internet a space highly conducive to crime and deviance. As we will discuss later, the ability of computer users to connect to the network without personal credentials being verified—being anonymous—made deception much easier and crime inevitable.

Thinking about Technology and Society

When a new technology is introduced into society—let's say for example a new application that connects individuals with cars to people who need transportation—the response by the media and many writers is to ask: "How will the technology impact society?" or "How will the technology change the way we do things?" For everyday discussions of technology, this is a perfectly valid way of talking about and thinking about new technology.

However, most scholars of technology believe that there is an interplay between what a technology can do, often called the "affordances" of a technology, and the values and goals of individuals (Bijker, Hughes, & Pinch, 2012; MacKenzie & Wajcman, 1999). Technology does not simply "impact" society. The makers of a technology will have a use in mind when they initially design it and introduce it to the public. But after its introduction, people often find new uses for the technology (see Figure 1.1).

For example, the initial thoughts of Twitter developer Jack Dorsey were to create a new version of the citizens band, or CB radio, for the Internet age. Its original purpose was to allow small groups to maintain contact with each other. Twitter has indeed become a kind of mobile, quick messaging system that is similar to how truckers used CB radio.

But Twitter has become much more than what its founders dreamed it would be. Groups with specific values and goals began using Twitter in ways that helped them achieve their goals. Twitter is now a public platform to publicize causes such as police brutality and sexual violence against women (Gill & Orgad, 2018; Graham & Smith, 2016; Mendes, Ringrose, & Keller, 2018; Royal & Hill, 2018). Groups seeking revolutionary changes in their countries have used Twitter to communicate their cause and organize on a mass scale. It has not all been positive for Twitter. The platform has also taken criticism as a space where racist, sexist, and homophobic ideas proliferate.

The point here is that a technology rarely ever impacts society in a simple, one-way fashion. Instead, a technology is designed with a series of affordances that the designer believes will lead to a given usage (Davis & Chouinard, 2016; Graves, 2007; Shaw, 2017). However, the goals and values of individuals will create new uses from these original affordances. Consequently, the patterns that develop around a technology after it is produced are hard to anticipate.

Figure 1.1   Mobile driving services such as Uber (shown) and Lyft are relatively new applications that link people who need transportation with people willing to provide that service. One way of thinking about these applications is to ask how they change the way we travel in cities. However, a more nuanced way of thinking about these applications is to ask the additional question of how do people modify and adapt the technology to their personal goals (https://marketresearchupdates.com/2019/03/06/grab-reportedly-valued-14-billion-investment-softbanks-vision-fund/).

We import this understanding of technology into our exploration of cybercrime and cyberdeviance. For example, we should not only ask "How do algorithms impact practices in the criminal justice system?" This is a good starting question because indeed algorithms have already changed aspects of the criminal justice system in the form of predictive policing and risk assessment in sentencing. However, we must also ask a more difficult, but more rewarding question: "How do the values and goals of people influence the way algorithms are used in the criminal justice system?"

Criminal behavior via technology is often the result of people taking technology designed for one purpose, and finding new, illegal uses for the technology. Take **asymmetric key cryptography**. Asymmetric key cryptography makes it possible to share a message over a distance without two people physically meeting. A mathematically related key is made and split into two separate keys. One key is used for decrypting a message and is kept private by the user. The second key is used to encrypt messages and is made public. Anyone who wishes to send a private message can use the public key to encrypt a message, and then send it to the person with the public key. There are many benign or positive applications of asymmetric key cryptography, with militaries, governments, and banks all needing to send secure messages through computer networks. But it can also be used by terrorists, child pornography distributors, and other cybercriminals who wish to share sensitive information as well.

Interconnected Technologies

Complicating our thinking about technology is the fact that the Internet is not just one technology, but several interconnected technologies that produce the experience of being online. As an example, if law enforcement is looking to collect evidence for a case they will probably not look "on the Internet." Instead, they will look on a suspect's hard drive. They will request information about the suspect's social media activity from the social media company (information stored on its databases). They may examine the log files on the suspect's home router. All these technologies work together to produce interconnected computer networks—the Internet.

The Internet is a complex ecosystem of technologies that produces an environment for social interaction. This environment is produced through several layers of technology. This includes the infrastructure through which computers communicate (e.g. copper wires, fiber-optic cables), the machines that house computer processors (e.g. smartphones, desktops, and increasingly household appliances), and the software applications or "apps" that power the machines. This complexity can be bewildering to some, as each year a new way of using the Internet and computer technology is invented. At one time computers were connected through phone lines. Within a few years, the Internet had shifted from this "dial-up" service to faster fiber-optic connections. Or more recently, Wi-Fi connections are moving from 4G capability to 5G capability. Similarly, someone who was an Internet user in 2000 would not have had a "social media" account such as Facebook or Myspace or would have used Geographic Information System (GIS) mapping technology on their phone to help them navigate a new city.

Because it is hard to predict what will happen with a technology, and because the Internet is not one piece of technology but a collection of technologies, we believe it is necessary to introduce some heuristic tools to make our analysis of cybercrime easier. First, we explain what is meant by a digital environment. Second, we discuss the four categories of cybercrime that we will explore in more detail in future chapters—cybertrespass, cyberpornography, cyberviolence, and cyberdeception (Wall, 2001).

Along with simplifying an analysis of cybercrime, an added benefit of using this approach is that the knowledge gained will retain its value longer. As we have mentioned previously, technology changes rapidly. However, the digital environment model will retain its value because most technologies will fall into one of the layers. Similarly, new ways of committing criminal acts in the digital environment are being invented by people every day but the typology of cybertrespass, cyberpornography, cyberviolence, and cyberdeception will still be useful.

The Digital Environment

Entire subdisciplines in academia are devoted to social behavior in a given space. There are subdisciplines focused on "urban sociology" (Gottdiener, Hutchison, & Ryan, 2015) and "rural criminology" (DeKeseredy & Donnermeyer, 2014). An underlying assumption in these subdisciplines is that distinct social dynamics occur in the space, place, or environment under study. Scholars of urban sociology understand that a person who moves from a small town to a city will experience a different set of social structures. They will experience positive aspects—culture, access to high-paying jobs, a highly skilled population. They will also experience negative aspects—traffic, crime, and concentrated poverty. These aspects make city life qualitatively different than living in a small town. Urban sociologists must then try to understand the social patterns associated with this qualitatively different environment.

The same approach can be taken with the space created by Internet-enabled, networked computers—the digital environment. Networked computing has created a space where distinct social patterns take place, including crime and deviance. These patterns are likely different than the patterns that occur offline, in the physical environment.

A LAYERED ENVIRONMENT

Computer scientists and engineers often conceptualize technological systems as layered systems. In a layered system, a large task is broken down into smaller tasks organized by layer. Consider the TCP/IP layered system used for internet traffic:

- Application—Responsible for standardizing data from different sources and provides a user interface. Web browsers, social media applications, video applications, voice applications, and more are examples of technologies in the application layer.
- Transport—Responsible for the verification of data and the exchanging of data between specific endpoints within a network. The transport layer can also be called the "host to host" layer because the technologies in this layer control direct connections between user computers. The protocol most often used in this is the Transmission Control Protocol (TCP). An example of a technology in the transport layer is a modem.
- Network layer—Responsible for the exchanging of data packets across networks (e.g. a user with service from Verizon and a user with service from Sprint). This layer is also called the Internet layer. Most technologies in this layer use the Internet Protocol (IP) developed during the early stages of computer networking. Routers are technologies in the network layer.
- Link—Responsible for transporting data from one network to another. This includes broadband technologies and Wi-Fi technologies. It is the physical link between networks.

Two characteristics of layering systems are important here. First, technologies in one layer receive an input from the layer directly below it and use that input to produce an output for technologies directly above it. The transport layer (a router) receives data from the network layer (a modem), and then produces output for the application layer (Netflix on your smart TV). Second, technologies can be designed for completing functions in one layer without considering the technologies in another if they use the proper protocol. A company can begin manufacturing modems without having to make special modems for each kind of router produced, because all routers use the IP.

The notion of layering is meant to aid computer scientists, computer engineers, and software designers as they design technologies. However, we can apply it to the social scientist's concern for behavior in the digital environment. Table 1.1 shows a layered model of digital environment with brief descriptions and several examples of the technologies or activities occurring in each layer.

In the paragraphs that follow we describe in more detail the technologies and activities within these layers. We approach these paragraphs with the assumption that the social science student may not be as conversant in internet technologies as they would like to be. Consequently,

Table 1.1   The Layers of the Digital Environment

Type of Layer	Description	Examples
Human	The connections and communications between users	Identity construction, radicalization
Content	The information that is produced and shared on the Internet	Racist or sexist content, fake news, filter bubbles, cultural production
Application	Programs that allow users to perform operations on a computer	Social media, e-health, websites, search engines, word processing programs, database programs
Operating system	The software that manages the operation of applications on a computer	Windows, Mac OS, Linux, Android
Hardware	The machines that compute and manipulate data	Laptops, tablets, mobile phones, Internet enabled devices
Infrastructure	The technologies that transmit data between machines	Fiber-optic cables, Wi-Fi connections, dial-up

we provide a broad historical and technological understanding within each layer. We only introduce some important individuals and technologies here. The student can then explore further if they wish to do so.

Infrastructure Layer. The infrastructure layer comprises the cables, satellites, and cell phone towers that transmit data. Internet service providers build and maintain these networks and sell access to these networks to computer users through subscription services. Initially, computers were connected through phone lines, on what was called dial-up services. A computer connected to the phone through a modem, and "dialed" the Internet Service Provider. In essence, your computer was making a call and tying up a phone line. Dial-up connections had a theoretical maximum data transfer speed of 56 kilobytes (56kb) per second. One of the most well-known Internet Service Providers during this early period was America Online, or AOL.

There are few dial-up users left in the United States, with most internet subscribers accessing the network through a broadband connection. Broadband connections are much faster than dial-up, and new innovations continue to increase data transfer speeds. Digital subscriber lines (DSL) use the phone lines already connected to a location but do not tie up the phone line. A second type of broadband connection is through the cable lines that bring TV service to the residence. These and other types of connections are much faster, with maximum data transfer speeds at least 5 million bytes per second (5Mbps). These transfer speeds are fast enough for streaming movies and video games.

Hardware Layer. Technologies in the hardware layer are the devices that house some variation of a computer processor. These technologies compute and store data received from the technologies in the infrastructure layer. For most of the Internet age, this layer has been composed of desktop, laptops, and computer servers within companies and organizations. However, as with data transmission speeds, there has been a rapid and continuous evolution in the size and power of computer processors. Computer processors are small enough to fit into all manner of hardware and have the requisite processing power to perform high-level functions. The most obvious example is the use of computers in cell phones (making them smart phones). At this point in the evolution of smart phones they can be described more accurately as computers with the ability to call someone.

Society has also moved towards the **Internet of things**, which we can understand as everyday appliances and wearable technologies (things) being equipped with computer processors and connected to the Internet. One's coffeemaker, television, central heating and air system, and automobile are equipped with computer hardware connected to the Internet (see Figure 1.2).

Operating Systems Layer. As computers became more powerful and could perform multiple operations simultaneously, the need arose for computer code that could manage multiple jobs at once. Modern computers can perform hundreds of tasks at the same time. Operating systems are software that help manage multiple tasks on a computer. Use the "task manager" on your computer to see just how many tasks (also called jobs) your computer is currently running. Some operating systems for desktops and laptops are Microsoft Windows, Mac OS, and Linux. Operating systems for mobile phones and tablets include Android OS, iPhone OS, and Blackberry OS. We don't tend to think of operating systems as software, because operating systems are usually sold bundled with the hardware. For many computer users, the Windows operating system and a Dell PC are one in the same. Or, a MacBook Pro and a macOS are also seen as the same technology. However, tech-savvy computer users can add an additional operating system to their computers or replace the pre-installed operating system with a new one.

Operating systems make it easier for third parties to write software for computers. A piece of software can be written for the more generalized operating system instead of having to write software for a particular machine. An app developer, for example, can write a program for the

Figure 1.2 Smart coffeemakers are technologies in the hardware layer that receive inputs from the infrastructure layer. In the case of this coffeemaker, there is no incoming inputs—the Wi-Fi signal is not in operation.

By Zuzu [CC BY-SA 3.0 (https://creativecommons.org/licenses/by-sa/3.0) or GFDL (www.gnu.org/copyleft/fdl.html)], from Wikimedia Commons.

Android operating system and be confident that the application will perform on any device the operating system runs on—from wearable technology like a GPS device to a mobile phone to a tablet.

Application Layer. The next layer, the application layer, is comprised of software that allow users to perform operations or jobs on a computer. The application layer of the digital environment is generally where we see the most human–computer interaction. People experience a computer through their use of Facebook, for example. Other examples of applications include word processing programs such as MS Word, web browsers such as Opera, and video-calling programs like Viber.

Technologies in the application layer are important because they make it possible for many people to use computers. Before modern computer applications with Graphical User Interfaces (GUIs), most computing was done through users typing in specific instructions using programming languages from Command Line Interfaces (CLIs). Most people do not have the time or interest in learning command line computer languages, and it wasn't until the development of applications with GUIs that many people began entering into the digital environment.

Two historically significant applications are search engines and web browsers. Search engines are the programs that index web pages and list those pages when a person searches for a given set of search terms. Google became one of the dominant technology companies because its Google search webpage was powered by the Pagerank algorithm (Thelwall, 2003). Pagerank was so useful and popular to computer users that the Google search engine became by far the most dominant search engine in the digital environment. Web browsers, such as Firefox and Chrome, are GUIs that make it easier for a computer user to access web pages on the Internet.

Content Layer. The content layer is composed of what we see or hear in the digital environment. Humans take the inputs from the application layer and produce content or experiences for other users. Examples are the tweets from Twitter, the likes from Facebook, and the search results from Google. Other examples include podcasts, videos, graphs, and charts. Most social science research analyzes data from the content layer (as well as the human layer). This includes issues of relevance for cybercriminology. It is in this layer that the text describing women or people of color as inferior—hate speech—is produced. It is also in this layer where people are presented news that is misleading—fake news. People can also manipulate content to deceive others into divulging personal information for identity theft or for hacking into a computer.

Earlier in the chapter, we made the point that the relationship between technology and culture is not a one-way relationship. People adopt and adapt technologies to their specific needs. This is innovation, and it is prevalent in the content layers. People continue to invent new ways of presenting content in the digital environment. For example, each year, new hashtags or emojis become a part of a society's lexicon —#Blacklivesmatter, #Bluelivesmatter, and so on.

Human Interaction Layer. In the human layer individual users interpret and act upon inputs from the content layer. The human layer is the layer of meaning-making and behavior. When social scientists measure the amount of time someone spends online, their attitudes about technology, or the meanings they attribute to what they see or hear online, they are measuring phenomena in the human layer.

Meaning-making is an important aspect of the digital environment. Meaning is made from the interpretation of content. The tweets on Twitter are not only a series of symbols. The words, images, emoticons, and memes in a tweet carry cultural markers and signifiers that are interpreted by the person who is taking in the inputs. This interpretation is a calculation or manipulation based upon the culturally based mental algorithm of the reader. The hashtag #MeToo will have a different meaning for a teenage boy in Korea than a 30-something woman in Canada.

The interpretation of content in the human layer is important for social scientists. Criminals and deviants not only manipulate technology (hacking for example) but also manipulate content. How individuals respond to that contact may determine if they are victims or not. Consider cyberbullying. How people respond to taunts, insults, and hate speech online is a matter of interpretation. Some people may ignore the content they see or be indifferent to it. Others can see similar content and have a severely negative reaction leading to depression or suicidal ideation.

Crimes by Layer

The primary function of discussing layering is to explain how several technologies work together to produce the online experience. In this sense, it simplifies. Layering can also help organize one's thoughts about cybercrime because crime and deviance occur in each layer.

One of the four categories of cybercrime we will discuss is cyberpornography. One type of cybercrime within that category is the distribution of child pornography. The commission of a crime such as the distribution of child pornography involves all layers. The offender must have access to the Internet (infrastructure layer). Often the offender finds a way to circumvent the surveillance capabilities of an Internet Service Provider through a virtual private network or some other anonymizing technology. The hardware layer is involved, as some type of machine—usually a home computer—is used to go online. The offender will be using one of the three main operating systems to run his or her hardware. Software in the application layer gives the offender the ability to edit a photo, encrypt that photo, and then share it with others. Finally, we get to the content and human layers. The production and possession of child pornography (content layer) and distribution of child pornography (human layer) is a criminal offense.

Layering also has import for practical computer investigations. The crime of possessing and distributing child pornography can again be used to make this point. During an investigation, inculpatory or exculpatory evidence can be found in each layer. Law enforcement can issue a search warrant to Internet Service Providers as IP addresses can be used as evidence. For example, if a suspect did not use a virtual private network, their IP address activity may link them to a website or email correspondence involving pornographic images (infrastructure layer). Once a computer is seized, an experienced forensic examiner can find evidence linking the suspect to the crime. Photographs may be stored on the hard drive of the machine (hardware layer), encryption keys or passwords to incriminating email addresses can be found on the operating system registries (operating system layer), and in the folders associated with software applications (software layer). With regards to software, software companies often store information on their servers about an offender and law enforcement can access this information with a proper warrant. Even though many computer investigations of child pornography rely on forensic examinations of hardware, some of the most high-profile cases have relied on investigators going undercover online and collecting evidence through text and images on websites and emails (content layer) and through incriminating conversations with offenders (human layer).

The Categories of Cybercrime

There are many ways of categorizing types of cybercrime. For example, one way has been to place crimes into two broad categories—crimes in which the computer is used as a tool, and crimes in which a computer is a target. This is a useful typology, but it can be too broad. The typology we use in this text is David Wall's four-category typology of cybertrespass, cyberpornography, cyberviolence, and cyberdeception (see Figure 1.3). This typology is a common one and is used often in cybercrime literature. In the following paragraphs, we define each type of cybercrime and give examples. In future chapters, we will explore these categories with more detail.

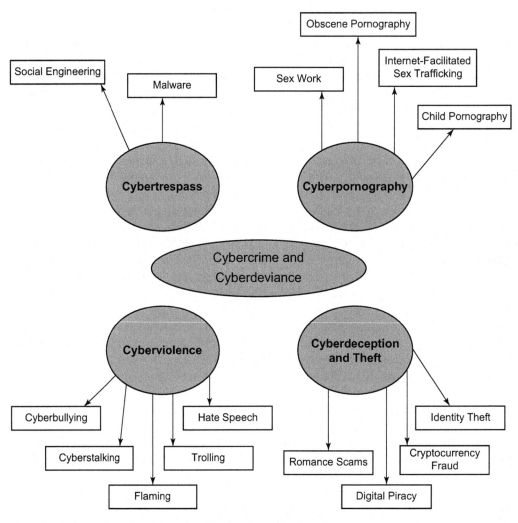

Figure 1.3 David Wall's four categories of cybercrime with examples.

CYBERTRESPASS

Cybertrespass is the "unauthorized crossing of the boundaries of computer systems into spaces where rights of ownership or title have already been established" (Wall, 2001, 3). For practical purposes, cybertrespass is synonymous with hacking (Taylor, 1999). Gaining access to a computer network at a university without permission, finding a way into a company's database, and unlocking a personal laptop by finding the password are all examples of cybertrespass.

Hacking is arguably the most talked about cybercrime in the media. A major news story about a company or organization being hacked appears every few months or so in the United States. These hacks are often called "data breaches," and the purpose of crossing unauthorized boundaries (cybertrespass) is ultimately to gain access to valuable data. Some companies experiencing high-profile data breaches include:

- Yahoo—a 2014 data breach exposed all 3 billion of its user accounts. In terms of the total number of people affected, the Yahoo data breach was the largest in history.
- Equifax—in 2017 the credit bureau was hacked, exposing the personal information of around 148 million customers. The Equifax data breach was especially worrisome because of the sensitivity of the information their databases housed: social security numbers, birth dates, addresses, and in some cases credit card numbers and driver's license numbers.
- Ashley Madison—the hack of this dating site exposed the information of 32 million users. This information included credit card numbers, names, and addresses. Because of the nature of Ashley Madison—a dating site for adulterers—many customers were concerned about their activities being exposed.

CYBERDECEPTION AND THEFT

Cyberdeception describes "the different types of acquisitive harm that can take place" in the digital environment (Wall, 2001, 4). This type of cybercrime covers all aspects of deception, fraud, and theft in the digital environment.

One type of theft is the stealing of intellectual property in the form of movies, music, and software. This property is understood as intellectual because the property is not material but based on someone's idea and creativity. Movies and music are the most common forms of intellectual property, but algorithms, computer code, and logos are other examples of products of the mind that are the property of a person or company. The theft of intellectual property is one of the more common instances of cybercrime. This is often called digital piracy in everyday language (Herings, Peeters, & Yang, 2018; Smallridge & Roberts, 2013).

Another type of theft is the stealing of information. The theft of information is usually the end game, with the means for data theft being hacking. After gaining unauthorized access to a computer network a hacker may decide to download information from a person's computer or a company's database. Indeed, in the examples given previously of Yahoo, Equifax, and Ashley Madison, the emphasis is less on the breach, but instead on the consequences of data theft. It is important, however, to not conflate cybertrespass and cyberdeception/theft. It is a crime to gain unauthorized access even if nothing is stolen or altered.

While theft is readily understood as a crime in most cases, deception is more ambiguous. Some forms of deception may be frowned upon and labeled. Other forms of deception are so serious they are criminalized and come with serious penalties. Misrepresenting oneself on dating websites, for example, does not reach the level of a punishable offense. It is a fact of life that individuals construct public images of themselves that are at variance with their private selves. To say to a potential romantic partner that one "loves taking walks on the beach" when one actually dislikes sand is bad behavior but not a crime. However, when those false pretenses are used to extract money or resources from someone, this then becomes a punishable offense. Many people are defrauded each year through these "romance scams" (Kopp, Layton, Sillitoe, & Gondal, 2015; Whitty & Buchanan, 2012).

CYBERPORNOGRAPHY

Cyberpornography, as defined by Wall, is "the publication or trading of sexually expressive materials" in the digital environment (Wall, 2001, 6). As Wall has noted, pornography has been a catalyst for the growth of the Internet. Men were interested in consuming pornography and this created an early base of Internet users. Pornography producers, looking to monetize men's interest in sexual imagery, developed online credit card transactions and streaming video. The pornography industry also pioneered innovations such as monthly membership fees for access to sites and the concept of "upselling" where a customer is sold related services once they have joined a site (e.g. a customer pays $10 per month for one site and is offered access to a second site for an additional $5 per month).

As we will discuss in Chapter 3 on cyberpornography, most forms of pornography are legal and in the United States a high bar must be passed before the production, distribution, or consumption of pornography is prohibited. For this reason, a large portion of criminological analysis surrounding cyberpornography is about its deviant characteristics. The topic of pornography engenders strong debate between many groups in society, and it is usually suffused with moral overtones (Paasonen, 2015). Many feminists, parents, and conservative groups want to restrict pornography. They see pornography as exploiting women or reducing women to sexual objects. They also see pornography as lowering the moral standards of society and teaching children improper sexual behaviors. Meanwhile, civil liberties groups, citizens with an interest in preserving free speech, and people who openly enjoy pornography support its production and consumption. However, these debates about the morality of pornography do not extend to child pornography. Child pornography, also called child sexual abuse images, is universally condemned within the United States and internationally, and researchers have studied the dynamics of this crime extensively (Martin & Alaggia, 2013; Merdian et al., 2016; Merdian, Curtis, Thakker, Wilson, & Boer, 2013).

In this textbook, we have extended Wall's definition beyond the publication and trading of materials—images, videos, text messages. We also place sexual services facilitated in the digital environment in the category of cyberpornography. Internet-facilitated sex trafficking is an example of a sexual service using digital technologies to facilitate a crime (Bromfield, 2016;

Farrell, Owens, & McDevitt, 2014; Leary, 2014). As we will discuss later, sex traffickers use websites for marketing purposes, use cryptocurrencies to launder money, and use text messaging to organize and coordinate their activities.

CYBERVIOLENCE

Cyberviolence describes the

> violent impact of the cyberactivities of another upon an individual or a social or political grouping. Whilst such activities do not have to have a direct physical manifestation, the victim nevertheless feels the violence of the act and can bear long-term psychological scars as a consequence.
>
> (Wall, 2001, 6)

The subjective feeling of harm—either actual or threatened—is what determines if a behavior is categorized as cyberviolence. As such, a wide range of behaviors falls under the category of cyberviolence.

The type of cyberviolence that arguably garners the most media attention is cyberbullying (Hinduja & Patchin, 2008; Madlock & Westerman, 2011; Payne & Hutzell, 2017). **Cyberbullying** can be defined as: "any behavior performed through electronic or digital media by individuals or groups that repeatedly communicates hostile or aggressive messages intended to inflict harm or discomfort on others" (Tokunaga, 2010, 278). Examples of cyberbullying include posting insults on a victim's social media page, sending hateful text messages to a victim, or sharing via the Internet embarrassing or degrading images of a victim.

Over the past several decades, many young people have committed suicide entirely or in part because they have been cyberbullied. Variations of hurtful communications, including trolling, flaming, and hate speech are also instances of cyberviolence because the receiver of the communications experiences psychological harm.

For most of the Internet age, cyberviolence was primarily limited to psychological violence, and the victims were individual computer users. This is because so many pieces of hardware that perform essential societal functions are now connected to the Internet (i.e. are in the digital environment). The damaging of this hardware can lead to a disruption of services, panic, and even death. Consider the amount of chaos that could be caused if the computers that control a city's water system are either damaged or destroyed. Modern nations must now protect their computer networks from these types of attacks.

Summary

This chapter describes two organizing ideas: the digital environment and the four types of cybercrime. The discussion of the digital environment helps the student to understand how various technologies work together to produce the experience of being online. The application of layering—imported from computer science and modified for use within a social science context—illustrates the functions of each technology, up to and including the function of human content generation and behaviors.

David Wall's cybercrime typology also helps organize one's thinking. There are numerous examples of cybercrime, and Wall's typology organizes them into four types—cybertrespass, cyberdeception/theft, cyberpornography, and cyberviolence. This typology, it should be stressed, is not the only useful one used by social scientists. However, it is more than adequate for an introductory text and, like the digital environment, provides a means of understanding and integrating new forms of cybercrime as they arise.

Vocabulary

1. **Application Layer**—A layer of technologies in the digital environment comprised of the software that allows users to perform operations or jobs on a computing device
2. **Asymmetric Key Cryptography**—A system of encryption in which information is made and split into a public and a private key. The public key is made available on websites and databases and is used to encrypt new information. The encrypted information can then be sent to the owner of the private key who can then decrypt the information. Only the owner of the private key can decrypt information encrypted by the public key. In this way, a person can send private communications to someone without ever meeting them.
3. **Content Layer**—The layer in the digital environment that houses the content that computer users see and hear.
4. **Cyberbullying**—Any behavior performed through electronic or digital media by individuals or groups that repeatedly communicates hostile or aggressive messages intended to inflict harm or discomfort on others
5. **Cyberdeception**—The different types of acquisitive harm that can take place in the digital environment.
6. **Cyberpornography**—The publication or trading of sexually expressive materials in the digital environment.
7. **Cybertrespass**—The unauthorized crossing of the boundaries of computer systems into spaces where rights of ownership or title have already been established.
8. **Cyberviolence**—The violent impact of the cyberactivities of another upon an individual or a social or political grouping.
9. **E-commerce**—The buying and selling of goods and services online.
10. **Graphical User Interface (GUI)**—An interface that allows the computer user to interact with a computer through visual displays such as icons or images, instead of using text-based commands.
11. **Hardware Layer**—The layer in the digital environment composed of machines housing a computer processor.
12. **Human Layer**—The layer in the digital environment where humans interpret content and interact with each other.

13. **Infrastructure Layer**—The layer in the digital environment composed of technologies that transmit data between machines.
14. **Internet of things**—Everyday appliances and wearable technologies (things) being equipped with computer processors and connected to the Internet.

Study Questions

TRUE/FALSE

1. The "digital environment" refers to the space created by Internet-enabled, networked computers.
2. Networked computing has created a space where distinct social patterns take place, including crime and deviance.
3. The layer of the digital environment comprised of the technologies that transmit data between machines is referred to as the hardware layer.
4. The content layer in the digital environment is composed of what we see and hear.
5. Cyberdeception refers to unauthorized crossing of the boundaries of computer systems into spaces where rights of ownership or title have already been established.
6. The pornography industry pioneered innovations such as monthly membership fees for access to sites and the concept of "upselling."
7. The subjective feeling of harm is what determines if a behavior is categorized as cyberviolence.
8. The hashtag #FootballFriday will have the same meaning for a teenage boy in Virginia and an elderly woman in Canada.
9. The use of malware is an example of cyberdeception.
10. The pornography industry has been an important innovator in the digital environment.

MULTIPLE CHOICE

11. In the digital environment, the _____ layer refers to programs that allow users to perform operations on a computer.
    a. Human
    b. Content
    c. Application
    d. Operating System
12. _____ is the layer of the digital environment represented by identity construction and radicalization.
    a. Human
    b. Infrastructure
    c. Content
    d. Hardware

13. Hashtags like #MeToo have different meanings depending upon the various demographic and cultural distinctions of the Internet audience. This is an illustration of the _____ layer in the digital environment.
    a. Human
    b. Infrastructure
    c. Content
    d. Hardware
14. _____ is arguably the most heavily discussed and policed cybercrime.
    a. Identity theft
    b. Hacking
    c. Flaming
    d. Trolling
15. In cyberviolence, variations of hurtful communications include:
    a. Trolling, flaming, and phishing
    b. Cyberdeception, cybertheft, and cyberpornography
    c. Trolling, flaming, and hate speech
    d. Flaming, cyberdeception, and hacking
16. The affordances of a technology refer to:
    a. the design features of the technology
    b. how profitable the technology will be on the market
    c. how much the technology costs
    d. the amount of time it takes for a technology to become popular
17. Which of these sentences best describes the relationship between technology and criminal behavior?
    a. Technology is usually produced for positive purposes, however, people adapt the technology to criminal purposes
    b. Criminals tend to avoid technology because of its complexity
    c. Young people who may initially be on the path to criminality find a positive outlet in developing new technology
    d. Crime has decreased in society because governments use technology to surveil criminals
18. The Internet of things refers to:
    a. household appliances and personal devices connected to the Internet
    b. interconnected computer networks
    c. the series of devices used by law enforcement to monitor criminal activity
    d. the computers used by people in their homes
19. One of these are software that help manage the multiple tasks on a computer:
    a. Operating systems
    b. Social media
    c. Broadband
    d. Encryption
20. According to your text, what was the importance of GUIs?
    a. GUIs made it possible for more people to enter the digital environment
    b. GUIs are the interface between government and civilians
    c. GUIs are the interface between businesses and civilians
    d. The use of GUIs increased the chances that someone would be victimized

Critical Thinking Exercise

The advent of the Internet dates back to the early 1990s—merely a few decades old. How would you explain the Internet to a student like yourself in an earlier time period (e.g. the 1970s)?

This chapter raises the concept of the "Internet of things." Consider the implications of this in your own life. What daily activities in your own life can you think of that incorporate the use of an Internet-enabled device? What activities *do not* incorporate the use of Internet-enabled devices?

Do you intentionally disable Internet capability for certain items when performing certain tasks? If so, which tasks and why?

NOTES

1 See (Hafner & Lyon, 2006) for a more detailed history of Internet development
2 DARPA was originally called the Advanced Research Projects Agency.

REFERENCES

Bijker, W. E., Hughes, T. P., & Pinch, T. (Eds.). (2012). *The social construction of technological systems: New directions in the sociology and history of technology* (Anniversary ed). Cambridge, MA: MIT Press.

Bromfield, N. F. (2016). Sex slavery and sex trafficking of women in the United States: Historical and contemporary parallels, policies, and perspectives in social work. *Affilia, 31*(1), 129–139. doi: 10.1177/0886109915616437

Davis, J. L., & Chouinard, J. B. (2016). Theorizing affordances: From request to refuse. *Bulletin of Science, Technology & Society, 36*(4), 241–248. doi:10.1177/0270467617714944

DeKeseredy, W. S., & Donnermeyer, J. F. (2014). *Rural criminology*. Abingdon, Oxon: Routledge, Taylor & Francis Group.

Farrell, A., Owens, C., & McDevitt, J. (2014). New laws but few cases: Understanding the challenges to the investigation and prosecution of human trafficking cases. *Crime, Law and Social Change, 61*(2), 139–168. doi:10.1007/s10611-013-9442-1

Gill, R., & Orgad, S. (2018). The shifting terrain of sex and power: From the 'sexualization of culture' to # MeToo. *Sexualities, 21*(8), 1313–1324. doi:10.1177/1363460718794647

Gottdiener, M., Hutchison, R., & Ryan, M. T. (2015). *The new urban sociology* (5th ed.). Boulder, CO: Westview Press.

Graham, R., & Smith, 'Shawn. (2016). The content of our #characters: Black twitter as counterpublic. *Sociology of Race and Ethnicity, 2*(4), 433–449. doi:10.1177/2332649216639067

Graves, L. (2007). The affordances of blogging: A case study in culture and technological effects. *Journal of Communication Inquiry, 31*(4), 331–346. doi:10.1177/0196859907305446

Hafner, K., & Lyon, M. (2006). *Where wizards stay up late: The origins of the internet* (1. Simon & Schuster paperback ed). New York: Simon & Schuster Paperbacks.

Herings, P. J.-J., Peeters, R., & Yang, M. S. (2018). Piracy on the internet: Accommodate it or fight it? A dynamic approach. *European Journal of Operational Research, 266*(1), 328–339. doi:10.1016/j.ejor.2017.09.011

Hinduja, S., & Patchin, J. W. (2008). Cyberbullying: An exploratory analysis of factors related to offending and victimization. *Deviant Behavior, 29*(2), 129–156. doi:10.1080/01639620701457816

Kopp, C., Layton, R., Sillitoe, J., & Gondal, I.. (2015). The role of love stories in romance scams: A qualitative analysis of fraudulent profiles. *International Journal of Cyber Criminology, 9*(2), 205–217. doi:10.5281/zenodo.56227

Leary, M. G. (2014). Fighting fire with fire: Technology in child sex trafficking. *Duke Journal of Gender Law & Policy, 21*(2), 289–323.

MacKenzie, D. A., & Wajcman, J. (Eds.). (1999). *The social shaping of technology* (2nd ed.). Buckingham [Eng.] ; Philadelphia, PA: Open University Press.

Madlock, P. E., & Westerman, D. (2011). Hurtful cyber-teasing and violence: Who's laughing out loud? *Journal of Interpersonal Violence, 26*(17), 3542–3560.

Martin, J., & Alaggia, R. (2013). Sexual abuse images in cyberspace: Expanding the ecology of the child. *Journal of Child Sexual Abuse, 22*(4), 398–415. doi:10.1080/10538712.2013.781091

Mendes, K., Ringrose, J., & Keller, J. (2018). #MeToo and the promise and pitfalls of challenging rape culture through digital feminist activism. *European Journal of Women's Studies, 25*(2), 236–246. doi:10.1177/1350506818765318

Merdian, Hannah Lena, Curtis, C., Thakker, J., Wilson, N., & Boer, D. P. (2013). The three dimensions of online child pornography offending. *Journal of Sexual Aggression, 19*(1), 121–132. doi:10.1080/13552600.2011.611898

Merdian, Hannah L., Moghaddam, N., Boer, D. P., Wilson, N., Thakker, J., Curtis, C., & Dawson, D. (2016). Fantasy-driven versus contact-driven users of child sexual exploitation material: Offender classification and implications for their risk assessment. *Sexual Abuse, 30*(3), 230–253.

Paasonen, S. (2015). Online pornography. In J. D. Wright (Ed.), *International encyclopedia of the social & behavioral sciences* (pp. 217–222). London: Elsevier. doi:10.1016/B978-0-08-097086-8.64109-0

Payne, A. A., & Hutzell, K. L. (2017). Old wine, new bottle? Comparing interpersonal bullying and cyberbullying victimization. *Youth & Society, 49*(8), 1149–1178. doi:10.1177/0044118X15617401

Royal, C., & Hill, M. L. (2018). Fight the power: Making #blacklivesmatter in urban education: Introduction to the special issue. *Urban Education, 53*(2), 143–144. doi:10.1177/0042085917747123

Shaw, A. (2017). Encoding and decoding affordances: Stuart Hall and interactive media technologies. *Media, Culture & Society, 39*(4), 592–602. doi:10.1177/0163443717692741

Smallridge, J. L., & Roberts, J. R. (2013). Crime specific neutralizations: An empirical examination of four types of digital piracy. *International Journal of Cyber Criminology, 7*(2), 125–140.

Taylor, P. A. (1999). *Hackers: Crime in the digital sublime.* London; New York: Routledge.

Thelwall, M. (2003). Can Google's PageRank be used to find the most important academic Web pages? *Journal of Documentation, 59*(2), 205–217. doi:10.1108/00220410310463491

Tokunaga, R. S. (2010). Following you home from school: A critical review and synthesis of research on cyberbullying victimization. *Computers in Human Behavior, 26*(3), 277–287. https://doi.org/10.1016/j.chb.2009.11.014

Wall, D. (Ed.). (2001). *Crime and the internet.* New York: Routledge.

Whitty, M. T., & Buchanan, T. (2012). The online romance scam: A serious cybercrime. *Cyberpsychology, Behavior, and Social Networking, 15*(3), 181–183. doi:10.1089/cyber.2011.0352

Chapter 2

Cybertrespass

Introduction

This chapter explores the crime of cybertrespass, commonly called "hacking." Cybertrespass refers to "the unauthorized crossing of the boundaries of computer systems into spaces where rights of ownership or title have been already established" (Wall, 2001, 3). Cybertrespass is grounded on the notion that areas of the digital environment are pieces of real estate that someone owns. Like real estate or property in the physical environment, the owner can grant or restrict access. People who gain unauthorized access are committing cybertrespass.

Gaining unauthorized access can be illustrated with a simple example. Consider someone owning a professional website that displays their educational credentials, a blog, and work samples. This front-end information is public, and unless otherwise stated can be accessed, copied, and distributed without any special credentials from a user. This front end is like the front yard of a home which is considered public.

The website will also have a back end containing various types of data including analytics about who comes to the website, drafts of unpublished posts, and uploaded files that have not been posted to the front end. This back-end information is considered private because access to that information is restricted to only those who have the appropriate credentials. This is like the inside of a house where only someone with a key may enter. These credentials (or key) are usually a username and password.

We can extend this understanding to other layers of the digital environment. All layers of the digital environment use procedures that restrict access to only users with the appropriate credentials, and imply no trespassing. The development and implementation of these procedures encompass the profession of cybersecurity. Table 2.1 lists some of these practices.

Cybersecurity personnel are the trained professionals who identify vulnerabilities and exploits and attempt to address them. **Vulnerabilities** are potential ways of gaining

Table 2.1   The Layers of the Digital Environment and Unauthorized Access

Type of Layer	*Description*	*Practices Preventing Unauthorized Access (Cybersecurity)*

Human	The connections and communications between users	• Education about:
		  • Social engineering techniques
		  • Proper password creation and storage
		  • Encrypted communications

Content	The information that is produced and shared on the Internet	• Trash cans and dumpsters in restricted locations • Encrypting content • Safe social media practices
Application	Programs that allow users to perform operations on a computer	• Passwords and other methods of authentication • Downloading and installing security patches • Restricting downloading of apps to select personnel
Operating System	The software that manages the operation of applications on a computer	• Passwords • Antivirus software • Downloading and installing security patches
Hardware	The machines that compute and manipulate data	• Closed-circuit television (CCTV) • Transparent (windowed) walls around data centers • Encrypted hard drives • Admin passwords
Infrastructure	The technologies that transmit data between machines	• Password for Wi-Fi or network access • Network firewalls

unauthorized access, while **exploits** are actual attempts at leveraging those vulnerabilities. A **virus** for example, may be written for a particular operating system such as Windows 8. This virus may allow the hacker to collect sensitive data from all the machines it is downloaded onto. The potential of the virus to compromise the operating system is a vulnerability. An exploit is when a hacker attempts to get a computer user in a network to download the actual virus through an email.

A cybersecurity professional will attempt to anticipate and protect their property from these vulnerabilities. For example, she may need to ensure that all possible updates from Microsoft are downloaded and installed (the vulnerability may have been discovered and a fix or "**patch**" for that vulnerability can be installed). She may also work to inform and educate the authorized users of common social engineering techniques such as phishing emails. Moreover, she will constantly monitor the network for vulnerabilities and exploits using common tools such as Wireshark (analyzes the data passing through a network) and Algosec (analyzes the effectiveness of a firewall).

Cybersecurity professionals must also think about protecting the areas around hardware. A hacker may attempt to gain access by installing hardware or software physically. An example of this is keyloggers that can be installed onto keyboards and record the keystrokes of users. A hacker can install a keylogger that collects usernames and passwords. Along with installing hardware, hackers can also gain unauthorized access by looking through trash and dumpsters for information that can help them decipher passwords.

Demystifying Hacking

So how do cybercriminology and the actions of non-cyber law enforcement personnel fit into the discussion on cybertrespass? Unlike less technologically advanced cybercrimes to be discussed in later chapters, cybertrespass appears to be the domain of cybersecurity professionals and computer scientists. The protection of computer networks is indeed a highly technical and specialized field. However, this does not exempt cybercriminologists and law enforcement personnel from addressing hacking. There are at least three ways in which their competencies and knowledge base can be applied to the understanding of cybertrespass:

1. Law and Policy—Understanding the impacts of various federal and state laws prohibiting unauthorized access. This also includes the writing of laws and social policies. Hacking is a complex activity, and legislation must be crafted with care such that victims are appropriately protected, and the punishments meted out to offenders are just.
2. Investigations—The investigation and apprehension of hackers. Most law enforcement agencies employ cybersecurity professionals or officers trained in cybersecurity. However, cybersecurity has historically been a defensive activity. Law enforcement can be more proactive and attempt to identify and disrupt hacker activities *before* there is an attempt at a breach.
3. Research—Academics who study cybercriminology are trying to understand the psychology and sociology of hackers. They are also working to understand the tendencies of organizations and individuals that increase their likelihood of victimization. These are human behaviors that are connected, but distinct from the technological aspects of hacking. They require a social science focus.

This orientation to cybertrespass is no different from other domains of criminal activity that require specialized knowledge. Consider a new synthesized illegal drug that has become available on the black market. Criminologists will be interested in the buying and selling of the drug. They will also be concerned about the likely violence and social disorder associated with the drug trade.

However, they will only have a surface understanding of the chemistry of the drug or the physiological impacts of the drug on its users. This does not mean they cannot apply their training or skills to the phenomena. It means that they must collaborate with scientists and medical professionals to inform their policy-making, criminal investigations, and research.

The Computer Fraud and Abuse Act

Cybertrespass is prohibited at the federal level by the Computer Fraud and Abuse Act (CFAA). The CFAA was originally passed in 1986 and prohibits (1) the unauthorized access of a computer, or (2) exceeding authorized access; and damaging a computer or accessing information from a protected computer. Since 1986, the CFAA has been revised and updated numerous times. However, these two prohibitions remain at the core of the legislation. Also, each state will have its own series of laws prohibiting cybertrespass, yet most hacking crimes are investigated and prosecuted by federal agencies because of the interstate and international nature of hacking.

The key term, authorization, is not clearly defined by the CFAA but has come to mean a reasonable expectation of privileges. For example, there is a reasonable expectation that a computer user can request access to Amazon's website. There is no reasonable expectation that a user can access any of Amazon's customer databases through a manipulation of code. Exceeding authorization is defined as "to access a computer with authorization and to use such access to obtain or alter information in the computer that the accesser is not entitled so to obtain or alter."[1]

A computer user may have access to a computer network, but is only authorized to perform certain functions. For example, a student can use their email and password to log into the university network on their college campus, and view the information associated with their account. However, their access is generally restricted. They are not allowed to alter the data associated with their grades. Nor are they allowed to download certain types of software onto a computer they do not own, although they can log into that computer. Finding ways to gain access to exceed their authorized roles constitutes hacking.

The term "protected computer" has receded in importance over time. A protected computer is one used by a financial institution or the United States government, or for interstate commerce or communication. These computers were considered worthy of special consideration given the data they likely housed. In the 21st century, most computers are involved in either interstate communication or commerce. Most computers are connected to the Internet where clients and servers are almost always in different geographic locations. At this time in the development of networked computing, all computers are essentially protected computers.

The CFAA has been modified numerous times since its original passage. As of this writing, the penalties for violating sections of the CFAA are:

- For the first offense:
  - Imprisonment for not more than one year and/or
  - A fine of not more than $100,000 ($200,000 for organizations) for the first offense
- For subsequent offenses:
  - Imprisonment for not more than ten years and/or
  - A fine of not more than $250,000 ($500,000 for organizations)

The first person prosecuted under the CFAA was Robert Tappan Morris in 1988. Morris, at the time a first-year graduate student, created the first known computer worm. Although a student at Cornell, Morris released the worm via a floppy disk on a computer at the Massachusetts Institute of Technology to avoid detection. The "Morris Worm," as it would eventually be called, spread quickly, infecting numerous Internet-connected university computers. Morris was sentenced to three years' probation, community service, and a fine of $10,050 dollars.

Another, more recent example is Andrew "weev" Auernheimer. Auernheimer, at the time a 26 year old from Fayetteville, Arkansas, was charged with hacking into AT&T's website and obtaining the personal data of more than 100,000 iPad owners. Auernheimer and a colleague had discovered a security hole in AT&T's website, allowing them to access the data. In 2013, Auernheimer was sentenced to 41 months in federal prison and ordered to pay $73,000 in restitution.

CRITIQUES OF THE COMPUTER FRAUD AND ABUSE ACT

The use of the CFAA by the federal government has come under scrutiny by legal scholars and advocacy groups. The first critique is the imprecise usages of "authorization" and "exceeding authorization." This vagueness means that prosecutors can stretch the term to cover any number of actions. For example, David Nosal, an executive recruiter, was convicted of conspiracy to gain unauthorized access to a computer system. Nosal, in an attempt to start his own firm, paid and cajoled current employees of his former company for trade secrets. Nosal was sentenced to one year and one day in prison in 2014. The problem with the conviction is that at no time did Nosal hack into someone's account, a computer, or a network, and yet he was charged with exceeding authorization. Most would agree that Nosal had committed some type of crime, but many would dispute the charge that he committed some type of hacking. As the title of a *Wired* magazine article written during the time read, "Man Convicted of Hacking Despite Not Hacking."[2]

The second critique is that the penalties for violating the CFAA are too severe. The most well-known illustration of this is the case of Aaron Swartz. Swartz was an active member of the computer programming and hacking community and had developed the code for RSS (Rich Site Summary). Swartz had also contributed to the organization of the sharing site Creative Commons. In January, 2011, Swartz was arrested for downloading about 4.8 million documents from the digital library JSTOR using a guest account. He was charged with two counts of wire fraud and eleven violations of the Computer Fraud and Abuse Act. The cumulative maximum penalty was $1 million in fines and 35 years in prison. Swartz was offered a plea bargain for six months in prison, which he declined. In January, 2013, Swartz committed suicide. In the wake of Swartz's death, advocacy groups such as the Electronic Frontier Foundation argued that the penalties were far too harsh for the crime committed.

Exploring Hacking

FROM HEROES TO HOOLIGANS

One area in which criminologists and other social scientists have contributed to an understanding of cybertrespass is by exploring the culture and motivations of hackers (Jecan, 2011; Jordan, 2008, 2017; Nikitina, 2012; Nissenbaum, 2004; Taylor, 1999). The term "hacking" has its origination in the 1960s at the Massachusetts Institute of Technology, and was generally a positive label:

> To anyone attending the Massachusetts Institute of Technology during the 1950s and 60s, a hack was simply an elegant or inspired solution to any given problem. Many of the early MIT

hacks tended to be practical jokes. One of the most extravagant saw a replica of a campus police car put on top of the Institute's Great Dome. Over time, the word became associated with the burgeoning computer programming scene, at MIT and beyond. For these early pioneers, a hack was a feat of programming prowess.[3]

The students at the Massachusetts Institute of Technology during this time were working within a subculture in which a "hack" meant finding a better, more efficient, or cleverer way of using something or accomplishing a goal. In *Hackers: Heroes of the Computer Revolution* (1984) Levy describes the early culture of hacking and hackers. Levy identified a series of beliefs that he describes as the **hacker ethic**. These include:

- Access to technology and information should be unfettered
- Political structures should be decentralized
- Computers can improve one's life

Levy's characterization is not unique. For example, Yar (2005) argued that hacker culture can be organized around four characteristics:

- The right to freely access and exchange knowledge and information
- A belief in the capacity of science and technology to enhance individuals' lives
- A distrust of political, military, and corporate authorities
- A resistance to mainstream lifestyles, attitudes, and social hierarchies

Cornell University information scientist Helen Nissenbaum (2004) argues that hackers have gone from "heroes to hooligans" in Western society. Nissenbaum is describing a gradual change from seeing hackers as being beneficial influences on technological innovation to dangerous agents capable of obstructing businesses and governments. As mentioned in Chapter 1, the original users of the Internet, from 1960 to the mid-1990s, were primarily academics, people in the military, and some financial institutions. The percentage of the population using the Internet at this time was small and there were few economic transactions.

The type of users and the type of activities changed in the 1990s with the deregulation of the Internet. More users went online. The average user was no longer an academic or computer scientist but a non-tech person using the Internet for entertainment and communication. People began putting more of their personal information online. Commerce became an important aspect of the online experience with people buying more things online and conducting financial transactions online.

These changes meant that "hacks" and the people who did them were dangerous. The desire to tinker with technology ran counter to the desire to control and exploit computer technology for economic gain. It also raised the fears of everyday users who believed that the archetypal "hacker in a basement" would find a way to steal their money or identity.

Scholars stress that hacker practices are not primarily unlawful and reducing hacker motivations to those of a criminal nature is imprecise and crude (Holt, Freilich, & Chermak, 2017; Steinmetz, 2015; Turgeman-Goldschmidt, 2005, 2008). Yet, despite the variety of hacker practices and motivations, it is clear that the characteristics of hacker culture described above can be paths to deviant and criminal behavior. The *anti*-authoritarian bent of hackers means that the rules and policies of law enforcement, government, and businesses are often rejected. Rules regarding information, for example, are routinely ignored. Consistently, hackers have found ways to gain access to sensitive government documents or intellectual property and share this data publicly.

TYPES OF HACKERS

Hackers can be divided into five categories based upon their motives and skill level (see Table 2.2). The major demarcation line is between hackers who are technologically sophisticated and hackers who are not. Some individuals who wish to get into computer systems do not have the ability to manipulate computer technology at high levels. They do not have the computer programming and networking expertise to find vulnerabilities in the software, hardware, or infrastructure layers. Instead, they focus their energies in the content and human layers of the digital environment. These individuals can be considered "low-tech" hackers, of which the two types are social engineers and script kiddies. A second group of individuals are "high-tech" hackers and possess higher-level computing and networking skills. These individuals have knowledge of common programming languages such as C+ or Java, for example. These are the types of hackers that tend to capture the imaginations of everyday citizens and appear in media and movies. The archetypal high-tech hacker is a socially awkward, highly intelligent young white male who invests an inordinate amount of time in front of a computer screen. Indeed, the case studies we use in this text are primarily of white males. So there is some accuracy in this generalization. However, this image is not *completely* accurate, as is the case with most criminal generalizations. People of color, women, older people, and individuals with a wide range of personalities have been arrested and jailed for high-tech hacking.

Social Engineers and Script Kiddies

Social engineers and script kiddies are low-tech hackers. Social engineers have minimal computer programming skills—or at any rate do not use them to hack. Their strategies for cybertrespassing revolve around getting others to provide access to their networks by directly manipulating a victim or by finding indirect ways into a system. One tactic is to send emails that purport to

Table 2.2 Types of Hackers

Names	Technological Skill	Motives
Social Engineers	Low Tech	Criminal
Script Kiddies		
Black Hat	High Tech	
Gray Hat		Contingent
White Hat		Beneficial

be from legitimate companies or authorities, asking for personal information. This tactic, called **phishing**, has proven to be very effective. Phishing can be very low-tech, as when social engineers use it. However, it can also be very sophisticated as we will discuss in a later section. Two other ways include **shoulder surfing**, looking over the shoulder of someone as they key in their personal information, and **dumpster diving**, looking through the discarded documents of a target. Dumpster diving is often a preparatory technique for high-tech hackers, as they can gain information about how to infiltrate the computer networks of a business. However, it can also be used by social engineers to find discarded passwords or personal information that will allow them to guess passwords.

AN INSTANCE OF SOCIAL ENGINEERING: "CRACKAS WITH ATTITUDE"

An excerpt from an FBI press release on September 8, 2016[4] reads:

> *ALEXANDRIA, Va.—Andrew Otto Boggs, aka "INCURSIO," 22, of North Wilkesboro, North Carolina, and Justin Gray Liverman, aka "D3F4ULT," 24, of Morehead City, North Carolina, were arrested today on charges related to their alleged roles in the computer hacking of several senior U.S. government officials and U.S. government computer systems.*
>
> *According to charging documents filed with the court, Boggs and Liverman conspired with members of a hacking group that called itself "Crackas With Attitude." From about October 2015 to February 2016, the group used "social engineering" hacking techniques, including victim impersonation, to gain unlawful access to the personal online accounts of senior U.S. government officials, their families, and several U.S. government computer systems. In some instances, members of the conspiracy uploaded private information that they obtained from victims' personal accounts to public websites; made harassing phone calls to victims and their family members; and defaced victims' social media accounts. At least three other members of the conspiracy are located in the United Kingdom and are being investigated by the Crown Prosecution Service.*

There are several elements of this case worth discussing. First, this case illustrates the ability of someone using social engineering to gain unauthorized access to accounts. This case is even more startling considering the victims. Among the high-ranking government officials were the then CIA director John Brennan, then National Intelligence Director James R. Clapper, and then FBI Deputy Director Mark Giuliano. One would imagine that these officials would be extra vigilant given their governmental roles as heads of security agencies. The officials' accounts were accessed by one of the members of the collective posing as a technician from Verizon—a British teenager called "Cracka."

Second, it illustrates the harm that hacking of any kind can cause. Liverman, with access to Mark Giuliano's contact information, began texting the Deputy Director with harassing messages about his wife and family. Using stolen credentials, the collective accessed the Law Enforcement Enterprise Portal and posted personal details about Miami, Florida police officers.

The "Crackas with Attitudes" have been brought to justice. Boggs and Liverman pleaded guilty in 2017. Boggs was sentenced to two years in prison, while Liverman received a five-year sentence. In 2018, "Cracka," whose real name is Kane Gamble, received two years in prison.

Script kiddies are unskilled hackers who find tools and technologies already produced by more skilled hackers and use them to gain unauthorized access to computer networks. The label is meant to be demeaning and comes from the practice of a person finding code or a script and then using it in a juvenile way to hack. There are numerous hacker forums and websites where individuals with criminal intent can find worms, viruses, or other malware. Script kiddies can also buy hardware such as keyloggers and credit card scammers on these online forums. One recent trend is for script kiddies to be actual kids, or young people.[5] Across all dimensions of criminal behavior and across cultures, young people are more likely to engage in deviant or criminal acts. In the past, the young people who could hack were exceptional in their ability to write computer code and understand computer networks. However, the bar to entry into hacking has been lowered by the availability of exploit tool kits found on the dark web.

White, Black, and Gray Hat Hackers

High-tech hackers can be divided into three types—black hat, white hat, and gray hat (Holt, 2010). The labels are inspired by the tropes of Western movies, where the good guys wore white clothes and the bad guys wore black clothes.

Black hat hackers find vulnerabilities in software and networks and exploit them for malicious purposes. Money is a major motivation. However, many black hat hackers hack for political or ideological reasons. For example, they may hack into databases or emails and release sensitive information to the public in the furtherance of a political goal. Recall the hacker values described previously, such as "information should be free" and a "mistrust of authorities." These values lead to hackers often breaking into the systems of large corporations or businesses, stealing data, and making that data available to the public. The motivation in these cases is not economic, but instead based on political or ideological motives.

White hat hackers attempt to break into computer networks in order identify the vulnerabilities and patch them. The term often attached to this practice is "ethical hacking." When working for security firms or law enforcement, white hat hackers may attempt to identify black hat hackers or anticipate their movements.

Gray hat hackers occupy a middle position. They are often freelancers looking to identify exploits and vulnerabilities. Once they find these exploits, they sell their information to either law-abiding corporations or governments, or on the black market to criminals. Gray hat hackers may even sell their software or hardware to script kiddies.

Gaining Unauthorized Access

We separate cybertrespass into two stages. First there is the act of gaining unauthorized access, followed by what happens after unauthorized access is gained (see Figure 2.1). In this section we discuss gaining unauthorized access.

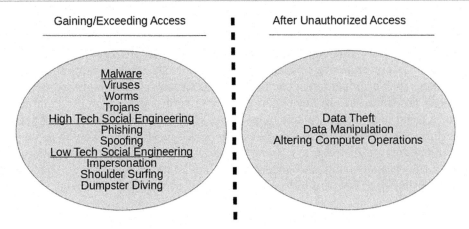

Figure 2.1 Gaining unauthorized access and actions taken after access is gained.

Hackers have developed and employed many tools and techniques for gaining unauthorized access or exceeding authorized access. Below is a brief description of these tools and techniques. We begin with three types of malicious software, or malware—viruses, worms, and Trojans. We end the section by discussing various social engineering techniques.

VIRUSES

Viruses are pieces of malware that infect a computer and change the functionality of the computer or programs running on that computer. Viruses are embedded in other files and need interaction from a human user to drop their "payload" (executable action) and replicate. Viruses can be direct-action viruses and will immediately perform the desired action once installed. They may also be memory-resident viruses and will remain inactive until the user performs a desired action. Memory-resident viruses are often called "time-bomb" viruses. Viruses are usually of three types:

- Macro viruses—Viruses that infect the macro languages of software applications such as MS Word or MS Excel. The programming language is Visual Basic for Applications (VBA), and the program created is called a macro. Macros bundle a series of steps into one operation that can be executed by a user with one click. For example, businesses may want to use an Excel macro to insert an empty space after every row in the document, and then save the document. A macro can be written in VBA or recorded by a user and the code saved for future use. A macro virus infects the VBA code in a macro, and then infects all the files that use the macro.
- File infector (or file injector)—these viruses infect data files such as MS Word documents and mp3 files, or executable files with .SYS or .EXE extensions. Once the virus has been activated it attaches itself to a section of the file (front, middle, or end).

If the virus is attached to the beginning or end of a file, the file may still work normally. Viruses that attach themselves to the middle of a file may do so by overwriting a portion of the file, making the file unstable or even unusable. Some file infector viruses do not attach themselves to other program files but are instead bundled in email attachments.

- Boot sector viruses—these viruses infect the boot sector of a computer's hard drive. The boot sector of the hard drive contains the programs used to start the operating system. Because the virus is installed here, it can perform its action before antivirus software has been booted up. Boot sector viruses are usually installed when a user installs bootable media into a computer (USB, floppy disk, CD).

WORMS

Worms can be understood as self-replicating malware that performs its actions without the intervention of a user. Once a worm has gained entry into a computer network—through an email or hyperlink—it will spread or replicate without any additional user interaction. Worms are self-contained programs and do not need to attach themselves to programs or files, and operate surreptitiously within the computer system.

Unlike viruses, worms usually do not have a "payload." However, they are very damaging because they recruit computer memory to replicate and spread, slowing down computing speed. As a result, one indicator of an infected machine is that it is running slower than usual or crashes repeatedly. Worms are also damaging because they can clog the connections between networks, simulating the same difficulties observed in a denial of service attack (discussed next). The common ways in which worms spread are through vulnerabilities in the protocols in a computer network, through emails, and through the sharing of infected portable media.

TROJANS

Trojans are named after the mythological Trojan Horse used to smuggle Greek soldiers during the Trojan War. Subterfuge is the defining characteristic of computer Trojans. Trojans appear to the user to be legitimate software. Once the user clicks on the software, the Trojan's payload is installed onto the computer. Trojans are not characteristically designed to replicate across computer or systems or to interfere with the normal operations of the computer. These behaviors would alert a user or cybersecurity professional to the presence of the Trojan, which would defeat its purpose. By being undetected, Trojans allow a hacker to perform unwanted functions unbeknown to computer users. Trojans can be used to:

- Create backdoors for remote control of a user's computer
- Control a user's computer for denial of service attacks
- Install a keylogger onto a computer to record the keystrokes of a user

SOCIAL ENGINEERING TECHNIQUES

Social engineering can be called "hacking the wetware" (Applegate, 2009), **wetware** being a term used to describe the human brain and its psychological processes. Hackers use social engineering techniques to gather initial information before more technological means are used to hack into a system, or to get a user to willingly give up access to their computer or network (e.g. giving usernames, passwords, and identification numbers).

Social engineering can be divided into two distinct but intertwined types—technological and psychological. Technological social engineering occurs when someone leverages technology for the purposes of gaining personal information. Phishing is the prime example of this—an email is sent that purports to be legitimate, but after being clicked releases malware (Hutchings & Hayes, 2008; Konradt, Schilling, & Werners, 2016). We can see how the technological and psychological are intertwined through phishing. A good phishing email exploits human psychology in order for the target to take the bait. Phishing has evolved over the years to incorporate other technologies in the digital environment. Vishing is phishing via telephone, where a hacker attempts to fool a target into providing sensitive information. Meanwhile, smishing is phishing via text message, with links or phone numbers being sent to cell phones.

Spoofing is also a type of technological social engineering. Spoofing refers to falsifying the origin of communication, thereby misleading or deceiving the receiver of the communication. In the case of social engineering, the receiver of the false communication is a computer user; however, spoofing can also be done by deceiving computers and computer systems.

One common type of spoofing is email spoofing. Email spoofing occurs when the identifying attributes of a sent email are falsified. These attributes include from what email address the message is sent, to whom the message is sent, the path along which the email traveled from sender to recipient, and the IP address of the computer from which the email was sent. Most scammers use software often called "ratware" to change some of these identifying attributes.

Another type of spoofing is web spoofing. In web spoofing, a website is created that approximates the look of a more well-known website. The URL for the fake website may also be quite similar. For example, a spoofed website may use a logo similar to that of the iconic half-eaten apple used for the Apple Corporation, and a URL of www.apple.com. The purpose of such websites is usually to trick someone to input personal information.

Social engineers also exploit human psychology. One of the more common techniques is to impersonate a government official. This tactic works because people are socialized into listening to authority figures. The United States' Internet Crime Complaint Center reported government impersonation as being the 15th most commonly reported crime in 2015, with 11,832 complaints. This is most certainly an undercount, as many people are not aware that they have been duped, they are too embarrassed to admit they have been scammed, or they do not know that the crime complaint center is available.

Other types of human-centered social engineering include shoulder surfing and dumpster diving. Shoulder surfing refers to the act of looking over a target's shoulder as they key in personal information. Shoulder surfing has also been called visual hacking and can be done at close range by literally looking over someone's shoulder or at a distance using binoculars. In response, companies have developed strategies to protect users from shoulder surfing attacks. Some newer laptops have a privacy mode that makes it difficult to view the screen at an angle, thereby discouraging shoulder surfing, and cell phone users can buy screen protectors that approximate the same effect.

Dumpster diving refers to the act of searching for discarded information about a potential target. The term dumpster is metaphorical, signifying the fact that the search is for discarded information that has been thrown away or neglected. As such, a hacker will look for discarded information in any number of areas—both physical and digital. Information can be found, for example, in trash bins as well as old hard drives. Dumpster diving is a precursor to more sophisticated forms of social engineering or hacking. An organizational chart or phone list could be the information needed to make a phishing email look more legitimate.

After Unauthorized Access

After gaining access to a network, hackers then commit a wide variety of crimes. Some of these crimes can also be placed within the category of cyberdeception/theft and cyberviolence—categories we will explore later. For example, the hacking into a database in order to steal credit card data is initially cybertrespass, but the goal is to use the credit card numbers or sell them on the black market, which is cybertheft. Similarly, the hacking into someone's Facebook account (cybertrespass) and then using it to publicly shame them can easily fit within cyberviolence. What we present here are a series of actions that are more tightly connected to the trespass—namely, data theft, data alteration, and sabotage of computer functions. Crimes such as credit card fraud, cyberbullying, and identity theft are discussed in different chapters.

DATA THEFT

The hacks that have gotten the most media coverage have been those in which hackers have stolen credit card or financial information. The Target hack of 2013 resulted in an estimated 40 million credit and debit card information stolen, as well the names, addresses, phone numbers, and email addresses of around 70 million customers. In 2017, the credit rating company Equifax was hacked, resulting in the theft of social security numbers, addresses, and other identifying information from over 140 million customers.

The theft of data is not always motivated by economic gain. Data theft can also be politically motivated. Nations are perpetually spying on each other. In 2015, the United States government computer systems were hacked with over 21 million people's records stolen, including 19.7 million people who had been subject to a government background check. The theft was the largest cyberattack on government systems to that date, and industry professionals believe that China was the perpetrator.[6]

DATA MANIPULATION

An emerging action committed after unauthorized access is the manipulation of data. For example, a hacker can gain access to a sensitive document or software application and modify records or values. Data manipulation could be more effective than theft because the intrusion can be difficult to detect. This is because cybersecurity professionals often detect intrusions when massive amounts of data are detected leaving the network. Data being extracted from a network is called **exfiltration**. Data manipulation does not require the exfiltration of data.

One form of data manipulation is encrypting someone's data without their authorization. A particular type of malware, called **ransomware**, encrypts a victim's files and demands payment for them to be decrypted. A ransomware attack can be especially difficult for the victim and for law enforcement. Once a computer is infected, it is practically impossible to reverse the infection as decrypting files without a decryption key can be extremely difficult. Other types of attacks, by contrast, can be combatted with software that can clean a system of the malware. Furthermore, payment is demanded in the form of cryptocurrency. Cryptocurrency is difficult to trace making it hard for law enforcement to identify the perpetrators.

Data manipulation can be rather simple. Consider, for example, a student who has managed to get the password to their professor's college account. They can then go into the grading system using the professor's credentials and change their grades. In essence, they have manipulated the data that is associated with their account.

ALTERING COMPUTER OPERATIONS

Hackers can alter the way in which a computer or network operates. **Distributed denial of service (DDoS)** attacks are examples in which a hacker alters the functionality of a computer. DDoS attacks are carried out by a hacker who first spreads a malware across a number of computers, taking control of them. These infected computers are called "bots." A collection of bots, together called a botnet, can then be controlled by the hacker, who uses these infected computers *en masse* to send numerous requests to a website or server. The victim's machines or servers shut down under the strain of the traffic.

As computers become more integrated into everyday machines and appliances, the altering of computer functions will become a greater issue. Individuals and families are beginning to use computer networks to turn on home power and lights, operate ovens and stoves, and drive cars. These machines and appliances—or more specifically the internet-enabled computers that animate them—can be hacked and manipulated. This creates a potentially dangerous situation that will need to be addressed in the future.

Summary

In this chapter, the topic of cybertrespass was explored. Cybertrespass, commonly called hacking, refers to "the unauthorized crossing of the boundaries of computer systems into spaces where rights of ownership or title have been already established" (Wall, 2001, 3). Hacking is the most technologically sophisticated cybercrime, often requiring in-depth knowledge of computer programming and computer networking. In each layer of the digital environment, cybersecurity professionals must develop and enact strategies to protect computers and their users from hackers.

This sophistication does not mean that criminology and law enforcement personnel are not important to understanding cybertrespass. Criminologists can apply social science theory and methods to understanding at least three aspects of cybertrespass. Both criminologists and law enforcement personnel can understand the impacts of laws and policies, help develop effective criminal investigation practices, and they can conduct research on aspects of hacking.

One area in which criminologists have contributed to understanding cybertrespass is by exploring the culture and motivations of hackers. Hacker practices are not by themselves illegal or harmful. However, as the Internet became available to more people in the 1990s, the tinkering nature of hackers became threatening to business and user safety.

There are two stages of cybertrespass. The first stage of cybertrespass is gaining unauthorized access. This can be done through malware—viruses, worms, or Trojans. It can also be done through various social engineering techniques. The second stage of cybertrespass is committing criminal acts after unauthorized access. This includes stealing data, manipulating data, and altering computer operations.

Vocabulary

1. **Black Hat Hackers**—Hackers who find vulnerabilities in software and networks and exploit them for malicious purposes.
2. **Directed Denial of Service Attacks**—A form of attack in which a collection of infected computers send numerous requests to a server. The victim's server is slowed or shut down under the strain of the traffic.
3. **Dumpster Diving**—The hacker tactic of looking through discarded documents for clues that can be used for social engineering or developing spoofed communications.
4. **Exploits**—An attempt by a criminal to gain access to a computer or network.
5. **Exfiltration**—The stage in which data is removed from a network.
6. **Gray Hat Hackers**—Freelance hackers looking to identify vulnerabilities and exploits. They may sell their knowledge to cybersecurity professionals, use their knowledge for malicious purposes, or sell their knowledge to black hat hackers.
7. **Hacker Ethic**—A collection of values and beliefs that are often associated with members of the hacking community.
8. **Patch**—Updates to a computer program. Within the context of cybercrime, patches are meant to fix vulnerabilities in a computer or network.
9. **Phishing**—A tactic used by hackers in which emails that purport to be from legitimate companies or authorities are sent to a target asking for personal information.
10. **Ransomware**—A form of malware that encrypts a victim's files for the purpose of holding the files ransom.

11. **Script Kiddies**—Unskilled hackers who find tools and technologies already produced by more skilled hackers and use them to gain unauthorized access to computer networks.
12. **Social Engineers**—Low-tech hackers who use social and psychological tools to manipulate a computer user to provide access to their networks or to find indirect ways into a system.
13. **Spoofing**—Falsifying the origins of a communication thereby misleading or deceiving the receiver of the communication.
14. **Trojans**—Malware that appears to the user to be legitimate software but hides malicious code.
15. **Vulnerabilities**—Potential ways of gaining unauthorized access to a computer or network.
16. **Virus**—Malware that infects a computer and changes the functionality of the computer or programs running on that computer. Viruses are embedded in other files and need interaction from a human user to act.
17. **White Hat Hackers**—Hackers, often cybersecurity professionals, who attempt to break into computer networks in order identify the vulnerabilities and patch them.
18. **Wetware**—A term used to describe the human brain and its psychological processes.
19. **Worms**—Self-replicating malware that performs its actions without the intervention of a user.

Study Questions

TRUE/FALSE

1. The term *authorization* is clearly defined in the Computer Fraud and Abuse Act of 1986.
    a. True
    b. False
2. A common critique of the CFAA is that its penalties are too severe.
    a. True
    b. False
3. Hackers would generally be considered purveyors of the rules and policies of law enforcement, government, and business.
    a. True
    b. False
4. Social engineers have a high degree of computer programming skill.
    a. True
    b. False
5. Social engineers have a high degree of skill in getting others to provide access to their networks through direct victim manipulation or indirect ways into a system.
    a. True
    b. False

6. Unlike file infector viruses, macro viruses are used by hackers to attack specific programs.
   a. True
   b. False
7. Social engineering can be divided into two categories—technological and physiological.
   a. True
   b. False
8. Phishing—the act of sending an email that purports to be legitimate, but after being clicked releases malware—is an example of technological engineering to gain access to personal information.
   a. True
   b. False
9. Spoofing is another type of psychological social engineering.
   a. True
   b. False
10. A vulnerability one finds oneself subject to when checking social media accounts in a public café is the occasional stranger peeking over one's shoulder to view private content. This is considered a form of social engineering.
    a. True
    b. False
11. The Target hack of 2013 is best categorized as a form of data manipulation.
    a. True
    b. False
12. Black hat hackers gain unauthorized access to computer networks for political reasons.
    a. True
    b. False
13. Compared to 15 years ago, it is easier for young people with no computer skills to hack into computer systems.
    a. True
    b. False
14. Installing a virus on a computer can be called "hacking the wetware."
    a. True
    b. False

MULTIPLE CHOICE

15. On the matter of computer authorization, which of the following best represents the general understanding of *reasonable access*?
    a. Accessing eBay.com's customer databases through a manipulation of code or malware
    b. Using your student email and password to log into computer networks on your college campus

    c. Altering data associated with a student's grades

    d. Downloading software onto a computer that you do not own (i.e. a university-owned computer)

16. The term *hacking* originated at _____.

    a. Harvard University

    b. Massachusetts Institute of Technology

    c. Columbia University

    d. Old Dominion University

17. Each of the following is a part of the hacker ethic Levy originally defined EXCEPT:

    a. Access to technology and information should be free

    b. The future lies in artificial intelligence

    c. A distrust of political, military, and corporate authorities

    d. Computers can improve one's life

18. Hacker culture tends to be:

    a. Antiauthoritarian

    b. Iconoclastic

    c. Technocentric

    d. All of the above

19. Hackers with high technical skill and criminal motives would be considered

    _____.

    a. Social engineers

    b. Script kiddies

    c. White hat

    d. Black hat

20. Social engineers tend to employ at least one of the following tactics EXCEPT:

    a. Shoulder surfing

    b. Virus development

    c. Dumpster diving

    d. Phishing

21. You've just been hired by a prestigious financial firm to identify and secure vulnerabilities in their online account management system. Part of your work entails attempting to hack into the firm's systems anonymously to test their security measures. The best label for what you do would be:

    a. White hat

    b. Black hat

    c. Gray hat

    d. Script kiddy/kiddies

22. The use of "ratware" is most often connected with the act of _____.

    a. dumpster diving

    b. shoulder surfing

    c. directed denial of service attacks

    d. e-mail spoofing

23. In an email spoofing attack, which of the following typically occurs?
    a. Falsification of email address origin
    b. Falsification of email address recipient
    c. Falsification of the sender's IP address
    d. All of the above
24. As a potential hacker, if I want to directly take over a user's computer without being noticed, my *best* option would be to use a _____.
    a. bot
    b. Trojan
    c. virus
    d. worm
25. Which of these cybersecurity practices is used to protect the application layer of the digital environment?
    a. Downloading and installing security patches
    b. Closed-circuit television
    c. Firewalls
    d. Encryption
26. Which of these cybersecurity practices is used to protect the human layer of the digital environment?
    a. Education about creating passwords
    b. Restricting downloading of apps to select personnel
    c. Encrypted hard drives
    d. Firewalls
27. Which of these is not one of the three ways in which cybercriminologists can apply their knowledge to hacking?
    a. Developing encryption algorithms
    b. Investigating cybercrimes
    c. Understanding the effects of laws and policy
    d. Conducting criminological research on cybercrime
28. The CFAA was originally passed in _____.
    a. 1969
    b. 1986
    c. 1993
    d. 2003
29. Which of these, according to the CFAA, are protected computers?
    a. A home computer connected to the Internet
    b. A computer in Naval Station Norfolk
    c. A computer at a Bank of America location
    d. All of the above
30. The first person prosecuted under the CFAA was _____.
    a. Robert Morris
    b. Aaron Swartz

      c. Graham Tucker
      d. Tucker Graham

31. One of the concerns raised about the CFAA is that _____.
      a. the meaning of the term "authorization" is unclear
      b. the penalties are too lenient
      c. federal law enforcement rarely enforce it
      d. state or local law enforcement rarely enforce it

32. At one point in the history of hacking did the term "hack" take on a negative meaning?
      a. When businesses began operating online
      b. When Kim Kardashian "broke" the Internet
      c. At the end of the Cold War
      d. When the National Science Foundation invested in the growth of infrastructure

33. What is one way, as mentioned in the text, that manufacturers are attempting to combat shoulder surfing?
      a. Laptops have a setting that makes it difficult for someone to view the screen at an angle
      b. Laptops are designed with "hats" that hide the screen from hackers
      c. Newer laptops are being designed with more narrow screens to reduce the viewing area
      d. All of the above

34. Which of these is NOT one of the actions that hackers take after gaining unauthorized access as discussed in the text?
      a. Invite other hackers to explore the network
      b. Altering computer operations
      c. Stealing data
      d. Changing data

Critical Thinking Exercise

In 2014, unknown hackers attacked Apple's proprietary iCloud servers and compromised the data security of both Apple computing devices (i.e. Apple Macs, MacBooks, iPhones, and iPads) and operating software connected to the server network in stealing hundreds of images of celebrities—many of an explicit and sensitive nature. While the original source of the hack effort remains unknown, the images were subsequently released on the 4chan imageboard, and then later on broader online community spaces like Imgur and Reddit. The event, now infamously known as "The Fappening" or "Celebgate" represents a benchmark moment of the 21st century among cybercriminologists, social scholars, and the general public for the various questions and considerations it raised pertaining to the vulnerability of iCloud and similar cloud networks, as well as the extent of rights of privacy and even the Fourth Amendment itself.

    While some would argue that a great wrong was committed against the various celebrities that had their content stolen, others could and have argued that the various victims (in light of the increased public exposure and interest inevitably linked to their celebrity status) must claim some responsibility for storing risqué photos and videos of themselves without properly securing the digital devices containing the content or the network those devices were connected to. The latter has grown somewhat in popularity since the initial event as proponents contend that both celebrities and non-celebrities alike should be more aware of the vulnerabilities associated with their digital devices and cloud accounts as a result of the notoriety of The Fappening.

- Recalling Table 2.1 (*The Layers of the Digital Environment and Unauthorized Access*), which layers would you say were compromised in the above-mentioned hacking effort? For each layer, explain the nature of the compromise you think occurred.
- Many wondered (and still do) who was at fault for this unprecedented instance of cyber-trespass. Where do you stand? Do the hack victims share all, some, or none of the blame? Explain.
- What of Apple's position in the event? What role, if any, do they hold? Explain.

NOTES

1 www.law.cornell.edu/wex/computer_and_internet_fraud
2 www.wired.com/2013/04/man-convicted-of-hacking-despite-no-hacking/
3 www.bbc.com/news/technology-13686141
4 www.justice.gov/usao-edva/pr/two-men-arrested-allegedly-hacking-senior-us-government-officials
5 www.bbc.com/news/technology-39654092
6 www.nytimes.com/2015/07/10/us/office-of-personnel-management-hackers-got-data-of-millions.html

REFERENCES

Applegate, S. D. (2009). Social engineering: Hacking the wetware! *Information Security Journal: A Global Perspective*, *18*(1), 40–46. doi:10.1080/19393550802623214

Holt, T. J. (2010). Examining the role of technology in the formation of deviant subcultures. *Social Science Computer Review*, *28*(4), 466–481. doi:10.1177/0894439309351344

Holt, T. J., Freilich, J. D., & Chermak, S. M. (2017). Exploring the subculture of ideologically motivated cyber-attackers. *Journal of Contemporary Criminal Justice*, *33*(3), 212–233.

Hutchings, A., & Hayes, H. (2008). Routine activity theory and phishing victimisation: Who gets caught in the net. *Current Issues in Criminal Justice*, *20*, 433.

Jecan, V. (2011). Hacking hollywood: Discussing hackers' reactions to three popular films. *Journal of Media Research*, *4*(2), 95–114.

Jordan, T. (2008). *Hacking: Digital media and technological determinism*. Cambridge, MA: Polity Press.

Jordan, T. (2017). A genealogy of hacking. *Convergence: The International Journal of Research into New Media Technologies*, *23*(5), 528–544. doi:10.1177/1354856516640710

Konradt, C., Schilling, A., & Werners, B. (2016). Phishing: An economic analysis of cybercrime perpetrators. *Computers & Security*, *58*, 39–46. doi:10.1016/j.cose.2015.12.001

Levy, S. (1984). *Hackers: Heroes of the computer revolution* (1st ed.). Garden City, NY: Anchor Press/Doubleday.

Nikitina, S. (2012). Hackers as tricksters of the digital age: creativity in hacker culture. *The Journal of Popular Culture,* 45(1), 133–152.

Nissenbaum, H. (2004). Hackers and the contested ontology of cyberspace. *New Media & Society,* 6(2), 195–217. doi:10.1177/1461444804041445

Steinmetz, K. F. (2015). Craft(y)ness: An ethnographic study of hacking. *British Journal of Criminology,* 55(1), 125–145. doi:10.1093/bjc/azu061

Taylor, P. A. (1999). *Hackers: Crime in the digital sublime.* London; New York: Routledge.

Turgeman-Goldschmidt, O. (2005). Hackers' accounts: Hacking as a social entertainment. *Social Science Computer Review,* 23(1), 8–23. doi:10.1177/0894439304271529

Turgeman-Goldschmidt, O. (2008). Meanings that hackers assign to their being a hacker. *International Journal of Cyber Criminology,* 2(2), 382.

Wall, D. (Ed.). (2001). *Crime and the internet.* New York: Routledge.

Yar, M. (2005). Computer hacking: Just another case of juvenile delinquency? *The Howard Journal of Crime and Justice,* 44(4), 387–399.

Chapter 3

Cyberpornography

Introduction

Cyberpornography, as defined by Wall, is the publication or trading of sexually expressive materials in the digital environment (Wall, 2001). There is a wide range of sexually expressive materials in the digital environment. On the one hand, pornography consumption has become a commonplace aspect of the digital environment. Pornography is consumed legally on websites like PornHub and RedTube. On the other hand, criminalized pornography, most often in the form of child pornography, is also an aspect of the digital environment. Child pornography is often distributed via anonymous darknets that make it difficult for law enforcement to identify and apprehend the offenders. In between these two extremes is cyberpornography that is criminal or deviant depending upon the context. As we will discuss later, most pornography is legal in the United States, however boundaries can be crossed. If sexual material is deemed obscene, it is criminalized. Similarly, the sharing of sexual material—sexting—is criminalized to varying degrees state by state.

We will extend Wall's definition and discuss not only the publication and trading of sexual materials—images, videos, text messages—but also *the trading of sexualized bodies*. We also discuss sex work in this chapter. The digital environment has become an integral component of how sex work is bought and sold. Sex workers are increasingly turning to the digital environment to sell their services virtually, or as a means of meeting potential customers for an encounter in the physical environment. Some sex work is done voluntarily, however sex trafficking is on the rise. Sex traffickers use the Internet to lure young men and women into the sex trade, to coordinate their activities, and to find customers.

Types of Cyberpornography

The original definition of cyberpornography is the "publication or trading of sexually expressive materials." However, we have expanded this definition to also include the trading of bodies. This broader definition allows us to place a wider range of phenomena under the rubric of cyberpornography. We list those that will be discussed in this chapter, and give brief descriptions:

- **Child Pornography** (possession and distribution)—Child pornography is defined as the visual depiction of sexually explicit conduct involving a minor. In the United States, this is anyone under the age of 18. The possession and distribution of child pornography is prohibited.
- **Internet Facilitated Sex Trafficking**—Sex trafficking refers to the recruitment, harboring, transportation, provision, obtaining, patronizing, or soliciting of a person for the purpose of a commercial sex act.[1] Much of sex trafficking has been facilitated by the Internet, including contacting and grooming victims, and finding potential buyers of sexual services.
- **Obscene Pornography**—Obscene pornography refers to sexually explicit material that is labeled as filthy within a given cultural context. Most pornography is protected by the United States' relatively strong free-speech laws. However, "hardcore" pornography is often considered obscene and subject to regulation.
- **Sexting**—Sexting is the transmission of sexually explicit material usually by mobile phone. The severity of this offense varies by the age of the sender, receiver, and person depicted in the image, with harsher penalties given to adults.
- **Sex Work**—refers to the exchange of sexual services for money or goods. In this exchange there is usually someone producing the service—the sex worker, and someone consuming the service—a male "john" or female "jane." In the digital environment, the production of these sexual services and who can consume these services has expanded greatly.

Pornography Consumption in the Digital Environment

RATES OF CONSUMPTION

Data on rates of pornography consumption—how much is viewed, who is viewing, when, and where—is difficult to acquire. There are taboos in most societies about watching pornography, and people are reluctant to discuss the activity. However, there is little doubt that the consumption of pornography is prevalent and financially lucrative for producers. As Dines and Jensen write:

> While statistics are difficult to collect on Internet pornography use, studies suggest the Internet generates $2.5 billion of the $57-billion-a-year global pornography industry.

With 4.2 billion Web sites and 372 million pornography pages, there are 72 million visitors to porn Web sites annually, and 25% (68 million) of total search engine requests are for pornographic materials.

(2)

Businesses and tech companies often collect information about pornography consumption. This data is often computer-centric, and may not tell us much about the characteristics or motivations of the people who are consuming pornography. For example, the security firm Webroot[2] writes that:

- Every second 28,258 users are watching pornography on the Internet
- Every second $3,075.64 is being spent on pornography on the Internet
- Every second 372 people are typing the word "adult" into search engines
- 40 million American people regularly visit porn sites
- 35% of all internet downloads are related to pornography
- One-third of porn viewers are women
- Every 39 minutes a new pornography video is being created in the United States
- About 200,000 Americans are "porn addicts"

We can also get a sense of the popularity of pornography by comparing popular porn sites with popular non-pornographic sites. Table 3.1 compares the web traffic of three porn sites with other popular sites. As expected, Google receives the most traffic of any site in the United States or the world, and Twitter and Netflix are also popular. Pornhub—a free porn site that hosts videos in a format like YouTube—receives a high amount of traffic, with a US rank of 15 and a global rank of 27. Pornhub receives more traffic than Walmart, the nation's largest retailer and Hulu, a popular streaming service. We also included Chaturbate, which

Table 3.1 Comparing Traffic Statistics of Popular Porn Sites with Other Popular Sites*

Site	US Rank	Global Rank
Google.com	1	1
Twitter.com	7	11
Netflix.com	12	26
Pornhub.com (free porn site)	15	27
Walmart.com	37	169
Hulu.com	40	241
Chaturbate.com (sex cam site)	56	107
NFL.com	113	831
Brazzers.com (pay porn site)	810	934
Whitehouse.gov	2903	9705

*Data collected from Alexa.com on 9/8/2018

receives more traffic than the official website for the United States' most popular sport, and Brazzer's, a porn site that receives more traffic than the website representing the American government. These numbers suggest that pornography consumption is a commonplace aspect of US society.

Legislating Pornography in the Digital Environment

THE MILLER TEST AND CRIMINALIZING PORNOGRAPHY

One can think of pornography through a lens of deviance—violating social norms, and a lens of criminality—violating formal laws. However, criminal cases against the production and consumption of pornography are rare. When they do occur they involve extreme sexual acts or exploitation of children. Most pornography is legal in the United States because of the strong free-speech protections afforded by the United States Constitution. Indecent materials, of which most pornography is understood to be, are protected as free speech. *Obscene* materials, however, can be regulated and prohibited by the government. Packard gives a distinction between indecency and obscenity: "In general *indecency* encompasses profanity, references to excretory organs, nudity, and implied sexual behavior. *Obscenity* refers to explicit depictions of actual sexual conduct, masturbation, violent sexual abuse, and child pornography" (2013).

Courts apply a three-pronged test for obscenity, originating from *Miller v. California* (1973):

1. *An average person, applying contemporary community standards, must find that the material, as a whole, appeals to the prurient interest.* In other words, is the material considered sexually explicit by the standards of the community?
2. *The material must depict or describe, in a patently offensive way, sexual conduct specifically defined by applicable law.* Does the material show an explicit act of sex?
3. *The material, taken as a whole, must lack serious literary, artistic, political, or scientific value.* Does the material have any societal value other than for sexual consumption?

This three-pronged test, called the "Miller Test," places a high bar for the prohibition of pornography. Few sexual materials can be clearly categorized as obscene. A primary reason is because of the third prong of Miller's test: pornography can be understood as having artistic value. Pornographic material can be understood as a recorded artistic performance, placing it into the same category as other recorded performances such as movies, television shows, and public lectures.

A second problem is the "community standards" argument, or the first prong of the test. The Miller Test has traditionally placed the burden on deciding what is obscene on local communities. In one sense, this is a reasonable orientation to take, especially in an analog world. The purpose of regulating pornography is to protect the sensibilities and respect the tastes of the people who may be exposed to it. Who better to know what is obscene than the communities themselves?

This logic breaks down in a digital environment. Consider a tech company with home offices in Seattle, Washington hosting content on servers in Alexandria, Virginia and someone watching videos in Burlington, Vermont. What community's standards should be taken into account to judge obscenity? Seattle, Alexandria, or Burlington?

In a 2009 case, *United States v. Kilbride*, porn spammers Jeffrey Kilbride and James Schaffer were convicted of spam violations and obscenity charges. The court ruled that a national community standard must be applied to pornography on the Internet. This ruling however, was for the Ninth Circuit. In *United States v. Little*, Paul Little, otherwise known as "Max Hardcore," produced pornography in California but was indicted in Florida. In this 2010 case the Eleventh Circuit rejected the national community standard and instead upheld the community standards argument—judging Little on the standards of Florida. Little was sentenced to 48 months in prison. In sum, the courts have not settled on a definitive understanding of what community standards means in the digital environment.

Although it is difficult to determine what is obscene, and therefore subject to regulation, there are some general guidelines. Animal porn is considered obscene, and the production and distribution of it is prohibited. Porn in which scenes of violence or rape are depicted is considered obscene and is illegal to produce and distribute. Finally, the production, distribution, and consumption of images of a sexual nature involving children are also prohibited.

Impacts of Pornography Consumption

Scholars and community leaders have raised several concerns about the impact of online pornography consumption. The narrative has focused primarily on its negative impacts. These impacts include:

- Pornography addiction
- Perceptions of women
- Normalizing risky sexual behaviors

PORNOGRAPHY ADDICTION

Whether or not high rates of pornography consumption warrant the label "addiction" is still a matter of debate for scholars and practitioners. Some suggest that the notion of pornography addiction is overhyped (Ley, 2012). Ley, Prause, and Finn (2014) in their review of pornography addiction studies, concluded that the studies asserting clinical addiction were inadequately designed and therefore misleading. Voros (2009) argues that calling pornography consumption an addiction is ultimately a moral judgment that, in Western societies, is powered by Judeo-Christian values.

Williams (2017) questions the research done on pornography consumption and argues that the use of the addiction label is premature. He argues:

> [In] the growing popularity among clinicians and the public in applying an addiction framework to sexuality issues, such application is not yet warranted and seems to reflect entrenched sociocultural biases. Competent social workers do not need to use the term addiction in order to help their clients resolve a range of potential problems associated with sexuality. Simply referring to 'problematic sexual behavior' will do, at least for now.
>
> (621)

Yet another viewpoint is that the individuals who seek help for pornography addiction are not always consuming more pornography than others, but instead have stronger moral strictures against pornography usage. In other words, they *perceive* themselves as having an addiction because they have been taught that consuming porn is a deviant behavior (Grubbs, Wilt, Exline, Pargament, & Kraus, 2018).

Conversely, other scholars suggest that pornography addiction is a medical disorder that can require treatment (Wilson, 2015). Analogies are drawn to the addiction of Internet gaming, which the American Psychiatric Association recognizes as a "condition for further study":

> The studies suggest that when these individuals are engrossed in Internet games, certain pathways in their brains are triggered in the same direct and intense way that a drug addict's brain is affected by a particular substance. The gaming prompts a neurological response that influences feelings of pleasure and reward, and the result, in the extreme, is manifested as addictive behavior.
>
> (Internet Gaming Disorder, American Psychiatric Association)

Scholars who argue that pornography consumption can reach the level of addiction argue that repeated consumption of pornography alters brain functioning to the point in which the behavior impacts negatively how a person functions in life (Love, Laier, Brand, Hatch, & Hajela, 2015).

Concerns about pornography addiction need to be put into a social and historical context. Sociologist Peter Conrad (2007), in his book *The Medicalization of Society*, argued that alcoholism, ADHD, menopause, and erectile dysfunction as life problems have been redefined as requiring medical treatment. Conrad does not address pornography directly; however, one could apply the same logic. The desire to consume sexual images has always been an aspect of human society, and one can question the notion that it has become a problem that needs to be treated clinically.

PERCEPTIONS OF WOMEN

Pornography is primarily consumed by men. For the vast majority of pornography, the express purpose is to show women as ready and willing to perform sexual activity. Thus, there is a concern that excessive pornography consumption can negatively impact men's perception of women. Scholars have identified at least three potential impacts:

1. *Men are more likely to accept rape myths.* **Rape myths** are "attitudes and beliefs that are generally false but are widely and persistently held, and that serve to deny and justify male sexual aggression against women" (Lonsway & Fitzgerald, 1994). One common myth is that women lie about rape. Sexual activity was initially consensual, the myth goes, but because of remorse or fear of recrimination a woman will assert that the activity was not consensual. Another common rape myth is that only certain kinds of women—presumably women who are socially marginal—are raped. A variant of the rape myth is that women feign disinterest in sexual activity until being "conquered by men."

2. *Men are more likely to be sexually callous towards women.* Men may presume that the purpose of the sexual act is for women to please them. They may ignore or downplay the sexual desires and needs of their female partners.

3. *Men are more likely to reduce women to sexual objects.* Men who watch large amounts of pornography may begin to see women only as potential sexual partners. This objectification lowers the status of women in men's eyes to things to be used.

Many of the assertions about the impacts of pornography are based upon work that was done on pornographic materials produced with older media and consumed offline (DVDs, VHS). Newer research exploring pornographic materials in the digital environment has produced a view that is more nuanced. Some research has found that the majority of videos in their sample could be classified as degrading to women, which supports the idea that viewing pornography produces attitudes in men about sex that are unfavorable to women (Gorman, Monk-Turner, & Fish, 2010). Vannier, Currie, and O'Sullivan(2014) found, like Gorman and colleagues, that male actors were more often depicted as dominant. However, their research also found that women and men were portrayed equally in terms of sexual experience, occupational status, and the initiation of sexual activity. They also found that male actors were more likely to appear nude than female actors. Klaassen and Peter (2015), in the most extensive study at the time of writing this text, also found a great deal of complexity in what is shown in pornographic videos. Their research showed that both men and women were objectified in pornography, only in different ways. Like Vannier and colleagues they found equality in terms of professional status, but men were depicted more often as dominant.

RISKY SEXUAL BEHAVIOR

Some scholars have argued that one impact of excessive pornography use is an increase in risky sexual behaviors. Risky sexual behaviors are behaviors that pose an unintended negative health outcome. These negative outcomes include teen pregnancy and acquiring a sexually transmitted disease. People, especially the young who are still learning how to interact with a potential sexual partner, may uncritically accept the behavior they see in pornography as a realistic description of sexual activity. Watching pornography can suggest what should and should not happen in a sexual encounter, how individuals should respond to the events in a sexual encounter, and the expected outcome of adopting a particular action during a sexual encounter (Huesmann, 1986).

Pornography models several types of risky sexual behavior. Pornographic material depicts scenes of multiple sex partners, sexual activity between strangers, and sexual activity without a condom. Watching these scenes can give a person sexual scripts that they then use in everyday encounters (Sun, Bridges, Johnson, & Ezzell, 2016). There is some evidence linking the watching of pornography to risky sexual behavior. A study using a national sample of Americans showed that pornography consumption was positively associated with having sex with multiple partners, engaging in paid sex, and having had extramarital sex (Wright & Randall, 2012).

The Distribution and Consumption of Online Child Pornography

CHILD SEXUAL ABUSE IMAGES

Many scholars and policymakers prefer to use the term **child sexual abuse images**, or CSAIs instead of child pornography. In other words, the images and videos are pornographic depictions of abuse, not pornographic depictions of sexual activity. Using the term CSAIs shifts the focus from the consumer of the images to the actual victims—children. The United States Department of Justice recognizes this fact:

> Experts and victims agree that victims depicted in child pornography often suffer a lifetime of re-victimization by knowing the images of their sexual abuse are on the Internet forever. The children exploited in these images must live with the permanency, longevity, and circulation of such a record of their sexual victimization. This often creates lasting psychological damage to the child, including disruptions in sexual development, self-image, and developing trusting relationships with others in the future.
>
> (www.justice.gov/criminal-ceos/child-pornography)

Although the utility of using the term CSAI is acknowledged, this textbook uses child pornography because it is still the term used most often by citizens, policy-makers, and law enforcement in an American context.

THE AMOUNT OF CHILD PORNOGRAPHY IN THE DIGITAL ENVIRONMENT

It is difficult to know how much child pornography is present in the digital environment. Most of the images of children are encrypted or shared on darknets like Tor and Freenet (see Figure 3.1).

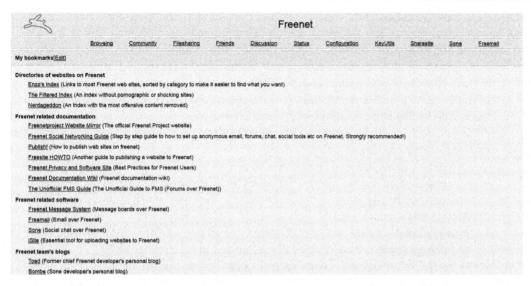

Figure 3.1   Freenet is an anonymous peer-to-peer network—a "darknet." Most content on darknet technologies like Freenet are not pornographic. However, the anonymizing abilities of darknet technologies make them a prime tool for people wishing to consume and distribute child pornography. Below is a screenshot from the home page of Freenet. Pornography is so prevalent on Freenet that indexes are constructed that filter out offensive content.

Despite these difficulties, researchers who have explored darknets have found a high prevalence of child pornography (Jardine, 2016; Owen & Savage, 2015). In one study exploring a year's worth of child pornography sharing on a peer-to-peer network, researchers found that on an average day, 122,687 known child pornography files were shared (Wolak, Liberatore, & Levine, 2014).

PROFILING CHILD PORNOGRAPHY OFFENDERS

According to Houtepen and colleagues (2014), some broad characteristics of child pornography offenders (CPOs) can be identified. They are primarily white, between the ages of 25 and 50 years, and compared to child sexual abusers, more likely to be employed. They have above average intelligence, and 30% of known CPOs have completed some form of higher education. They often have jobs that either require little to no social interaction or where they have daily contact with children. CPOs are less likely to be employed in jobs requiring consistent interaction with adults, such as college professor, police officer, or bank manager.

One assumption about CPOs is that their consumption of images is either a temporary substitute or a gateway to child contact—the consumption of images will inevitably lead to actual child abuse. Indeed, a study done in 2007 showed that at least 80% of CPOs are active child molesters (Schell, Martin, Hung, & Rueda, 2007).

However, some recent research has questioned this tight link between the consumption of images and child contact. Henshaw, Ogloff, and Clough (2017) write that a large percentage of

CPOs do not move to actual child contact, are not deviant or criminal in other ways, and as a result have a rather normal life. Merdian, Curtis, Thakker, Wilson, and Boer (2013) argue that there are three dimensions to online child pornography offending:

1. *Fantasy-driven versus contact-driven.* CPOs that were fantasy-driven had a wide array of motivations for consuming child pornography. CPOs who were contact-driven were those who had had an encounter with a child in the past.
2. *Different motivations for fantasy-driven CPO.* There are several motivations for CPOs who were driven by fantasy:
   - Pedophilic motivation—These CPOs have a sexual interest in children
   - General deviant sexual interest—These CPOs are sexually deviant in general, and are not specifically interested in children (e.g. they may also be interested in bestiality, sadomasochism, etc.)
   - Financial motivation—These CPOs are interested in profiting from the sale of child pornography and are not necessarily interested in children sexually
   - Other—CPOs can have a wide range of motivations that are not easily categorized. Some are simply collectors of pornography, and others simply wish to defy the legal codes against consuming child pornography
3. *Low or high networking.* Some CPOs consume child pornography in isolation, while others consume child pornography in a social context that reinforces their behavior. Low-networking CPOs tend to consume smaller amounts of child pornography, and are not linked to other forms of deviance or child contact. However, high-networking CPOs are more serious offenders. High-networking CPOs are often involved in online victim grooming.

Research providing evidence of several types of CPOs allows society to move away from the common stereotypes seen in the media. CPOs on fictionalized crime shows such as *Law and Order* or *Luther* are often depicted as maladjusted, awkward, or otherwise "creepy" individuals who have uncontrollable desires for child sexual contact. Research shows that this is only a small percentage of the population. As a result, law enforcement and policy-makers will need to adjust their investigations and their policies to this reality. For example, because the link between the consumption of images and actual child contact is not as clear as once imagined, it may be necessary to treat individuals who have only ever consumed images differently than those who have had actual contact. There may be preventative or therapeutic measures available for offenders of the first type that may prevent them from graduating to more serious contact-related offenses.

Sexting

DEFINING SEXTING

Sexting in the broadest sense is the sharing of sexually explicit material. The archetypal example of sexting is two people in a current or future sexual relationship sharing sexual images of each other via text messages on their mobile phone (i.e. "sext"). There are numerous variations that are also considered sexting. Sexting does not need to be done by mobile phone. The material can be shared via email or instant message. It is the sharing that matters. Moreover, sexting does not have to be only the sharing of images. Sharing words, video, and audio of a sexual nature are also considered forms of sexting. Finally, it does not need to be the sharing of personal material. If an image of a third party is shared with a confidant, this may also be considered sexting. In this last scenario, charges of **revenge porn** may also be brought if the third party did not agree to the sharing.

When exploring the phenomenon of sexting, a question can be asked: Who is the actual sexter? Consider an exchange where one person asks another to send them a sexually explicit image. The image is then sent and opened. Who, then, is the sexter? Is it the transmitter of the image, the receiver, or both? This matters in an academic sense, because how sexting is defined determines its rate of prevalence. In a review of sexting literature, Barrense-Dias, Berchtold, Surís, and Akre (2017) report that prevalence ranged from 7.1% to 60% for passive sexting—those who ask for and receive sexts, and 2.5% to 27.6% for active sexting—those who send sexts. Also, it may determine how a sexter is profiled. Active sexters may be different demographically and psychologically than passive sexters.

WHO SEXTS?

Research has identified demographic trends associated with sexting. Young people, as one would expect, are more likely to both send and receive text messages of a sexual nature. There are gender differences in sexting. Klettke, Hallford, and Mellor (2014) found that girls send more sexually explicit texts than boys. They suggest that this may be because females perceive pressure to send texts of a sexual nature.

In a study of Canadian and American cell phone users, Galovan, Drouin, and McDaniel (2018) showed that sexters can be divided into four groups distinguished by who sends, who receives, and whether it is words, pictures, or both. Non-sexters were 71.5%, or about a quarter of those surveyed. This group did not send words or pictures. About 14.5% were word-only sexters. This group sent word only sexts a few times a week, but rarely sent pictures. A third group, labeled frequent sexters (8.5%), sent and received both texts and images a few times a week. A fourth group was labeled "hyper sexters." Hyper sexters were 5.5% of the sample, and reported that they sent and received sexually explicit text messages and pictures every day.

CHALLENGES IN ADDRESSING SEXTING

On the one hand, sexting can be seen as a harmless activity between two people who wish to share intimate details of their lives. On the other hand, scholars have identified some negative consequences to sexting. Klettke and colleagues (2014) argue,

A clear finding that emerged was that sexting is associated with a higher likelihood of being sexually active, as well as engagement in a range of sexual risk behaviours, such as having unprotected sex and consuming alcohol and drugs prior to sexual activity.

In other words, sexting may be an indicator of other deviant behaviors. There may also be mental health problems associated with sexting, as research has linked sexting to depression (Van Ouytsel et al., 2017) and contemplating suicide (Dake, Price, Maziarz, & Ward, 2012). Therefore, although some may see sexting as a relatively harmless activity, its presence may be a sign of more serious issues.

A second challenge with addressing sexting is that it can be illegal and in some localities prosecuted as the distribution of child pornography. This is because the images shared in sexting fit the strict legal definition of child pornography—a sexual image of a minor. Therefore, possession and distribution is illegal. Traditionally, there has been no exception for who has taken or distributed the image. For example, a 17-year-old boy in Washington State was convicted of child pornography charges for sending an image of his penis to an adult woman.[3] A question can be asked: What if the image is of an adult? In those cases, where both sender and receiver are adults, there is no crime. However, if the image is of an adult and it was sent to a minor, then the adult can be charged in most states with committing a lewd act towards a minor.

Some legal scholars and child advocates argue that an application of child pornography law in this manner is not in the spirit it was intended. Child pornography laws, they argue, were meant to protect children and not prosecute them. Some states recognize the misapplication of child pornography to cases of sexting and have created specific statutes dealing with sexting. As of 2013, 23 states had passed statutes that address sexting more appropriate to the offense (Spooner & Vaughn, 2016). In cases where new sext-specific laws were not passed, several states have reduced sexting among minors from a felony to a misdemeanor. In other states, sexting is penalized with community and counseling.

Sex Work

SEX WORK IN THE DIGITAL ENVIRONMENT

In the physical environment, distinctions are often made between different types of sex work and the spaces in which this work happens. Sex work in the physical environment is stratified by how much freedom the sex worker has and how much money they make from their labor. Street prostitutes occupy the bottom strata. They tend to work in urban or low-income areas and exhibit less control over their time of work and the amount of money gained from their services. They are also more likely to be physically abused. Workers in massage parlors have some discretion over the clients they service, work in safer environments, and garner a larger percentage of the money from their services. Escorts are the most privileged sex workers and occupy the top stratum. They exercise the greatest amount of freedom and control in when and where they perform their services, and usually receive more compensation for their services.

Scholars of sex work in the digital environment also appreciate the complex ways in which sexual services are bought and sold. The digital environment is used as a way of facilitating connections between clients and workers, after which sex happens in offline environments. It is also used to sell digitized sexual services in the form of videos and live shows. Another way in which sex work is facilitated in the digital environment is through the advertising of services and the reviewing of services rendered by clients. Cunningham and colleagues (2017) have produced a typology of the varied ways in which sex work occurs in the digital environment (Table 3.2).

Table 3.2 identifies a multitude of spaces within the digital environment where sexual services are produced, displayed, bought, and reviewed. These spaces complicate our understanding of cyberpornography and sex work. Consider the forums where sex workers who, presumably

Table 3.2   Typology of Sex Work Spaces in the Digital Environment

Escort directories	Websites that allow sex workers who offer in-person direct sex work to create profiles to advertise their services.
Webcam platforms	Sites dedicated to the facilitation of webcam shows that provide an interface between the webcam models and the customers.
Multi-service adult entertainment platforms	Websites that offer a range of different services within the one site including providing advertising for escorts, webcam shows, and instant message.
Dating and hook-up platforms with commercial advertising	Websites/applications that facilitate connection between people for personal relationships and unpaid sexual encounters but some have commercial advertising space where sex workers can advertise their services.
Dating and hook-up platforms without commercial advertising	Websites/applications that facilitate connection between people for personal relationships and unpaid sexual encounters but prohibiting advertising for paid sex.
Customer review forums	Spaces where customers post messages about their experiences of buying sexual services including reviews of individual sex workers. They are also a marketing space for sex workers.
Agency websites	Websites run by third party agencies who act as intermediaries between sex workers who provide direct in-person services and their clients. The agencies are responsible for the running of the websites, which are used to advertise different sex workers working for the agency.
Individual sex worker websites	Websites used to market individual sex workers who work independently, created and managed by sex workers or by web designers/IT specialists on their behalf.
Classified websites	Advertising spaces/forums that allow individuals to post user-generated advertisements for a range of goods and services. Some classified sites permit sex work advertising and have dedicated and separate space for these while others prohibit it altogether.
Social media platforms	Sex workers engage with social media (for marketing, networking, and peer support) in a range of ways and to varying degrees.
Sex worker forums	Sex worker-led spaces where sex workers can network, get information and advice, and peer support.
Content delivery platforms	Dedicated platforms that host and sell user-generated adult content online.

(Modified from Cunningham et al., 2017.)

on a voluntary basis, congregate and share information. This is not an instance that can easily be labeled as exploitative. Moreover, the digital environment presents more options for sexual interactions. The actions skirt the boundaries between criminality, deviance, and legal behavior. Consider Chaturbate, which is described by Cover as:

> an online site which allows people to narrowcast webcams from private home or work-places to a broad, international audience. It operates … by serving at the interface between online dating, exhibitionist camming, real-time textual chat, and making recorded videos and images available, sometimes for a fee.
>
> (2015, 162)

Webcam modeling or "camming" is not illegal and is considered legal pornography, even if the modeling is done for a fee. The same acts done in the physical environment—a sex worker meeting a client in a hotel and performing sexual exhibitions—may be considered prostitution.

Internet Facilitated Sex Trafficking

UNDERSTANDING SEX TRAFFICKING

Sex trafficking is the buying, selling, and sexual exploitation of people. This requires varying levels of coercion and threats of physical violence. Although the digital environment is not the primary space of exploitation, traffickers use the digital environment as a way of facilitating the crime.

The phenomenon of human trafficking—which includes trafficking for sex—can be organized into three elements: the act, the means, and the purpose (see Figure 3.2):

1. The first element is the act: recruiting, transporting, transferring (moving from one mode of transport to another), harboring, or receiving a victim of human trafficking. These are acts that are necessary for global sex trafficking and can be performed by different actors in a trafficking organization.
2. To commit these criminal acts, traffickers use threats of force, deception, and money—the second element of human trafficking.
3. The third element is the ultimate purpose of the trafficking enterprise. This includes most notably prostitution or other forms of sexual exploitation. However, trafficking can also be for other purposes such as slavery and removal of organs.

SEX TRAFFICKING AND TECHNOLOGY

For this chapter, we are interested in human trafficking for the purposes of prostitution and other acts of sexual exploitation, and how the digital environment facilitates the act and provides

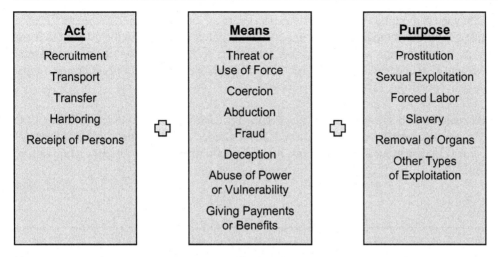

Figure 3.2 The three dimensions of human trafficking.

the means for that purpose. For the act of trafficking, the digital environment makes it easier to recruit victims. Victims can be found online and groomed. Traffickers can coordinate their activities amongst themselves across wide distances using mobile phones, making it easier to transfer, transport, and harbor victims. For the means of trafficking, the digital environment makes it easier to communicate with a victim through space and time. A trafficker can more easily and more often make threats, coerce, and deceive. With the growing use of cryptocurrencies such as bitcoin, it may be easier for traffickers to send and receive payments without risk of being detected by law enforcement.

Another way in which the digital environment facilitates sex trafficking is by hiding it from mainstream society. As Leary (2014) argues, "The migration of sex trafficking to a digital space can both make the crime more public, but also remove it from places where it has been traditionally recognized and identified." Traffickers can recruit victims and coordinate their activities within relatively secure spaces. Prior to the growth of the Internet, traffickers would have needed to venture into spaces which children or young women frequented, such as schools, parks, shopping malls, etc. Now, traffickers can enter online spaces anonymously and entice victims with promises of money and travel.

Arizona State University's Office of Sex Trafficking Intervention Research (STIR)[4] conducted a study exploring sex trafficking in the United States from 2010 to 2015. The study reported that instances of sex trafficking increased from 97 in 2010 to 360 in 2015. Importantly, 67.3% of the cases used some form of digital technology. Most notably, in 592 cases over that time span the website Backpage.com was used at some point in the process.

In a study of court cases from 2001 to 2011 by Mary GrawLeary (2014), technology played some role in approximately 78% of all cases. Leary argues that technology is most prevalent in the recruitment of victims and the connecting of purchasers and victims. Leary's research also highlights the response of law enforcement. Local and federal police units have moved their operations into the digital environment. Law enforcement set up investigations online to identify offenders. They surveil digital spaces where traffickers meet victims. They, like the traffickers, take advantage of online anonymity. They impersonate a potential victim in the attempt to learn the identity of the traffickers and impersonate traffickers to learn the identity of purchasers. Law enforcement also undertakes undercover sting operations conducted entirely online. Leary argues that these operations have met with success:

> it would seem that an aggressive and successful approach to intervention in child sex trafficking cases necessarily includes utilizing technologies such as false online advertisements, false child sex tourism companies, or posing as fictitious offenders in certain online communities.
>
> (2014, 289)

Conclusion

The cybercrimes discussed in this chapter run the gamut from those that society takes somewhat lightly like consuming pornography that violates "community standards," to those that society punishes harshly in the case of possessing child pornography or sex trafficking. There are also types of cyberpornography, such as sexting and web cam modeling, that are questionable in their criminality. Scholars and lawmakers disagree as to if and to what degree they should be punished. For these reasons, cyberpornography is a category of cybercrime heavily dependent on social context. As such, we can expect rapid changes in how we define, discuss, legislate, and educate people on cyberpornography in the future.

Vocabulary

1. **Child Pornography**—The visual depiction of sexually explicit conduct involving a minor.
2. **Child Sex Abuse Images**—An alternative term used to describe child pornography. This term is gaining wide acceptance because it places the emphasis on abuse and deemphasizes the sexual nature of child pornography.
3. **Internet Facilitated Sex Trafficking**—The recruitment, harboring, transportation, provision, obtaining, patronizing, or soliciting of a person for the purpose of a commercial sex act.
4. **Obscene Pornography**—Sexually explicit material that is labeled as filthy within a given cultural context.
5. **Rape Myths**—General false attitudes and beliefs that serve to deny and justify male sexual aggression against women.
6. **Revenge Porn**—The sharing of sexually explicit images of a former intimate partner without their knowledge or authorization.
7. **Sexting**—The transmission of sexually explicit material.
8. **Sex Work**—The exchange of sexual services for money or goods.

Study Questions

TRUE/FALSE

1. Some states have created statutes that distinguish sexting from child pornography.
   a. True
   b. False
2. Camming is a form of prostitution.
   a. True
   b. False
3. The Miller Test is easier to apply in the digital environment than the physical environment.
   a. True
   b. False
4. Some child pornography offenders have no interest in children sexually.
   a. True
   b. False
5. Pornography is shared on darknets like Tor.
   a. True
   b. False
6. Criminal cases in which the pornography is produced and consumed are rare and involve extreme sexual acts or exploitation of children.
   a. True
   b. False
7. Most pornography is illegal in the United States because of the free-speech protections afforded by the US Constitution.
   a. True
   b. False
8. According to Packard's distinction, indecency refers to explicit depictions of actual sexual conduct, masturbation, violent sexual abuse, and child pornography.
   a. True
   b. False
9. Scholars agree that pornographic consumption is an addiction.
   a. True
   b. False
10. Scholars who argue that pornography consumption qualifies as an addiction argue that repeated consumption of pornography alters brain functioning to the point in which the behavior becomes an addiction.
    a. True
    b. False
11. Internet pornography is consumed equally by men and women.
    a. True
    b. False

12. Some materials online can be pornographic and indecent, but not illegal by United States free-speech precedents.
    a. True
    b. False

MULTIPLE CHOICE

13. _____ can be understood as recorded sexual performances; thus, it falls within the same category as other recorded performances such as movies, television shows, and public lectures.
    a. Obscenity
    b. Indecency
    c. Pornography
    d. None of the above
14. Each of the following are theorized to be an effect of pornography consumption EXCEPT:
    a. Men are more likely to abuse drugs
    b. Men are more likely to reduce women to sexual objects
    c. Men are more likely to be sexually callous towards women
    d. Men are more likely to accept rape myths
15. The term CSAI refers to:
    a. Child support and investigation
    b. Child sexual abuse images
    c. Central support advocacy initiative
    d. Child sexual advocacy investigations
16. Broadly speaking, child pornography offenders online tend to be:
    a. White
    b. Above average in intellect
    c. Employed
    d. All of the above
17. In a recent court case, a photographer's website is deemed to violate _____ laws given the amount of photos that depict sexual conduct in a clearly offensive way and as specifically defined by applicable law.
    a. pornography
    b. indecency
    c. spoofing
    d. obscenity
18. How does the Internet facilitate sex trafficking?
    a. Deceiving victims
    b. Recruiting victims
    c. Finding customers
    d. All of the above

19. _____ are (is) attitudes and beliefs that are generally false but are widely and persistently held, and that serve to deny and justify male sexual aggression against women.
    a. Rape myths
    b. Sexual coercion
    c. Cyberdeception
    d. Cyberpornography
20. Unintended outcomes from sexual activity such as teen pregnancy and acquiring a sexually transmitted disease are posited by scholars to _____ with the viewing of pornography.
    a. increase
    b. decrease
    c. not be affected
21. Most child pornography offenders are _____.
    a. teenage men
    b. teenage women
    c. adult men
    d. adult women
22. Research done on child pornography offenders suggest that many offenders are motivated by _____.
    a. making money
    b. making a political statement
    c. developing a new application for pornography consumption
    d. all of the above
23. How do cryptocurrencies impact human trafficking?
    a. They make it easier for law enforcement to track the flow of money
    b. They make it easier for traffickers to send and receive money without being tracked
    c. They have no impact on human trafficking
24. Most pornography is protected under free speech. What is one reason for this?
    a. Pornography is protected by the CFAA
    b. Pornography can be understood as art
    c. Government cannot regulate the cultural products of a business
    d. Government cannot regulate expressions of sexuality
25. Child pornography offenders tend to be of _____ intelligence.
    a. above average
    b. average
    c. below average

Critical Thinking Exercise

In this chapter, the discussion of indecency versus obscenity is prominent. For each of the following materials that might appear on the Internet or otherwise be distributed digitally, offer an explanation of whether the act described is indecent or obscene and why:

- A person simulating a sex act using a stuffed animal as a prop
- A demonstration of a ballet performance where the dancers are partially nude
- Two people engaging in a sex act while wearing animal costumes
- Distributing a mass email among your friends that depicts cartoon images engaging in a sexual act

Former Supreme Court Justice Potter Stewart famously once said concerning obscenity, "I shall not today attempt further to define the kinds of material I understand to be embraced ... *but I know it when I see it* ..."

- With respect to the material discussed in this chapter, what do you suppose Justice Stewart meant by this statement?
- What do you think the criminal justice system's role is in defining indecency versus obscenity?
- How might Justice Stewart's statement be adapted to cyberpornography?

NOTES

1   www.law.cornell.edu/uscode/text/22/7102
2   www.webroot.com/us/en/home/resources/tips/digital-family-life/internet-pornography-by-the-numbers
3   www.independent.co.uk/news/world/americas/17-year-old-child-pornography-share-penis-picture-woman-eric-gray-washington-state-supreme-court-a7948866.html
4   socialwork.asu.edu/stir

REFERENCES

Barrense-Dias, Y., Berchtold, A., Surís, J.-C., & Akre, C.(2017). Sexting and the definition issue.*Journal of Adolescent Health, 61*(5), 544–554. doi:10.1016/j.jadohealth.2017.05.009

Conrad, P. (2007). *The medicalization of society: On the transformation of human conditions into treatable disorders.* Baltimore, MD: Johns Hopkins University Press.

Cover, R. (2015). Visual heteromasculinities online: Beyond binaries and sexual normativities in camera chat forums. *Men and Masculinities, 18*(2), 159–175. doi:10.1177/1097184X15584909

Cunningham, S., Sanders, T., Scoular, J., Campbell, R., Pitcher, J., Hill, K., ... Hamer, R. (2017). Behind the screen: Commercial sex, digital spaces and working online. *Technology in Society, 53,* 47–54. doi:10.1016/j.techsoc.2017.11.004

Dake, J. A., Price, J. H., Maziarz, L., & Ward, B.(2012). Prevalence and correlates of sexting behavior in adolescents.*American Journal of Sexuality Education, 7*(1), 1–15. doi:10.1080/15546128.2012.650959

Galovan, A. M., Drouin, M., & McDaniel, B. T. (2018). Sexting profiles in the United States and Canada: Implications for individual and relationship well-being. *Computers in Human Behavior, 79,* 19–29. doi:10.1016/j.chb.2017.10.017

Gorman, S., Monk-Turner, E., & Fish, J. N. (2010). Free adult internet web sites: How prevalent are degrading acts?*Gender Issues, 27*(3–4), 131–145. doi:10.1007/s12147-010-9095-7

Grubbs, J. B., Wilt, J. A., Exline, J. J., Pargament, K. I., & Kraus, S. W. (2018). Moral disapproval and perceived addiction to internet pornography: A longitudinal examination: Moral disapproval and perceived addiction. *Addiction, 113*(3), 496–506. doi:10.1111/add.14007

Henshaw, M., Ogloff, J. R., & Clough, J. A. (2017). Looking beyond the screen: A critical review of the literature on the online child pornography offender. *Sexual Abuse, 29*(5), 416–445.

Houtepen, J. A. B. M., Sijtsema, J. J., & Bogaerts, S. (2014). From child pornography offending to child sexual abuse: A review of child pornography offender characteristics and risks for cross-over. *Aggression and Violent Behavior, 19*(5), 466–473. https://doi.org/10.1016/j.avb.2014.07.011

Huesmann, L. R.(1986). Psychological processes promoting the relation between exposure to media violence and aggressive behavior by the viewer.*Journal of Social Issues, 42*(3), 125–139. doi:10.1111/j.1540-4560.1986.tb00246.x

Jardine, E. (2016). Tor, what is it good for? Political repression and the use of online anonymity-granting technologies.*New Media & Society, 20*(2), 435–452.

Klaassen, M. J. E., & Peter, J. (2015). Gender (In)equality in internet pornography: A content analysis of popular pornographic internet videos. *The Journal of Sex Research, 52*(7), 721–735. doi:10.1080/00224499.2014.976781

Klettke, B., Hallford, D. J., & Mellor, D. J. (2014). Sexting prevalence and correlates: A systematic literature review. *Clinical Psychology Review, 34*(1), 44–53. doi:10.1016/j.cpr.2013.10.007

Leary, M. G. (2014). Fighting fire with fire: Technology in child sex trafficking. *Duke Journal of Gender Law & Policy, 21*(2), 289–323.

Ley, D., Prause, N., & Finn, P. (2014). The emperor has no clothes: A review of the 'pornography addiction' model. *Current Sexual Health Reports, 6*(2), 94–105. doi:10.1007/s11930-014-0016-8

Ley, D. J. (2012). *The myth of sex addiction.* Lanham, MD: Rowman & Littlefield Publihsers, Inc.

Lonsway, K. A., & Fitzgerald, L. F.(1994). Rape myths. *Psychology of Women Quarterly, 18*(2), 133–164.

Love, T., Laier, C., Brand, M., Hatch, L., & Hajela, R. (2015). Neuroscience of internet pornography addiction: A review and update. *Behavioral Sciences, 5*(4), 388–433. doi:10.3390/bs5030388

Merdian, H. L., Curtis, C., Thakker, J., Wilson, N., & Boer, D. P. (2013). The three dimensions of online child pornography offending. *Journal of Sexual Aggression, 19*(1), 121–132. doi:10.1080/13552600.2011.611898

Owen, G., & Savage, N. (2015). *The Tor Dark Net* (Global Commission on Internet Governance Paper Series No. 20). Retrieved from https://www.cigionline.org/sites/default/files/no20_0.pdf

Packard, A. (2013). *Digital media law* (2nd ed.). Malden, MA: Wiley-Blackwell.

Schell, B. H., Martin, M. V., Hung, P. C. K., & Rueda, L. (2007). Cyber child pornography: A review paper of the social and legal issues and remedies—and a proposed technological solution. *Aggression and Violent Behavior, 12*(1), 45–63. doi:10.1016/j.avb.2006.03.003

Spooner, K., & Vaughn, M. (2016). Youth sexting: A legislative and constitutional analysis.*Journal of School Violence, 15*(2), 213–233. doi:10.1080/15388220.2014.974245

Sun, C., Bridges, A., Johnson, J. A., & Ezzell, M. B. (2016). Pornography and the male sexual script: An analysis of consumption and sexual relations. *Archives of Sexual Behavior, 45*(4), 983–994. doi:10.1007/s10508-014-0391-2

VanOuytsel, J., Torres, E., Choi, H. J., Ponnet, K., Walrave, M., & Temple, J. R. (2017). The associations between substance use, sexual behaviors, bullying, deviant behaviors, health, and cyber dating abuse perpetration. *The Journal of School Nursing, 33*(2), 116–122. doi:10.1177/1059840516683229

Vannier, S. A., Currie, A. B., & O'Sullivan, L. F. (2014). Schoolgirls and soccer moms: A content analysis of free "teen" and "MILF" online pornography. *The Journal of Sex Research, 51*(3), 253–264. doi:10.1080/00224499.2013.829795

Voros, F.(2009). L'invention de l'addiction à la pornographie.*Sexologies, 18*(4), 270–276. doi:10.1016/j.sexol.2009.09.008

Wall, D. (Ed.). (2001). *Crime and the internet.* New York: Routledge.

Williams, D. J. (2017). The framing of frequent sexual behavior and/or pornography viewing as addiction: Some concerns for social work. *Journal of Social Work*, 17(5), 616–623. doi:10.1177/1468017316644701

Wilson, G. (2015). *Your brain on porn: Internet pornography and the emerging science of addiction.* Margate, UK: Commonwealth Publishing.

Wolak, J., Liberatore, M., & Levine, B. N. (2014). Measuring a year of child pornography trafficking by U.S. computers on a peer-to-peer network. *Child Abuse & Neglect*, 38(2), 347–356. doi:10.1016/j.chiabu.2013.10.018

Wright, P. J., & Randall, A. K.(2012). Internet pornography exposure and risky sexual behavior among adult males in the United States.*Computers in Human Behavior*, 28(4), 1410–1416. doi:10.1016/j.chb.2012.03.003

Chapter 4

Cyberviolence

Introduction

Violent crime can be understood as crime in which a perpetrator harms or threatens to harm someone with physical force. The Federal Bureau of Investigation has historically identified and kept records of four types of violent crimes—murder and nonnegligent manslaughter, forcible rape, robbery, and aggravated assault. Other types of violent crimes include kidnapping, torture, harassment, and extortion.

What links these more well-understood types of violence to violence in the digital environment (i.e. cyberviolence) is the harm caused. People can be hurt by the content produced and distributed in the digital environment. Wall defines cyberviolence as:

> the violent impact of the cyberactivities of another upon an individual or social grouping. Whilst such activities do not have to have a direct physical manifestation, the victim nevertheless feels the violence of the act and can bear long-term psychological scars as a consequence.

> (1998)

We add to this definition by suggesting that cyberviolence can not only have long-term psychological scars, but also sociological ones. Cyberviolence is a category of cybercrimes in which it is common for entire groups of people to be victimized. Through hate speech, for example, women, minorities, or individuals belonging to alternative lifestyles can be demonized and demeaned with long-term consequences for how they are viewed in society. Or, through social shaming people with unpopular views can be demeaned to the point where they lose their jobs, relationships, and maybe take their life. In this chapter we will explore several forms of cyberviolence, including cyberbullying, cyberstalking, trolling, flaming, and hate speech.

Comparing Violence in the Physical Environment with Cyberviolence

There are several similarities between physical violent crime and cyberviolence. First, and most importantly, someone is hurt in both environments. Because the hurt in the digital environment is not physical does not mean that the damage is less. The argument can be made that because some acts of cyberviolence lead to lifelong psychological problems and even suicide, symbolic violence can be equally or *more* damaging than physical violence.

Consider the events surrounding the suicide of Brandy Vela. Vela was an 18-year-old high school student living in Texas. On the morning of November 29, 2016, she sent an email to her family saying that she was going to kill herself. Family members rushed home and saw her leaning against the wall with a gun to her chest. They could not convince her to put the gun down, and Brandy committed suicide. She had been receiving text messages from an untraceable cell phone saying hurtful things. Fake Facebook pages had been set up, using her photo, saying that she would "offer sex for free." In 2017, a former boyfriend and his current girlfriend were arrested and charged in association with Brandy's death.

A second similarity is that the violence committed in both environments is often powered by emotions. Domestic violence—someone battering their spouse—is often a spontaneous reaction of anger. Although movies and television dramas depict sexual assaults as premeditated acts coming from strangers, most sexual assaults are committed by an angered acquaintance of the victim attempting to assert dominance. The perpetrator believes they are entitled to sexual activity and react negatively when permission is not granted. Emotion also underpins acts of cyberviolence. As we will discuss below, flaming, trolling, hate speech, and cyberbullying are primarily ways of an individual or group lashing out against another individual or group.

Although there are similarities, there are also differences. One difference is the means by which harm is caused. The means by which violence is committed in the physical environment is primarily through one's own body or by some weapon that acts as an extension of the body. When someone physically attacks another person (assault) they are using their body to inflict harm.[1]

Even when there is no actual assault, but instead the fear of assault, the logic is that there is a credible threat from the perpetrator. The tools used in the commission of assault—weapons like handguns and knives—are extensions of the body. By contrast, the means by which cyberviolence is committed is through the mind, and the tools are the affordances (or design features) of technologies in the digital environment. These technologies are primarily found in the application layer, as these are the technologies used to produce content. Recall in Chapter 1 that cybercrime is often a product of people finding novel ways to use technologies. The same affordances of a platform like Twitter that allow people to congratulate others, can also be used to demean them.

All individuals can commit physical harm to another person. However, not everyone has equal ability or predisposition to do so. A small boy with a water pistol is not a credible threat of violence. They do not have the physical presence (they are a small child) or the weapons (a water pistol) to commit harm. However, as that child grows into a young man his physical presence alone will likely make him threatening to others who are smaller and weaker. Moreover, he will have the means to buy and use weapons. Additionally, he may have higher levels of testosterone than older males and females, making him more impulsive and willing to use physical force. It is these reasons—along with social conditions such as poverty and challenging home circumstances—that make young men the primary candidates for committing physical violence.

Similarly, all individuals can commit cyberviolence to some degree; however, everyone is not equally likely to have the means or predisposition to do so. Cyberviolence requires a facility with symbolic communication. Constructing a particularly biting post or reply on Facebook, a clever tweet, or finding an appropriate meme requires some level of social awareness and linguistic ability. Understanding the nuances of a software platform to the degree that your attacks can be more effective requires a degree of interest in the technology that others may not have.

Therefore, a second difference between physical violence and cyberviolence is likely the type of perpetrator. One area of focus from scholars has been gender differences. There is some evidence that girls are more likely to be both the perpetrators and victims of cyberbullying—one form of cyberviolence (Peterson & Densley, 2017). However, scholars are still gathering research on the causes of cyberviolence and what type of person is most likely to use the digital environment to harm others. Given the different means used, future research may show that the modal perpetrator of cyberviolence will be different than the modal perpetrator of physical violence.

Types of Cyberviolence

Violent crimes can be organized by who is the perpetrator and who is the victim. The violent crime of rape, for example, can be understood as an individual perpetrator committing an act of sexual violence towards an individual victim. Meanwhile, acts of terrorism are often individuals committing indiscriminate acts of violence against a group (nation, religious group, racial group, etc.). The violence associated with gang warfare can be understood as groups committing acts of physical violence against other groups. We use this way of thinking in order to organize the types of cyberviolence. In Table 4.1 we compare physical violence to cyberviolence, organizing type of crime by perpetrator and victim.

In this chapter we will focus on six types of cyberviolence:

- **Cyberbullying**—Tokunaga (2010) defines cyberbullying as "any behavior performed through electronic or digital media by individuals or groups that repeatedly communicates hostile or aggressive messages intended to inflict harm or discomfort on others" (278). Other definitions also include a power dimension, as attempts at cyberbullying are most harmful when committed by a person or group in a position of power over someone else. There have been numerous high-profile suicides that have been directly or indirectly caused by cyberbullying. There have also been several movies and television shows that dramatize cyberbullying. As a result, cyberbullying may be the most readily identified form of cyberviolence.

Table 4.1 Classification Scheme for Types of Violent Crimes

Perpetrator	Victim	Physical Violence	Cyberviolence
Individual	Individual	Homicide Battery Domestic violence Child abuse	Cyberbullying Cyberstalking Flaming Trolling
Group	Individual	Gang violence Hate crimes	Online shaming
Individual	Group	Terrorism	Trolling Hate speech
Group	Group	Warfare	Cyberwar

- **Flaming**—Flaming can be defined as the uninhibited expression of hostility, insults, and ridicule (Kayany, 1998). Flaming often occurs in spaces where controversial issues are being presented. Actions of flaming do not usually rise to the level of crime but are a form of cyberdeviance, where the flamer is usually crossing boundaries of expected behavior.
- **Trolling**—Trolling can be described as the act of generating conflict online, often for a meaningless prank. Another common definition of trolling is the practice of following someone on social media without interacting with them, but this action may be best described as a mild form of cyberstalking. Buckels, Trapnell, and Paulhus (2014) write,

  > trolls share many characteristics of the classic Joker villain: a modern variant of the Trickster archetype from ancient folklore … Much like the Joker, trolls operate as agents of chaos on the Internet, exploiting 'hot-button issues' to make users appear overly emotional or foolish in some manner.

  Like flaming, trolling is a type of cyberdeviance. What distinguishes trolling from flaming is that flaming is more spontaneous and powered by immediate emotions, while many trolls focus on the long-term impact of generating conflict.
- **Hate Speech**—Hate speech can be defined according to three elements (Matsuda, 1989): (1) the speech implies or states that the target group is inferior (racial, ethnic, sexual), (2) the speech is aimed at a group that has been historically oppressed or disadvantaged, and (3) the speech is intended to be harmful. Hate speech is usually aimed at a group—most often a racial or sexual minority. In the United States, speech depicting groups as inferior is generally protected under free speech laws, however there are strong social norms against the practice.
- **Cyberstalking**—Reyns, Henson, and Fisher (2011) define cyberstalking as "the repeated pursuit of an individual using electronic or Internet-capable devices" (1). If the cyberstalking consists of reading and commenting on a victim's Instagram posts and sending them unwanted emails, one could argue that these transgressions are somewhat minor and at any rate the perpetrator can be blocked. However, it is not the act itself, *but the*

fear and anxiety associated with the act that matters. In other words, if a person knows that someone is stalking them, this in itself is harmful even if the erstwhile stalker is ineffective. As such, cyberstalking can cause wide-ranging harm to the victim—they could be distracted and unable to concentrate at school or work or their stress levels may rise leading to additional health complications.

- **Online Shaming**—Online shaming refers to a group subjecting an individual to harassment, bullying, and condemnation because of some real or perceived transgression. Like trolling, flaming, and hate speech, online shaming is generally not considered a crime, although the pain and hurt caused by being shamed online can be significant.

Cyberbullying

The Center for Disease Control and Prevention's (CDC) 2013 Youth Risk Behavior Survey reported that at least 21% of girls and 8% of boys admitted to being bullied through electronic means, such as texting, email, instant messaging, and websites (David-Ferdon & Hertz, 2009). These rates can vary depending upon how cyberbullying is measured, however most definitions of cyberbullying include four components: (1) a repeated behavior, (2) the behavior is in the digital environment, (3) a power differential between offender and victim, and (4) the behavior is meant to harm. Tokunaga (2010) uses three of these components and defines cyberbullying as "any behavior performed through electronic or digital media by individuals or groups that repeatedly communicates hostile or aggressive messages intended to inflict harm or discomfort on others" (278).

There are differences between cyberbullying and traditional, physical bullying. First are the already-discussed differences in means of producing harm—physical versus symbolic. Another difference is that cyberbullying is less prevalent than traditional bullying. Ybarra, Boyd, Korchmaros, and Oppenheim (2012), in a study of American youth between the ages of 6 and 17, report that "Despite the rapid uptake of technologies, 'traditional' face-to-face communication still is the dominant mode of bullying." Dan Olweus, a major figure in the study of traditional bullying, writes that the interest in cyberbullying is largely media-driven, and that parents and practitioners need to focus more on traditional bullying (2012). But the fact that cyberbullying is not as prevalent as traditional bullying does not mean that cyberbullying is not a phenomenon of interest. Scholars, practitioners, and the public at large are aware of the harm cyberbullying can cause. Indeed, because cyberbullying affects young people disproportionately, and because the victims of cyberbullying have often been pushed to high-profile suicides, cyberbullying has garnered a large amount of media attention. Some notable incidents include:

- Megan Meier committed suicide on October 15, 2006. Meier, 13 at the time, had been cyberbullied by the parent of a schoolmate. The parent, Lori Drew, had created a fake Myspace account and used it to send derogatory communications to Meier.
- On April 8, 2012, Grace McComas took her own life after a bully labeled Grace a "snitch" on Twitter. The online attacks migrated to offline physical gossip. The combination of online and offline cyberbullying drove McComas to commit suicide.

- August Ames, an adult film actress, committed suicide on December 5, 2017 after receiving negative comments for a Twitter post in which she stated a refusal to work with actors who had done gay porn.
- Aspiring country singer Katy Summer, 15, committed suicide on May 21, 2018. Summer committed suicide because of the taunts about her kissing a boy at a party and the music she made.

MYTHS OF CYBERBULLYING

The Cyberbullying Research Center provides evidence-based tips and strategies on cyberbullying (see Figure 4.2) However, there are several myths about cyberbullying. Television shows and movies depict cyberbullying as a common occurrence in American high schools, the consequences of which are often suicide. However, these media portrayals are not grounded in the reality of cyberbullying and can be misleading to the public. Sabella, Patchin, and Hinduja (2013) point out several myths of cyberbullying. We list some of these myths:

1. *Everyone knows what cyberbullying is.* Although we have stated a working definition of cyberbullying above, researchers have not come to a consensus about what constitutes cyberbullying. As we put it, cyberbullying has been theorized to be composed of at least four components— (1) a repeated behavior, (2) the behavior is in the digital environment, (3) a power differential between offender and victim, and (4) the behavior is meant to harm. However, most discussions of cyberbullying do not include all four. For example, some discussions may not include repeated behavior. Is it cyberbullying if on only one evening a victim was sent insulting communication? This may best be understood as flaming. Similarly, suppose someone of less power—an unpopular student in a high school—sends derogatory communications to someone with more power—the captain of the cheerleading squad. Can we say this is truly bullying, or just an annoyance? This confusion is illustrated in a recent report published by the Pew Research Center (see Figure 4.1). The center reports that most teens surveyed were the victims of cyberbullying. However, what indicates cyberbullying does not include power differences and repeated communications. As a result, the report can claim that 59% of teens have been victims of cyberbullying.
2. *Cyberbullying causes suicide.* This myth is media driven. There are certainly cases, including those we highlighted previously. However, Sabella and colleagues (2013) note

> the vast majority of cyberbullying victims do not kill themselves, and those who do typically have experienced a constellation of stressors and other issues operating in their lives, making it difficult to isolate the influence of one specific personal or social problem as compared to others.
>
> (2705)

Cyberbullying is an issue that needs to be addressed, but when suicides occur it may be because the victim has experienced other harmful experiences or social dysfunctions.

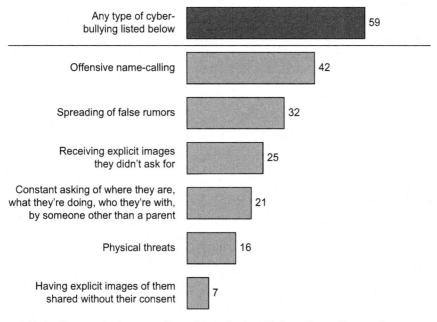

A majority of teens have been the target of cyberbullying, with name-calling and rumor-spreading being the most common forms of harassment

% of U.S. teens who say they have experienced__online or on their cellphone

Any type of cyber-bullying listed below	59
Offensive name-calling	42
Spreading of false rumors	32
Receiving explicit images they didn't ask for	25
Constant asking of where they are, what they're doing, who they're with, by someone other than a parent	21
Physical threats	16
Having explicit images of them shared without their consent	7

Note: Respondents were allowed to select multiple options. Those who did not give an answer or gave other response are not shown.

Source: Survey conducted March 7–April 10, 2018.
"A Majority of Teens Have Experienced Some Form of Cyberbullying"

PEW RESEARCH CENTER

Figure 4.1   2018 report from Pew Research Center on cyberbullying (www.pewinternet.org/2018/09/27/a-majority-of-teens-have-experienced-some-form-of-cyberbullying/).

Figure 4.2   A major resource for cyberbullying research is the Cyberbullying Research Center's website (https://cyberbullying.org/). The center and website, housed at Florida Atlantic University and directed by criminologists Justin Sameer Hinduja and Justin Patchin, provides research, basic facts, and tips about cyberbullying.

3. *Cyberbullying occurs more often now than traditional bullying.* The research shows that bullying in the physical environment is much more common than bullying in the digital environment. For example, Payne and Hutzell (2015) found that around 28% of students reported that they had been victims of traditional bullying, but only 9% of students reported that they had been victims of cyberbullying.

4. *Like traditional bullying, cyberbullying is a rite of passage all teens experience.* There is an understanding by some that dealing with mild forms of violence—insults, being picked on, being forced to conform, is a normal part of youth development. Many adults believe that navigating these experiences is a way to teach young people the adult skill of dealing with adversity. Said another way, social cruelty is a way of life, and one needs to get used to it and learn how to deal with it. The idea that young people must deal with adversity is not new, however: The notion that bullying or other types of violence should be acceptable because they teach someone how to live in the world is a myth.

5. *Cyberbullies are outcasts or just mean kids.* There is a sense, again coming from the media, that cyberbullies are hell-bent on destroying the lives of the victim. This does not seem to be the truth in most cases. Those who participate in cyberbullying are only trying to have some fun and are not attempting to inflict lasting harm. In this sense, cyberbullying for many kids is "a joke" where the perpetrator has no sense that his or her actions will permanently damage the victim.

6. *To stop cyberbullying, just turn off your computer or cell phone.* Parents may determine that the most effective way of shielding their children from cyberbullying is by taking them out of the digital environment. This, however, is not realistic for two reasons. First, the young person loses out on important life experiences. Post-industrial society requires that a person enter and navigate the digital environment. Young people must learn how to seek, interpret, and produce symbolic communication on the Internet. In the long run, restricting computer access only makes it harder for the young person to anticipate and defend against cyberbullying in the future. Second, this is practically impossible. The digital environment is made up of interconnected networks that are not under the control of individuals. A young person cannot avoid cyberbullying by turning off their cell phone or computer. Even if they turn off their phone, they will eventually have to check their email, be required to go online for school, or connect with family and friends through social media.

Trolling and Flaming

TROLLING

Trolling is the act of generating conflict online, often for a prank or to cause controversy. A major difference between trolling and flaming is that the troll often has no vested interest in the conflict-generating content they produce or have no relation to the victims they target. It is primarily a game or prank, encompassed in the catchphrase "doing it for the lulz," or doing it for the humor. Milner (2013) describes trolling through what he calls the logic of lulz. The logic of lulz, Milner argues, is to generate a "hyper-humorous, hyper-ironic, hyper-distanced mode of discourse" (89). Milner argues that trolls seek out normative discussions, ideas, and images and intentionally try to mock or subvert them. An example of this would be joining an online forum for people struggling with alcoholism, and repeatedly posting comments about the joys and health benefits of drinking beer.

Trolling can range from a harmless prank to an act that generates tremendous psychological harm. In 2011 Sean Duffy was sent to prison in the United Kingdom for Internet trolling. Many families set up Facebook tribute pages for their loved ones who have died. Duffy had posted derogatory messages on several of these pages. He also posted videos on YouTube mocking the deceased. On one tribute site to a young girl who died in a car crash, Duffy defaced a picture of her by adding stitches to her head and placing a caption under one picture reading "Used car for sale, one useless owner."[2] For these acts he was given an 18-week sentence. Duffy did not know the victims, and his actions appeared to be just for "the lulz."

In the United States, trolling can fall under existing laws of cyberstalking in some states. However, in the UK, trolling is more directly covered under the "Malicious Communications Act."[3] Thus, more accurate measures of the prevalence of trolling can be found in the United Kingdom. According to a 2015 story from the UK newspaper *The Daily Telegraph*, 1,209 people were convicted of trolling in 2014 compared to 143 in 2004—a 10-fold increase in a decade. It is likely that the rates are comparable in the United States[4] given comparable rates of internet penetration and usage in the two countries.

Flaming

Flaming can be defined as the uninhibited expression of hostility, insults, and ridicule (Kayany, 1998). Flaming often occurs on websites in which controversial issues are discussed, like the Huffington Post (see Table 4.2). Like face-to-face discussions that lead to raised voices and strong emotions, Internet users may express disagreement rudely and use profanity. Thus, a key difference between flaming and trolling is that a genuine interest underlies flaming motivations. A person who flames may themselves feel aggrieved because a sentiment was expressed that they strongly disagree with. A second difference between flaming and trolling is that flaming is an "in the moment" act and does not carry over to another context, or even to a subsequent post.

Flaming may have more wide-ranging societal implications than trolling. Inflamed passions are often the result of perceived cultural, ideological, or political differences that manifest themselves in online forums or social media. We are more likely to communicate harshly towards a person we believe to be of a different race, creed, or political affiliation—and thus not deserving of civility.

Table 4.2   The Huffington Post, Trolling and Flaming

The anonymity of the digital environment can be a positive for society. It allows citizens to speak openly about their concerns without fear of punishment from their government or other citizens. However, in some contexts, the anonymity allows people to troll and flame. Several news sites have either made comments possible only with a registered account, or suspended comments altogether. In 2013, The Huffington Post suspended anonymous comments on their site, and gave the justification below.

As of next month, Huffington Post users won't be able to create anonymous accounts to post on the site; going forward, their identities will be verified internally. HuffPost recognizes that many people are not in a professional or personal situation where attaching their name to a comment is feasible, and this change will not require users to identify themselves in connection with each comment. Rather, we will ask users to verify their identity when creating an account, which will reduce the number of drive-by or automated trolls ...

... Trolls have grown more vicious, more aggressive, and more ingenious. As a result, comment sections can degenerate into some of the darkest places on the Internet. At HuffPost, we publish nearly 9 million comments a month, but we've reached the point where roughly three-quarters of our incoming comments never see the light of day, either because they are flat-out spam or because they contain unpublishable levels of vitriol. And rather than participating in threads and promoting the best comments, our moderators are stuck policing the trolls with diminishing success.

Hate Speech

The term hate speech is used in everyday language to describe almost any critical comment towards a person or group. Expressing one's opinion about controversial issues such as same-sex marriage, racial inequality, or immigration can be considered hate speech. This is especially so when one's opinion is not shared by most of the population. However, hate speech has a more specific meaning in social science scholarship, and is composed of three elements (adapted from Matsuda, 1989): (1) the speech implies or states that the target group is inferior, (2) the speech is aimed at a group that has been historically oppressed or disadvantaged, and (3) the speech is intended to be harmful. This definition hinges on power differences—as the communication must be aimed at a historically oppressed group, and intent—the communication is a clear attempt at causing psychological harm. Examples of hate speech include:

- A website arguing that people of European ancestry are more intelligent than people of African ancestry
- A troll in an online forum replying to a person they think is Hispanic, saying that all Hispanics should go back to Mexico because they are all gang members
- Twitter comments aimed at a tweet celebrating the marriage of a gay couple, with the tweets calling the marriage "disgusting" or "sinful"

Evidence suggests that there is a large amount of hate speech online. Ofcom, the United Kingdom's communication regulatory agency, released a report in early 2017 stating that 1 in

3 Internet users between the ages of 12 and 15 reported seeing hate speech online in the previous year.[5]

In the United States, hate speech without a stated violent intent is not considered unlawful. Hate speech is protected under free-speech laws and prohibits *government agencies* from regulating what can and cannot be said. However, free-speech laws do not protect individuals from private companies regulating speech. Business may prohibit certain types of speech—such as preventing an employee from commenting on the plans of that business. They may also terminate employment if they deem the speech to be detrimental to their company's image.

Social norms are also outside of free-speech laws and dictate that hate speech is unwanted in most contexts. Comments about racial minorities, religious minorities, and women are usually met with opprobrium. Even comments from years past unearthed on social media can be a cause for public condemnation and other negative sanctions. Major League Baseball pitcher Josh Hader had to publicly apologize in 2018 for tweets he published in 2011 using racial epithets. Comedian Kevin Hart stepped down from hosting the 2019 Oscars because of anti-gay tweets he published between 2009 and 2011.

THE HARMS OF HATE SPEECH

Hate speech is prevalent in the digital environment. Indeed, an article in the *Washington Post* called the summer of 2018 "The Summer of Hate Speech."[6] However, in an American context free speech is valued highly, and protected by the First Amendment. There is a long-standing cultural and political tradition of letting people say what they want as long as they do not advocate (physical) violence. For example, in Germany it is a punishable offense to deny the Holocaust. In the United States Holocaust denial is a form of deviance, but not punishable by law.

Although most speech is permissible online in the United States, there is evidence that speech can cause harm in at least two ways. First, hate speech can lower the status of the group in the eyes of others. In this sense, hate speech is sociologically harmful. Hate speech can be used to paint a group as violent, unintelligent, or unpatriotic. This type of labeling can prepare members of dominant groups psychologically for more egregious types of behavior towards the minority group. In this sense, hate speech is a "gateway act" to discrimination, the supporting of harmful social policies, or physical violence. Numerous historical episodes show this pattern. The Third Reich in 1930s Germany, white supremacists in Jim Crow Era United States, and the Hutu majority in early 1990s Rwanda all used hate speech against a minority group. This speech was used to produce a sense of "otherness" in Jews, African-Americans, and the Tutsi minority, respectively. Once "otherized," dominant groups had the justification for discriminatory laws or committing acts of violence towards these groups.

Second, hate speech is psychologically harmful to the individuals within the groups it is directed at. In this sense, hate speech is functionally equivalent to the taunts and insults used by bullies. There are negative consequences to consuming content asserting one's person or group is inferior. Like cyberbullying, this can include psychological distress and lowering of self-esteem. For example, Gelber and McNamara (2016) explored the consequences of hate speech directed towards members of indigenous communities and minority groups in Australia. In their interviews, respondents reported the pain caused by hate speech (333):

- "To me the saddest thing is [there] not a recognition of the special status of what we add to this country. We don't take away from; we add … but it's always put up there as a negative, that Aboriginals don't add to the fabric of this country, that we don't—and … I think that it is painful … Yes, it does hurt and it strikes at your very being."
- "You can never, you can never repair damage in that content once it's been put out there. It lingers, it stays, it smells, it hangs around. You can't get rid of it and racism is racism, it builds and feeds on that."
- "Our kids also feel hopeless and ask why their parents as Muslims are doing something wrong."

The difference between hate speech and other forms of cyberviolence we have discussed is that hate speech is generally understood to be aimed at a group. Flaming, trolling, and cyberbullying are generally aimed at individuals, and it is easier to identify a clear victim. Nevertheless, hate speech is potentially more damaging for society because it can be a factor supporting discrimination and injustice towards large swaths of a population.

Cyberstalking

Stalking can generally be defined as an "ongoing course of conduct in which a person behaviorally intrudes upon another's life in a manner perceived to be threatening" (Nicastro et al., 2000, 69). When this intrusion occurs in the digital environment, we can consider this cyberstalking. Reyns and colleagues (2011), define cyberstalking as "the repeated pursuit of an individual using electronic or Internet-capable devices" (1). Cyberstalking is prevalent within romantic relationships (Marcum, Higgins, & Nicholson, 2017), and especially amongst young people who spend a lot of their time in the digital environment. Indeed, the connection between intimate relationships and stalking is strong enough that cyberstalking and "cyber dating abuse" are often used interchangeably (Marcum et al., 2017).

The potential for cyberstalking has increased over the years. This is because there are more ways of entering and communicating in the digital environment. For example, in the early 2000s, people entered the digital environment primarily through their home computers and used mainly emails for communication. Consequently, cyberstalking was somewhat limited to those devices, locations, and means of communication. Today, consider the number of ways in which a person can enter into the digital environment—phones, computers, laptops, appliances, automobiles, and wearable devices. Also consider the number of ways in which a person can communicate in the digital environment—email, text, and hundreds of social media applications. These ways of entering and communicating in the digital environment present more opportunities for a victim to be pursued and more ways in which a victim's life can be intruded upon. Examples of cyberstalking include:

- Seeking online communication in the form of emails, texting, social media correspondence, constantly from a victim.
- Collecting social media or other online information about a victim. This information could be photographs, replies, and comments by the victim, or other digital footprints such as likes, upvotes, and retweets.
- Logging into a victim's social networking accounts without their permission.
- Installing or activating GPS tracking devices on mobile devices without their permission.

There may be a belief that because cyberstalking does not involve a stalker having close physical contact with their victim and there is less danger of physical violence, the damage done to the victim is less. However, research suggests that the level of psychological distress experienced is the same for victims of both types of stalking (Short, Guppy, Hart, & Barnes, 2015):

the prevalence of PTSD following cyberstalking is comparable to other specific traumatic events such as sexual assault and combat. Moreover, what is clear is that the victims' reactions are of a negative nature and include fear, depression, stress, anxiety, lowered self-esteem and a loss of trust in other people.

(29)

Online Shaming

Online shaming refers to a group subjecting an individual to harassment, bullying, and condemnation because of some real or perceived transgression. The fundamental aspect of shaming, as described by Braithwaite, is the "societal processes of expressing social disapproval" (1989, 100). The perpetrators of online shaming are collections of individual users acting as a group. Research has shown that when individuals perceive themselves as being a part of the group, they lose their inhibitions, and become more vitriolic and nastier (Suler, 2004). Thus, the target of online shaming may be the recipient of particularly malicious comments that are out of proportion to the transgression.

There are at least two motivations for online shaming. One motivation is to teach a person what behaviors are unacceptable. In this way, shaming is about social control. Another motivation is to punish a person for an actual or perceived transgression. It may be that the transgression has not been properly addressed by law enforcement or another institution. In this way, online shaming is a type of vigilantism. By vigilantism we mean efforts by citizens to punish a person without the legal authority to do so.

The motives of social control and vigilantism are related, as both are about levying sanctions for bad behavior. However, we link shaming as social control primarily to cultural transgressions, and we link vigilantism to transgressions that are either criminal or that the group imagines *should* be criminalized. Another difference is the severity of sanctions. Online shaming as social control may never rise above the level of vitriolic comment—or a public outcry. This outcry may lead to punishment from other authorities; however, this punishment does not come from the shamers themselves. Vigilantes tend to undertake more severe forms of punishment, including hacking personal accounts in order to reveal personal information or making threats of physical violence. We discuss and give examples of these two forms of online shaming next.

ONLINE SHAMING AS SOCIAL CONTROL

A famous example of social shaming in which the purpose is to teach a person what is unacceptable behavior is the case of Justine Sacco.[7] Sacco was a public relations executive for a company called IAC. As she waited for her flight at London's Heathrow Airport, she began tweeting jokes:

- Weird German Dude: You're in First Class. It's 2014. Get some deodorant.—Inner monologue as I inhale BO. Thank God for pharmaceuticals.
- Chilly—cucumber sandwiches—bad teeth. Back in London!
- Going to Africa. Hope I don't get AIDS. Just kidding. I'm white!

After this last tweet, Sacco boarded her 11-hour flight, and went to sleep. At the time, Sacco had 170 followers, and her jokes could have easily melted into the Twittersphere. Unfortunately for Sacco, when she awoke, she realized that her third joke—about AIDS, Africa, and whiteness—was the number one trending tweet on Twitter. Sacco had crossed a boundary of social acceptance, and she was unfortunate in that other Twitter users—possibly those with a high number of followers—read and retweeted her joke.

Sacco experienced severe online shaming in the hours and days that followed. An article on Sacco by the *New York Times*[8] lists some of the responses to Sacco's tweet:

- "In light of @Justine-Sacco disgusting racist tweet, I'm donating to @care today" and "How did @JustineSacco get a PR job?! Her level of racist ignorance belongs on Fox News. #AIDS can affect anyone!"
- "I'm an IAC employee and I don't want @JustineSacco doing any communications on our behalf ever again. Ever."
- "This is an outrageous, offensive comment. Employee in question currently unreachable on an intl flight." [This tweet is from her employer, IAC.]
- "We are about to watch this @JustineSacco bitch get fired. In REAL time. Before she even KNOWS she's getting fired."

A popular hashtag was used to comment on Sacco—#HasJustineLandedYet, as people expressed pleasure in watching her lose her career. Sacco was eventually fired from IAC. Whatever one thinks about Sacco's poor taste in humor or even if one imagines that her jokes reveal unhealthy racial views, it is clear that Sacco experienced a high degree of stress because of online social shaming.

ONLINE SHAMING AS VIGILANTISM

Another motivation for online shaming is to punish a person for an actual or perceived transgression. Collections of individuals may decide to "right the wrong" using the tools they have available in the digital environment, what can be called digital vigilantism (Trottier, 2017). There are many reasons why groups decide to seek justice on their own:

- There may be no formal laws against the behavior in question
- Law enforcement may have historically ignored the transgression or place a low priority on it
- Law enforcement may be ineffective in bringing criminals to justice
- A person may have been convicted of a crime and punished, but the punishment does not meet the expectations of the group

In 2011, the Boston Bruins defeated the Vancouver Canucks in the Stanley Cup hockey finals. As the game drew to a close, riots broke out in downtown Vancouver, where the game was being played. The riots caused major damage to the city, and many people were injured. Arvanitidis (2016) describes the fate of Nathan Kotlyak. A photograph was taken by a bystander of Kotlyak attempting to light a police car on fire. The photograph was shared across numerous social media platforms. Eventually, Kotlyak was identified. Arvanitidis writes:

> The backlash he suffered from the public shortly after was immediate, merciless, and overwhelmingly public. As the photograph continued to make its way across the Internet, Kotylak found himself subjected to a torrent of verbal abuse, demands for punishment, and threats, until eventually he and his family were forced to flee their home following the publication of their home address online.
>
> (2016, 19)

Conclusion

Cybertrespass, and to a lesser degree cyberdeception/theft receives a lot of attention from the public because of the financial loss involved. Cyberpornography can also receive a lot of attention because of the salacious and heinous nature of the crimes. However, cyberpornography may be the type of cybercrime that has the most victims and causes the most societal damage. A significant amount of young people are cyberbullied and cyberstalked. Trolling and flaming are prevalent features of the digital environment, with almost every computer user having experienced aggressive or hostile communications on social media or discussion boards. Hate speech, a form of cyberviolence that is not prohibited in the United States, may ironically be the most damaging given its historical association to discrimination, unfair social policies, and even genocide.

Vocabulary

1. **Cyberbullying**—Behaviors facilitated by electronic or digital media that repeatedly communicate hostile messages intended to inflict harm or discomfort.
2. **Cyberstalking**—The repeated pursuit of an individual using electronic or Internet-capable devices.
3. **Flaming**—Uninhibited expression of hostility, insults, and ridicule.
4. **Hate Speech**—Speech intended to be harmful, that implies or states that a historically oppressed group is inferior.
5. **Trolling**—The act of generating conflict online, often for a prank or to cause controversy.
6. **Online Shaming**—A group subjecting an individual to harassment, bullying, and condemnation because of some real or perceived transgression.

Study Questions

TRUE/FALSE

1. Cyberviolence requires a facility with symbolic communication.
   a. True
   b. False
2. Scholars have speculated that men are more likely to commit cyberviolence than women.
   a. True
   b. False
3. Cyberbullying can cause suicide.
   a. True
   b. False
4. In the United States, hate speech is protected under free-speech laws.
   a. True
   b. False
5. Research suggests that cyberbullying is more prevalent than traditional bullying.
   a. True
   b. False
6. Well-behaved and well-adjusted kids do not participate in cyberbullying.
   a. True
   b. False
7. The act of trolling has led to jail sentences in some countries.
   a. True
   b. False
8. A tweet aimed at a gay person on Twitter saying that gay marriage is "disgusting" or "sinful" is hate speech as defined by your textbook.
   a. True
   b. False

9. Cyberstalking is often found in romantic relationships.
   a. True
   b. False
10. Logging into a victim's social networking accounts without their permission is a form of cyberstalking.
    a. True
    b. False
11. One reason why groups may try to online shame is because there may not be any formal laws in place to punish a certain behavior.
    a. True
    b. False

MULTIPLE CHOICE

12. One way that violence in the physical environment is similar to cyberviolence is because _____.
    a. both harm the victim
    b. the likely perpetrators are the same
    c. both require technical skill
    d. both require physical strength
13. One way that violence in the physical environment is similar to cyberviolence is because _____.
    a. the likely perpetrators are the same
    b. both require technical skill
    c. both are often powered by emotion
    d. both require physical strength
14. _____ is any behavior performed through electronic or digital media by individuals or groups that repeatedly communicate hostile or aggressive messages intended to inflict harm or discomfort on others.
    a. Cyberstalking
    b. Hate speech
    c. Phishing
    d. Cyberbullying
15. _____ often occurs in spaces where controversial issues are being presented.
    a. Cyberbullying
    b. Revenge porn
    c. Trolling
    d. Flaming
16. Given the conditions set forth in the chapter, why aren't white males likely victims of hate speech?
    a. People do not say bad things about white males
    b. White males are usually the ones voicing the hate speech
    c. They are not a historically oppressed group

17. _____ refers to a group subjecting an individual to harassment because of a transgression.
    a. Cyberbullying
    b. Hate speech
    c. Online shaming
    d. Flaming
18. What is one difference between flaming and trolling?
    a. Trolling is more spontaneous than flaming
    b. Trolling is more often done by females
    c. Flaming is more often done by females
    d. Flaming is more spontaneous than trolling
19. Which of these are consequences of being a victim of cyberstalking?
    a. Increased stress levels
    b. Inability to concentrate on tasks
    c. Both
    d. Neither
20. What are the myths associated with cyberbullying?
    a. Everyone has a clear understanding of what constitutes cyberbullying
    b. Cyberbullying is something that young people need to go through to become an adult
    c. People who are cyberbullied are likely to commit suicide
    d. All of the above
21. _____ are people who "do it for the lulz."
    a. Trolls
    b. Flamers
    c. Hackers
    d. Online shamers
22. Hate speech in the United States is lawful, and protected by free-speech laws. However, these laws do not protect a person from having their speech prohibited by _____.
    a. Local police
    b. Federal police
    c. Businesses
    d. Universities
23. One proposed harm of hate speech is that _____.
    a. it is a gateway act to discrimination and physical acts of violence
    b. it dumbs down American society
    c. it does not develop strong debating skills
    d. it causes physical harm to its victims
24. The likelihood that someone will be cyberstalked has _____ in recent years.
    a. increased
    b. decreased
    c. stayed the same
25. Which of these is a motivation for cyberstalking as discussed in the text?
    a. To show loyalty to the in-group
    b. To punish a person for something they have done

c. Economic reasons
d. To advocate for a political cause

Critical Thinking Exercise

When thinking of violent crime, it is easy to presume that the threat or actual harm committed upon the victim need be illustrated in some physical manner upon the victim (e.g. bodily bruises, erratic behavior). Yet, the indicators of cyberviolence victimization tend to contradict this presumption. Why might this be? What can we say about cyberviolence victimization that would support the idea that evidence of such victimization may not be as immediately apparent as violent victimization in a physical sense?

Does retweeting a negative hashtag (e.g. "#AGoodJew is a dead Jew," "#IfMyDaughterBroughtHomeABlack") count as hate speech? Does it count as an act of violence? Why/why not?

NOTES

1   Historically, assault has meant the intent to inflict harm, and battery meant the actual completion of the attempt of assault. However, we are using assault in its modern usage, in which assault means both the attempt and the successful completion of the attempt.
2   www.theguardian.com/uk/2011/sep/13/internet-troll-jailed-mocking-teenagers
3   www.legislation.gov.uk/ukpga/1988/27/contents
4   www.telegraph.co.uk/news/uknews/law-and-order/11627180/Five-internet-trolls-a-day-convicted-in-UK-as-figures-show-ten-fold-increase.html
5   www.ofcom.org.uk/research-and-data/media-literacy-research/childrens/children-parents-nov16
6   www.washingtonpost.com/technology/2018/08/30/summer-hate-speech/?utm_term=.6ce8f5e76146
7   www.nytimes.com/2015/02/15/magazine/how-one-stupid-tweet-ruined-justine-saccos-life.html
8   www.nytimes.com/2015/02/15/magazine/how-one-stupid-tweet-ruined-justine-saccos-life.html

REFERENCES

Arvanitidis, T. (2016). Publication bans in a Facebook age: How internet vigilantes have challenged the youth criminal justice act's "secrecy laws" following the 2011 Vancouver Stanley Cup Riot. *Canadian Graduate Journal of Sociology and Criminology*, 5(1), 18. doi:10.15353/cgjsc-rcessc.v5i1.142

Braithwaite, J. (1989). *Crime, shame, and reintegration.* Cambridge [Cambridgeshire]; New York: Cambridge University Press.

Buckels, E. E., Trapnell, P. D., & Paulhus, D. L. (2014). Trolls just want to have fun. *Personality and Individual Differences*, 67, 97–102. doi:10.1016/j.paid.2014.01.016

David-Ferdon, C., & Hertz, M. F. (2009). Electronic Media and Youth Violence: A CDC Issue Brief for Researchers. Centers for Disease Control and Prevention. Retrieved from http://eric.ed.gov/?id=ED511647

Gelber, K., & McNamara, L. (2016). Evidencing the harms of hate speech. *Social Identities, 22*(3), 324–341. doi:10.1080/13504630.2015.1128810

Kayany, J. M. (1998). Contexts of uninhibited online behavior: Flaming in social newsgroups on usenet. *Journal of the American Society for Information Science, 49*(12), 1135–1141. doi:10.1002/(SICI)1097-4571(1998)49:12<1135::AID-ASI8>3.0.CO;2-W

Marcum, C. D., Higgins, G. E., & Nicholson, J. (2017). I'm watching you: Cyberstalking behaviors of university students in romantic relationships. *American Journal of Criminal Justice, 42*(2), 373–388. doi:10.1007/s12103-016-9358-2

Matsuda, M. J. (1989). Public response to racist speech: Considering the victim's story. *Michigan Law Review, 87*(8), 2320. doi:10.2307/1289306

Milner, R. M. (2013). FCJ-156 hacking the social: Internet memes, identity antagonism, and the logic of lulz, 31.

Nicastro, A. M., Cousins, A. V., & Spitzberg, B. H. (2000). The tactical face of stalking. *Journal of Criminal Justice, 28*(1), 69–82. https://doi.org/10.1016/S0047-2352(99)00038-0

Olweus, D. (2012). Cyberbullying: An overrated phenomenon? *European Journal of Developmental Psychology, 9*(5), 520–538. doi:10.1080/17405629.2012.682358

Payne, A. A., & Hutzell, K. L. (2015). Old wine, new bottle? Comparing interpersonal bullying and cyberbullying victimization. *Youth & Society, 49*(8), 1149–1178.

Peterson, J., & Densley, J. (2017). Cyber violence: What do we know and where do we go from here? *Aggression and Violent Behavior, 34*, 193–200. doi:10.1016/j.avb.2017.01.012

Reyns, B. W., Henson, B., & Fisher, B. S. (2011). Being pursued online: Applying cyberlifestyle–routine activities theory to cyberstalking victimization. *Criminal Justice and Behavior, 38*(11), 1149–1169. doi:10.1177/0093854811421448

Sabella, R. A., Patchin, J. W., & Hinduja, S. (2013). Cyberbullying myths and realities. *Computers in Human Behavior, 29*(6), 2703–2711. doi:10.1016/j.chb.2013.06.040

Short, E., Guppy, A., Hart, J. A., & Barnes, J. (2015). The impact of cyberstalking. *Studies in Media and Communication, 3*(2), 23–37. doi:10.11114/smc.v3i2.970

Suler, J. (2004). The online disinhibition effect. *CyberPsychology & Behavior, 7*(3), 321–326. doi:10.1089/1094931041291295

Tokunaga, R. S. (2010). Following you home from school: A critical review and synthesis of research on cyberbullying victimization. *Computers in Human Behavior, 26*(3), 277–287. doi:10.1016/j.chb.2009.11.014

Trottier, D. (2017). Digital vigilantism as weaponisation of visibility. *Philosophy & Technology, 30*(1), 55–72. doi:10.1007/s13347-016-0216-4

Wall, D. S. (1998). Catching cybercriminals: Policing the internet. *International Review of Law, Computers & Technology, 12*(2), 201–218. doi:10.1080/13600869855397

Ybarra, M. L., Boyd, D., Korchmaros, J. D., & Oppenheim, J. K. (2012). Defining and measuring cyberbullying within the larger context of bullying victimization. *Journal of Adolescent Health, 51*(1), 53–58. doi:10.1016/j.jadohealth.2011.12.031

Chapter 5

Cyberdeception and Theft

Introduction

Cyberdeception and theft, as described by Wall, refers to "the different types of acquisitive harm that can take place" in the digital environment (2001, 4). Acquisitive crimes are those in which the offender gains materially from the crime. In a simpler sense, cyberdeception refers to the act of lying (deception) and stealing (theft) in the digital environment. In theory the two phenomena are distinct. Lying is commonplace in human relationships and is usually not a criminal offense, while theft is universally seen as a behavior that needs to be prohibited. However, the two phenomena are often linked. Criminals lie, construct elaborate fantasies, and embark on all types of subterfuges to steal money or information from a victim. Thus, for practical purposes, we can combine cyberdeception and theft.

Cyberdeception is distinct from the other categories of cybercrime in the wider array of both offenders and victims. Young people tend to be the perpetrators and victims of cyberviolence, the disadvantaged and poor are victims of child trafficking, and businesses or wealthy individuals are the target of cybertrespass. Cyberdeception, on the other hand, is a crime experienced by young and old, rich and poor.

There are at least two reasons for this. First, so much of commerce occurs through and by Internet-enabled technologies. The use of a credit card means that you are potentially a victim of credit card fraud or credit card skimming. Everyone who has an identification number of some kind (registration number, credit card number) and inputs this number in a website is a potential victim of identity theft. Buying goods online puts you in a position to be a victim of many crimes, including Internet auction fraud or unwittingly buying counterfeit goods. Second, there are numerous ways of deceiving someone in the digital environment, and these run from highly technical to more psychological. This expands the range of perpetrators. If someone does not have technical skill they can rely on social skills, and vice versa. It also expands the range of victims. A person may be aware of phishing or spoofed emails, for example, but fall victim to a romance scam because they are emotionally vulnerable.

Types of Cyberdeception and Theft

The ways in which someone can be defrauded online are far too many to list. One way of analyzing cyberdeception and theft is to look at the motivations behind the criminal or deviant behavior. Button and colleagues (2015) organize online frauds into two types—those motivated by the desire for money and those motivated by the desire for information (see Table 5.1). Any list is a tentative one, as individuals are continuously devising new schemes. However, the theft of money or information is a main way of organizing current and new schemes.

Table 5.1 Money vs. Information Motivation

Money Seeking Frauds

419 scams: The victim is contacted by someone claiming to be an official with a large sum of money. They are looking for someone to help them obtain the money, in return for which they offer to pay a substantial fee. To start the venture, however, they require a payment in advance from the victim.

Bogus inheritance scams: Victims are contacted and told they have inherited a large sum of money from a long-lost relative but need to pay fees in advance to release the money.

Bogus lottery: Victims are contacted and told they have won a lottery but need to pay a fee in advance to release the funds.

Bogus products: Goods and services advertised on online markets that are either defective or nonexistent.

Career opportunity scams: Jobs and training are offered online, usually for lucrative jobs, but the reality is there is no chance of work.

Clairvoyant and psychic scams: Victims are sent communications saying that something bad will happen to them unless they pay money.

Loan scams: Victims are sent demands for debt repayment with threats if they do not pay for nonexistent loans or scammers offer to renegotiate debts or amend adverse credit ratings.

Person in distress fraud: In some cases, people are targeted with a tragic story of a stranger and asked to send money, or in a variation, a person's email account is hacked and all their contacts are mailed to say they are in distress in a foreign country and could monies be wired urgently. This is often targeted at older computer users, and the fraudster purports to be a young relative in distress.

Romance frauds: There is a wide variety of different romance frauds, with the most common including the victim falling in love with usually a fake person and being tricked into sending gifts or money for emergencies or their costs of travel to meet them.

Share sale scams: Victims are convinced to buy worthless or overvalued shares using high pressure sales. The buying of these shares increases the values of the shares, at which time the fraudsters then sell their shares. This is also called a "pump and dump" scheme.

Personal Information Seeking Frauds

Fake websites and emails: The sending of fake emails (phishing) or the creation of fake websites (spoofing). These fraudulent communications and spaces are designed to harvest personal information in order to steal the identity of the computer users (identity theft).

Social networking: Fraudsters use fake identities to befriend individuals online and then harvest any online personal data displayed or trick them into parting with the information.

Malware: More sophisticated fraudsters use programs, viruses, and hacking to secure the personal information of a victim.

In this chapter we will narrow our focus to several well-known types of cyberdeception. These are:

- **Identity Theft**—Obtaining and using another person's personal data in some way that involves fraud or deception.
- **Phishing**—Sending fraudulent communications to obtain personal information.
- **Advance Fee Frauds**—Scams in which a fraudster leads a victim to believe that they will receive a large payment in the future for some present action—usually an "advance fee."
- **Romance Scams**—A fraudster develops a deceitful relationship with a victim to extract favors from the victim, usually in the form of monetary payments.
- **Selling of Counterfeit Goods**—The selling of merchandise that purports to be a product of a recognized brand company but is instead a copy of lesser value.
- **Pump and Dump Schemes**—A fraudster or group of fraudsters urges a victim to buy stocks to artificially inflate their value. They then sell the shares they own at the inflated price. The victim is left holding shares that are decreasing in value.
- **Digital Piracy**—The illegal acquisition of digital, copyrighted goods.
- **Cryptocurrency Fraud**—The fraudulent buying or selling of cryptocurrencies.

Identity Theft

Identify theft, also called identity fraud, is understood as all types of crime in which someone wrongfully obtains and uses another person's personal data in some way that involves fraud or deception. Most states have identity theft laws that prohibit the misuse of another person's identifying information. Although the term identity theft is of the 21st century, the process is not new:

> identity theft is as old as the concept of identity itself. As soon as identity acquired any sort of value, someone was going to want to steal it for nefarious purposes. Someone else's identity in ancient Egypt could gain you access to the presence, and influence, of a Pharaoh. If you were transported to the colonies in the 18th century, one way of getting back to England was to steal the identity of a sailor and blag [persuade/lie] your way onto a returning ship.
>
> (Kirk, 2014, 449)

In 2017, 17,636 people reported being victims of identity theft to the Internet Crime Complaint Center (IC3).[1] These victims reported a total loss of $66,815,298—an average loss of around $3,800. IC3 provides some understanding of how much money is lost per incident reported. However, the number of incidents reported is likely a low estimate because it is restricted to the people who contacted the center.

A more accurate estimate of the number of victims is provided by the Bureau of Justice Statistics National Crime Victimization Survey. The Bureau of Justice Statistics reported in 2014 that 17.6 million people were victims of identity theft.[2] This is a large number in comparison to other crimes. Consider that in the same year, 2014, the total number of people who were victims of burglary, motor vehicle theft, and theft totaled *together* 10.4 million.[3]

According to respondents to a survey conducted by the Identity Theft Resource Center,[4] victims lose not only money, but also time. Table 5.2 shows the most frequent actions taken by a victim of identity theft. It is noticeable that many of the more common responses were about the loss of time. Victims also experienced damages that extended beyond financial loss. Table 5.3 shows that victims of identity theft reported stress, lack of sleep, and headaches, and more.

In sum, the data presented in this section suggests that identity theft is a common crime that has wide-ranging impacts on those who are victimized. In the next section we discuss exactly what is "identity" in the digital environment.

PERSONALLY IDENTIFIABLE INFORMATION

Humans use observation to identify a person—usually their eyes to see physical features or mannerisms. They also use their ears to hear a person's voice, or their noses to smell. Individuals without sight may also rely on touch to identify a person. Once someone is identified, we then know how to interact with that person: to approach, to be guarded, to be friendly, etc. This happens at a subconscious level, and we are not necessarily cognizant of this process. We are only

Table 5.2   Most Frequent Responses to the Question: Did You Do Any of the Following as a Result of Your Identity Theft Case?*

Closed existing financial accounts	33%
Use online accounts less frequently or not at all	33%
Spent time away from other life experiences, like hobbies or a vacation	33%
Closed existing online accounts	27%
Borrowed money from family/friends	26%
Took time off from work	22%
Spend time away from family	22%

*Modified from the Identity Theft and Resource Center's "Identity Theft and Its Aftermath" 2017 report (www.ftc.gov/system/files/documents/public_comments/2017/10/00004-141444.pdf)

Table 5.3   Most Frequent Physical Reactions Because of Identity Theft Victimization*

Stress	64%
Sleep disturbances (unable to sleep, oversleeping, nightmares)	48%
An inability to concentrate/lack of focus	37%
Fatigue	35%
Headaches	34%

*Modified from the Identity Theft and Resource Center's "Identity Theft and Its Aftermath" 2017 report (www.ftc.gov/system/files/documents/public_comments/2017/10/00004-141444.pdf)

aware of the process when our senses cannot help us. For example, someone hears noises on the bottom floor of their home and call out to ask who it is. The response, or lack of one, will then determine how one should proceed.

Computers use information unique to each user—numbers, letters, dates, biometric information—to identify a person and then decide how to interact with that user. This information is of one of three types: something you know, something you are, or something you own (see Table 5.4). In a common scenario, a person goes to a banking website and is confronted with a screen asking for identifying information—a username and a password. The response, or lack of one, will then determine for the computer (the server owned by the bank) how to proceed.

This identifying information is called **personally identifiable information**, or PII. The act of stealing one's identity in the digital environment is ultimately the act of stealing a victim's PII. Some examples of PII include:

- Social security number
- Alien registration number
- Numbers issued by government organizations such as a school or the military
- Birthdate
- Address
- DNA
- Eye signature (retina display)

The requirement for PII is that it can distinguish one person from another. Some PII are by design meant to be unique, such as a social security number or military identification number. Other types of PII are not as effective at distinguishing individuals. Someone's name is technically a type of PII but because two people can have the same name it is not an effective identifier.

The more information a computer network can require for privileges the less likely someone will be able to steal the identity of a legitimate user. Thus, some computer networks use two forms of identification. This is usually something you know like a password, and something you own, like your mobile phone. This **two-factor authentication** is the norm at ATM machines, where a person must provide something they know (a username and password) and something they own (a credit card) to gain access.

As computer processing power and algorithms become more complex, computers are beginning to use other types of PII to distinguish people. For example, the ability of computers to

Table 5.4 Types and Examples of Personally Identifiable Information

Type of Personally Identifiable Information	Examples
Something you know	Passwords, answer questions (e.g. your mother's maiden name, the name of your favorite dog), birthdate
Something you are (biometric data)	Fingerprints, facial composition (through facial recognition software), voice (through voice recognition software), DNA
Something you own	Key, credit card, mobile phone

distinguish handwriting samples has improved to the point that handwriting is becoming an effective type of PII. Similarly, facial recognition software has become better at accurately identifying faces, and as such facial images are another potential type of PII. At the time of this writing, all new iPhones are equipped with Apple's version of facial recognition technology—Face ID.

Phishing

One of the main ways PII is stolen is through phishing. Phishing can be described as sending fraudulent communications—emails, text messages, and instant messages—to obtain personal information. In 2014, the American security firm RSA published a report stating that 2013 was a record year for phishing attacks globally. The report states that there were approximately 450,000 attacks with losses close to $6 billion.[5]

A common form of phishing is the sending of fraudulent emails that trick the receiver into providing PII. An example of a fraudulent email would be an email that purports to be from the victim's bank, asking the victim to either reply with information directly or click on a link. The email may use logos and wording that reminds the recipient of a prior legitimate communication from the bank. The link will then send the victim to a site that looks legitimate but is a harvester of PII. Although high-level coding skills are not needed, the fraudster must know how to design an email or website so that it looks legitimate.

THE SYSTEM OF PHISHING FRAUD

One successful phishing attempt can deceive thousands of people into unwittingly providing PII. Phishing is also, as discussed in Chapter 2, a means through which databases containing millions of customer entries are hacked. It is often the case that a successful phishing attempt may produce too much PII for one fraudster to use before the company or the customers realize they have been defrauded. Or, the individuals with the skills to develop convincing phishing communications are not always the individuals who are willing to use the stolen PII to steal money or information. Under these conditions a phishing system has developed on the dark web where PII is stolen, sold to third parties, and then used by those third parties to steal money or information.

There are at least four roles in this system—coders, fraudsters, brokers, and buyers. A model of the relationships between these roles, modified from Konradt and colleagues (2016), is presented in Figure 5.1. The flow of goods moves from coders who produce the fraudulent code, to fraudsters who then deploy the code and accumulate the PII, to brokers who arrange the space for transactions, to the buyers who then purchase the PII. A well-known example of a broker was the infamous Silk Road website on Tor, where buyers and sellers of a wide range of illegal goods met to complete illegal transactions. The broker often ensures the transaction—as the money is provided by the seller before the goods are shipped—and receives a small percentage of the sale for this service. The flow of cash moves in the opposite direction. The brokers receive a transaction fee for their services, which is a cost of business that is shared by both fraudster and buyer.

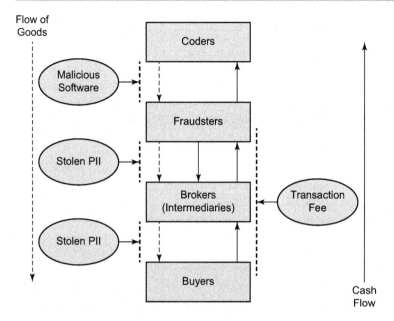

Figure 5.1   Roles and relationships in phishing fraud.

For example, a bundle of credit card numbers may sell for $300, plus a transaction fee of 7%, or $21. This fee is paid by the buyer; however, the fee is a "cost" for the fraudster as well as it increases the price of their product.

Advance Fee Frauds

Advance fee frauds are scams in which a fraudster leads a victim to believe that they will receive a large payment in the future if they perform some present action. The present action is usually the sending of money, hence the label "advance fee." However, fraudsters may sometimes ask for PII. For instance, the fraudster may ask the target to supply bank information so that they can wire a large sum of money into the target's account. The money will supposedly then be shared with the fraudster and target.

These frauds are also called confidence frauds as the fraudster must create a sense of confidence in the victim that the fraudster is being honest and truthful. These scams are most well known as Nigerian 419 scams, after the section of Nigerian law that it violates. In the early days of the public Internet, English-speaking scammers from West African nations were notorious for sending emails to targets in Western, English-speaking nations. Computer users have become warier of these scams; however, people are still defrauded on occasion.

Research done by Onyebadi and Park (2012) identified some common themes of advance fee fraud emails. One theme is that the emails are addressed to an unknown recipient—"Dear Sir/Madam." Onyebadi and Park argue that while this should be a red flag, this is often ignored by victims. Second, the fraudster attempts to establish credibility and engender trust in the target by sharing (false) personal information. This includes contact information such as email, telephone, or fax number. Third, each message details a circumstance in which a large sum of money is available, but to receive this money help is needed. The money has been gained through illegal dealings, an inheritance, or someone in a troubled circumstance looking to leave the country. Another theme is that the victim is promised a large financial reward for little or no investment. Here is an example of an email provided by Onyebadi and Park (2012):

> From 'Princess Fustina karom': 'I am a female student from University of Burkina faso, Ouagadougou. I am 23 yrs old ... my father died and left I and my junior brother behind. He was a king ... He left the sum of USD 7, 350, 000.00 dollars ... I am ready to pay 20% of the total amount to you if you help us in this transaction and another 10% interest of Annual After Income to you'.

A final theme identified by Onyebadi and Park is that the letters are not grammatically correct. At first glance, this would seem to be a clear indicator of the fraudulent nature of the email. However, one explanation provided by the researchers is that while the poor grammar may reveal the real handicaps in the scammer's language, it makes it possible for the victims to assume a sense of superiority: "the poor grammatical construction might be a part of the scammers' strategic deception of their potential victims, especially Europeans, into believing that they (scammers) are naive, uneducated and less intelligent folks who need supposedly wiser benefactors to help them" (195).

Romance Scams

Romance scams are scams in which online profiles are created or manipulated for developing a fraudulent relationship with the intended victim. The relationship is built to extract favors from the victim, usually in the form of monetary payments. In some cases, romance scams can be for the purposes of convincing a victim to traffic drugs, as in the case of Sharon Armstrong (see Table 5.5).

THE PROCESS OF ROMANCE SCAM VICTIMIZATION

Whitty (2013) used 20 semi-structured interviews with romance scam victims to develop a model of the romance scam victimization process (see Figure 5.2). The process begins with need or desire. The strong desire for companionship or love lowers the defenses of a potential victim. While data has been difficult to gather on romance scams, most research and most public instances of romance scams suggest that older females are the prime target. This is likely because as adults age, their romantic opportunities decrease, and this is especially so for women.

Table 5.5   The Story of Sharon Armstrong

In 2010, Sharon Armstrong, a high-ranking New Zealand government official, met a man named Frank on the dating website Match.com. Over the next six months, she and Frank exchanged over 7000 emails. In 2011, Ms. Armstrong and Frank agreed to meet in London, with Frank asking Ms. Armstrong to stop over in Buenos Aires, Argentina. Ms. Armstrong was to collect some documents in a suitcase from a colleague, a woman named Esperanza.

Ms. Armstrong was arrested by customs officers in the airport. She was transporting five kilograms of cocaine with a street value of over 1 million dollars. Ms. Armstrong was sentenced to four years and ten months in prison in Argentina and was released after two and a half years.

Since her release, Ms. Armstrong has become an advocate for more awareness of online fraudsters. She has written a book describing her experiences entitled *Organised Deception*. Ms. Armstrong's experiences are not unique, as many people fall victim to romance scams in which they are defrauded of money or asked to traffic drugs for drug cartels.

Source: www.sharonarmstrong.org/

The next steps involve social engineering. For instance, an "ideal profile" is constructed. This ideal profile is what the fraudster believes will attract the greatest number of victims.

One of the more interesting aspects of Whitty's study is the sales techniques used by fraudsters. For example, fraudsters test the waters, called the "foot in the door" technique, by asking the victim for small, trivial favors. If the victim complies, then larger sums of money are requested. Fraudsters also present a crisis in which there is little time to evaluate the validity of the request. This is analogous to salespersons offering a "limited time only" or "buy in the next two hours" sales promotion. These sales techniques can be understood as social engineering.

Another aspect of note is the alternative strategy employed by scammers where they sexually abuse or exploit their victims. Victims are asked to undress or masturbate in front of a camera. This is done for the enjoyment of the fraudster, or for future blackmailing. Whitty's study also illuminates the reason why people remain in scams even when they suspect foul play or to be re-victimized. Whitty argues that people may be aware that the person they are communicating with may be a scammer, but they are willing to play the long odds in the chance that the person is genuine. This is analogous to the person who plays the lottery, knowing the odds are exponentially long but is willing to risk a dollar or so.

Selling of Counterfeit Goods

One common type of cyberdeception is the sale of merchandise that purports to be a product of a recognized brand company (e.g. Rolex or Hermes) but is instead a copy, or "knock-off." For the fraudster, the selling of counterfeit goods is attractive because of the low levels of perceived risk and potentially high profits (D.S. Wall & Large, 2010). The primary victim in this fraud is usually the purchaser of the counterfeit product. They assume that they are getting an original of the same quality on discount, only to discover when the product arrives that their electronics or fashion accessories are of low quality and not produced by the brand company. However, there

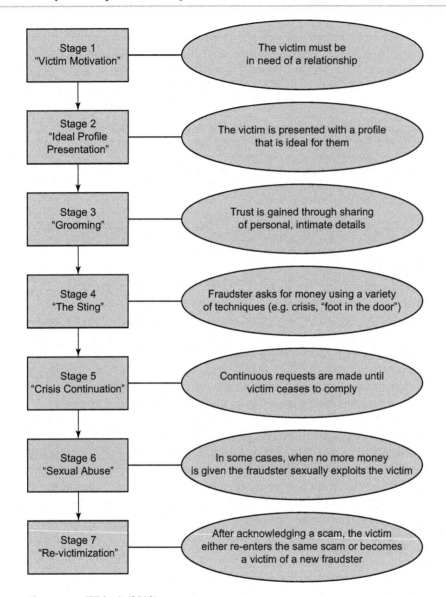

Figure 5.2   Whitty's (2013) romance scam process.

are occasions where the purchaser is aware that the product is a knock-off, but are comfortable with the low quality, especially for clothing, if they can convince others that it is the "real deal." Another victim is the company whose products are being counterfeited. They are losing profits because customers are buying "knock-offs" that take advantage of the name value they have produced.

Fraudsters contact victims in at least three ways. First, fraudsters may have their own website. Findings from research suggest that websites selling fakes were more likely registered in

China, and hosted in Estonia, Russia, or Sweden (Wadleigh, Drew, & Moore, 2015). Also, countries that have industries that are often the victims of counterfeiting are less likely to host counterfeit websites (Wadleigh et al., 2015). The hosting providers in France, a fashion capital, are less likely to host counterfeit shops. A second way is through online auction sites like eBay. Sellers can create fake accounts, or accounts not connected to their identity in the physical environment, and attempt to sell counterfeit goods. A third way is through direct emails or spamming. Fraudsters can purchase email lists from email aggregators, and then send email blasts to targets.

Heinonen and colleagues (2012) examine complaints submitted to the Internet Crime Complaint Center (IC3) for 2009 and 2010. They divide all complaints into auction fraud complaints (i.e. being defrauded on sites like eBay) and non-auction fraud complaints. Their study found that most complaints were for non-auction fraud and victims were contacted via email or through a website. Most of the fraudsters were from the United States, and most of the victims were male and over 30 years old. Heinonen and colleagues' study is informative but is limited. Only victims from the United States and who reported incidents to IC3 were analyzed. However, counterfeiting is a worldwide phenomenon and many victims do not report incidents to law enforcement.

Pump and Dump Schemes

Another type of fraud is a stock manipulation scheme commonly called "pump and dump." The scheme begins with a fraudster contacting potential investors to "pump" the stock. The investors are then conned into purchasing the stock by the misleading claims from fraudsters. The stock may be deemed the "next big thing" or "can't miss." When investors begin bidding for and buying shares of the stock, the price of the stock rises. The fraudsters then sell or "dump" their shares, netting a profit at the inflated value. This flooding of the market causes the value of the stock to fall, often below the original purchase price.

A traditional approach to pump and dump has been to contact investors by telephone or mail. However, the digital environment has made this scheme easier to execute because fraudsters have more means in which to communicate with investors. Social media platforms such as Twitter and Facebook can be a means through which fraudsters spread false claims about a stock. They can also spam potential investors through email.

Digital Piracy

Digital piracy can be described as "the purchase of counterfeit products at a discount to the price of the copyrighted product, and illegal file sharing of copyright material over peer-to-peer computer networks" (Hill, 2007, 9). More simply, it refers to the illegal acquisition of digital, copyrighted goods. A common example of digital piracy is recording a movie playing in a theater, and then selling "pirated" copies of the movie. The business can be profitable because, although the quality is often lower, the price of purchasing the pirated copy is a fraction of what it takes to purchase a movie ticket. Before internet usage became ubiquitous, pirated movies were often reproduced as physical copies on VHS tapes and CDs and sold in the physical environment.

A modified version of this practice occurs in the digital environment, with pirates making copies of a wide range of content, and then sharing it with millions of computer users through peer-to-peer file-sharing networks. These copies are made through tested methods such as recording movies in theaters, but more sophisticated thieves can rip content from subscription services like iTunes or from live TV and on-demand services.

Digital piracy impacts at least three groups. The first group impacted is the content producers. Content producers—the recording artists and individuals in the movie industry—fund their endeavors through selling their products to an audience. There is some disagreement as to how much digital piracy impacts these sales, but there is no doubt that many people elect to download illegal content instead of purchasing it for full price. Content distributors are also impacted by digital piracy. While Netflix and Amazon produce their own original content, their core business model has been to make content available and deliver that content to a paid user. Here again, there is some disagreement as to how much money these providers are losing, but many computer users will decide to watch illegal downloads instead of paying for a subscription. A third group may be the users who are consuming illegal content. There is some evidence that digital pirates may allow hackers to place malware on their sites. A user's computer will then be infected should they download the illegal content.

STATISTICS ON DIGITAL PIRACY

Although piracy is illegal, it carries little stigma. People are willing to report their piracy behaviors. As a result, several studies have been done that have measured the frequency of digital piracy.

Research commissioned by the United Kingdom's Intellectual Property Office in 2016 shows that copyright theft had decreased from previous years.[6] The report stated that the proportion of internet users 12 years or older consuming only legal content had increased from 41% to 44% from 2015. Computer users were opting for low-cost streaming services such as Netflix and Spotify instead of illegally downloading content, the report stated. This is a welcome trend for content producers and providers; however, this still leaves over half of the UK population illegally downloading some type of digital content. This same decline in piracy was reported in Australia. A government-commissioned study reported that

> over the first 3 months of 2016, 23% of Australian internet users aged 12+ consumed at least one item of online content unlawfully, which equates to approximately 4.6 million people. This was a significant drop from the 26% who had consumed unlawful content in 2015.[7]

In the United States, most of what we know about digital piracy at a national level comes from businesses or organizations associated with businesses. The Recording Industry Association of America (RIAA), the Motion Picture Association of America (MPAA), and the Business Software Alliance (BSA) routinely produce research showing the costs of digital piracy.

These reports need to be read with some skepticism, as these groups have an incentive to produce reports highlighting increases in piracy or new domains in which piracy may take place. The RIAA website's "2018 | Piracy Impact" page reports that that the United States economy loses $12.5 billion in total output because of music theft, and $422 million in tax revenues.[8] Similarly, a report promoted on the MPAA's website states that the elimination of piracy would increase movie revenues by $1.3bn per year.[9]

INTELLECTUAL PROPERTY AND COPYRIGHT

If someone stakes a claim to a good like a car or a mobile phone, and someone then takes that good, we can see that the good, or property, has shifted possession. The original person who claimed the property no longer has access to it. Or consider someone who has an apple, and that apple is stolen and eaten. The original owner no longer has the potential to use that product. In this sense, the ownership of cars, mobile phones, and even food is competitive in nature. If one person possesses it, the other does not. Economists call this type of good "rivalrous." For **rivalrous goods**, it is easy to identify when a property has been stolen and the original owner has been wronged.

Now consider a song, a movie, or a design that has been digitized and made available online. Or consider software code or a video game. These are not material goods, but intellectual goods. When ownership is claimed over them, they are intellectual properties. If a copy of these properties is made from the original and is shared, the original owner still has access to the property. Moreover, the original owner can still benefit from the property, by being entertained or by selling it for a profit. Economists call this type of good **non-rivalrous**. A considerable amount of the products that make up the digital environment have the quality of non-rivalry.

Table 5.6 shows a breakdown of the type of good by layer. The infrastructure and hardware layers are a combination of rivalrous, material properties and non-rivalrous, intellectual properties. Consider the theft of an iPad. The machine itself is a material, rivalrous good. However, its design is intellectual property—it can be copied by someone else and Apple still has possession of the design. All goods above the hardware layer are non-rivalrous. All operating systems and applications are ultimately computer code which can be copied. The content and the ideas in a user's head are also intellectual properties that can be copied.

This understanding of property is important for our interests in cybercrime and digital piracy for at least two reasons. First, it helps explain why people do not see this as theft because it is easier to rationalize piracy as not being theft. Someone can say—"Well, I just made a copy." This rationalization would not be available if the good was material and rivalrous. Second, it explains to some extent the ease by which people can commit acts of digital piracy. The barriers to copying and sharing property in the digital environment are low. The logistical barriers are low. A few clicks and one has copied a song that can be shared an infinite number of times. The economic barriers are low. There is little difference in price when copying the song once as opposed to one thousand times.

In theory, the property in the digital environment is naturally a non-rival good that is difficult to exclude from others. However, individuals can claim ownership over these non-material,

Table 5.6   Rivalrous and Non-rivalrous Goods in the Digital Environment

Layer	Description	Type of Good
Human	The ideas that have yet to be coded or digitized	Non-rivalrous
Content	The output from applications such as tweets, posts, audio, video; the digitized output of musicians, visual artists, and writers.	Non-rivalrous
Application	The computer code used to produce software like Skype, Pinterest, Facebook; the logos and branding associated with these companies	Non-rivalrous
Operating system	The computer code used to link applications with hardware (e.g. Windows, Linux)	Non-rivalrous
Hardware	The machines that individuals use to enter the digital environment; the design of the machines	Rivalrous/Non-rivalrous
Infrastructure	The connections between machines; the research used to increase data speeds (e.g. fiber-optic cables, Bluetooth)	Rivalrous/Non-Rivalrous

symbolic products via copyright. At its most basic level, a copyright establishes that the holder has the exclusive right to copy, or reproduce, a work. Packard (2013) summarizes the entirety of rights given to a copyright holder:

1. To reproduce the copyrighted work in copies
2. To prepare derivative works based upon the copyright
3. To distribute copies of the work for sale, or transfer ownership of copyright
4. To perform the work publicly
5. To display the work publicly
6. To perform the work by means of digital audio transmission

Copyright infringement, then, is the using of a copyrighted work in one of these six ways without either being the owner of a copyright or getting permission from the copyright owner.

WHY SO MUCH STEALING?

The stealing of copyrighted content is widespread and pervasive, especially amongst youth. The question is, what makes digital piracy so different? One reason is that it can be hard for someone who is illegally sharing files to link their actions to a definite victim. Movies, music, and other symbolic products are ultimately collaborations, and assuming that one person, the lead in the movie for example, is hurt by piracy can seem implausible. Even when one person can be identified as a clear victim—for example a solo music artist—the piracy can be rationalized by arguing that the victim is wealthy or famous and one song does no harm. Smallridge and Roberts (2013) argue that in addition to traditional techniques, digital pirates have developed piracy-specific techniques. One technique identified was "DRM defiance," where digital pirates rationalized their behavior by arguing that they were protesting the digital rights management code that prevents the copying or sharing of music.

In interviews with college students, Moore and McMullan (2009) showed that students tend to use at least one technique of neutralization when explaining their digital piracy. The most common technique used by the students was to deny injury. For example, one student in the study said:

> Artists will benefit from file sharing because my friends and I download music from the file sharing program and then we go out and purchase the CD. I listen to artists' songs off of the file sharing program and then I get more excited about seeing them perform live. I read somewhere that musicians make their money off concerts, so I think file sharing is actually helping the artists.
>
> (Moore & McMullan, 446)

Cryptocurrency and Fraud

In 2009, someone calling themselves Satoshi Nakamoto announced on the codesharing platform SourceForge: "Announcing the first release of Bitcoin, a new electronic cash system that uses a peer-to-peer network to prevent double-spending. It's completely decentralized with no server or central authority." Nakamoto's invention allowed people to use entries into a database as a medium of exchange. The program made by Nakamoto, Bitcoin, has become the most well-known cryptocurrency. There are others, including Ethereum, Litecoin, and Peercoin.

UNDERSTANDING CRYPTOCURRENCIES

Cryptocurrencies are, at their most straightforward, entries in a computer database. The database is a computer application that generates a set amount of currency that can then be shared and exchanged amongst everyone who has downloaded the software (or who uses a third party to help them manage the software). The currency, although nothing more than bits in a computer, can be used as a medium of exchange because it has the same qualities as paper money: They are in limited supply, the software prevents people from exchanging the same bits twice, and the currency can be divisible into smaller units (e.g. a person with one bitcoin can exchange 0.5 bitcoin).

We can show how cryptocurrencies are digitized versions of traditional currency by giving an example of one of the proposed uses of cryptocurrencies—aiding transactions in cash-deprived communities:

- Imagine John is ready to harvest his crop. He needs someone to help him harvest before the first frost.
- Ken has some ability in harvesting this particular crop and so is willing to provide his services for a fee.

- John offers Ken 0.30 *smartcoin* for a day's work. Ken knows about *smartcoin* and knows that he can take what John is offering and exchange it later for groceries at the market. The seller at the market accepts *smartcoin*.
- This is something of a negotiation, and Ken argues that he is better and faster than others at this job and asks for 0.50 *smartcoin*. They agree on 0.50 *smartcoin* for a day's work.
- After 5 days of work, John uses his mobile phone to send 2.50 *smartcoin* to Ken's mobile phone.
- Ken then goes to the market and uses his mobile phone to purchase 1.25 *smartcoin* worth of groceries and saves the rest.

Digital currencies can work in environments without established financial institutions or stable governments. Citizens in low-income countries may have Internet access but no access to paper money or have a lack of trust in banks. In these contexts, digital currencies can be used to exchange goods and services.

FRAUD AND CRYPTOCURRENCIES

Cryptocurrencies and their markets are especially susceptible to fraud. The technology underpinning cryptocurrencies is complicated and unfamiliar to most people. Even individuals with an advanced knowledge of computer technology or economics can be conned. Moreover, the strength of cryptocurrency markets—their decentralized and distributed nature, and their lack of regulation—also contribute to them being spaces for fraud. The fact that a central body is not organizing and regulating who can buy or sell, and a governmental authority cannot legitimate one currency over another, creates more opportunities for fraudsters.

Many cryptocurrencies are introduced to the market with much fanfare during their Initial Coin Offering (ICO). After individuals invest in the cryptocurrency by purchasing the currency with legitimate money (dollars, yen, etc.) the cryptocurrency is found to be fraudulent. A few examples:

- *Prodeum* purported to be a "blockchain for fruits and vegetables," and consumers could tell where their produce had originated. Environmentalists and green enthusiasts were interested in investing in the technology. After raising only $11, the company vanished. The scammers had used the identities of reputable personalities in the technology industry to legitimate their businesses.
- *Confido* had billed itself as being able to guarantee contracts between buyer and seller without the need for an escrow account. In what can be called an "exit scam," the startup disappeared after raising $375,000 from investors.
- *Centra Tech* claimed to provide a Mastercard and Visa debit card service that could instantly convert cryptocurrencies to cash. Buoyed by endorsements from celebrities such as the boxer Floyd Mayweather, the company raised $32 million. However, the company misrepresented themselves to the public and was brought up on charges. Stephanie Avakian, codirector of the SEC's enforcement division said in a statement:

"We allege that Centra sold investors on the promise of new digital technologies by using a sophisticated marketing campaign to spin a web of lies about their supposed partnerships with legitimate businesses."

A recent trend is the emergence of various "pump groups." This variation on the pump and dump scheme takes advantage of the lack of regulation and the trendiness of cryptocurrencies. Pump groups form in online chat rooms or discussion boards. Group leaders instruct the group when to buy a certain cryptocurrency. The intensity of transactions drives up the price of the cryptocurrency and becomes noticed by investors outside the group. Savvy scammers then pick the appropriate time to sell their currencies at the inflated price.

Conclusion

In this chapter we explored cyberdeception. Almost everyone in Western societies has an identity online that can be stolen. Similarly, almost everyone shops, or banks, or pays their bills online, and is thus susceptible to auction fraud, counterfeit fraud, and so on. Even in cases where people are vigilant in protecting their identities and are aware of the latest phishing attacks, they may still be susceptible to emotion-based scams such as romance scams and advance fee fraud. Thus, cyberdeception is a category of cybercrime in which a wide swath of people are potential victims, more so than cybertrespass, cyberpornography, or cyberviolence.

Vocabulary

1. **Advance Fee Frauds**—Scams in which a fraudster leads a victim to believe that they will receive a large payment in the future for a present action—usually an "advance fee."
2. **Cryptocurrencies**—A digital form of currency that is a recorded in shared and public databases, or ledger, called a block chain.
3. **Cryptocurrency Fraud**—The fraudulent buying or selling of cryptocurrencies.
4. **Copyright Infringement**—The using of a copyrighted work without either being the owner of a copyright or getting permission from the copyright owner.
5. **Digital Piracy**—The illegal acquisition of digital, copyrighted goods.
6. **Identity Theft**—Obtaining and using another person's personal data in some way that involves fraud or deception.
7. **Non-Rivalrous Goods**—Goods in which the provision or consumption by one party does not reduce the good's availability to another party.
8. **Personally Identifiable Information**—Information that can be used to distinguish and identity a computer user.
9. **Phishing**—Sending fraudulent communications to obtain personal information.
10. **Pump and Dump Schemes**—Fraudsters urge a victim to buy stocks to artificially inflate their value, and then sell the shares they own at the inflated price. The victim is left holding shares that are decreasing in value.

11. **Romance Scams**—A fraudster develops a deceitful relationship with a victim to extract favors from the victim, usually in the form of monetary payments.
12. **Rivalrous Goods**—Goods in which the provision or consumption by one party reduces the good's availability to another party
13. **Selling of Counterfeit Goods**—The selling of merchandise that purports to be a product of a recognized brand company but is instead a copy of lesser value.
14. **Two-Factor Authentication**—The process of identifying a computer user in which two separate types of identification are used.

Study Questions

TRUE OR FALSE

1. According to respondents to a survey conducted by the Identity Theft Resource Center, victims of identity theft lose not only money, but also time.
   a. True
   b. False
2. People have been stealing identities before the invention of the Internet.
   a. True
   b. False
3. One strategy by individuals attempting to commit confidence fraud is to establish credibility and engender trust in the target by sharing (false) personal information.
   a. True
   b. False
4. People who commit digital piracy are highly stigmatized in society.
   a. True
   b. False
5. One way in which fraudsters spread false information about pump and dump schemes is through social media platforms like Twitter.
   a. True
   b. False

MULTIPLE CHOICE

6. Officer Jenkins is giving a talk at a local church about cybercrime. He is trying to educate citizens about cybercrime. A resident asked him, "Officer Jenkins, what is the main thing I should think about when preparing myself for romance scams?" What should be Officer Jenkins' answer?
   a. Education is important. But most importantly, you have to be aware of your emotional state. No matter how smart you think you are, if you are emotionally vulnerable you can be swindled by a clever fraudster.

    b. Most citizens—especially older citizens—are unaware that people are out there trying to scam them. Learn as much as you can about scams and pay attention to the alerts that come from our department. If you learn as much as possible, you will be able to detect romance scams.

7. Which of these scenarios below best represents two-factor authentication?
    a. Entering a password and answering a challenge question (e.g. what is your father's birthday?)
    b. Using your fingerprint and your voice
    c. Inserting a credit card and receiving a notification on your mobile phone
    d. None of the above

8. Isabell has written a program that uses an algorithm to provide personal dating tips. She has copyrighted that program. She is selling the program on Google Play and through the Apple Store at $1.99 per download. Which of these is copyright theft?
    a. Nancy builds on top of Jared's work to produce a newer version of the program
    b. Aaron has bought a version of Isabell's program and is sharing copies of it with friends
    c. Neither A or B
    d. Both A and B

9. Consider an Amazon Kindle Tablet in which the owner has downloaded a series of movies onto the tablet. One of those movies is *The Hunger Games*. What is the non-rivalrous good?
    a. The tablet
    b. The movies on the tablet (e.g. *The Hunger Games*)
    c. Neither A or B
    d. Both A and B

10. In your text, what are the two major motivations for cyberdeception?
    a. Money
    b. Information
    c. Revenge
    d. Thrill
    e. Fear

11. _____ is understood as all types of crime in which someone wrongfully obtains and uses another person's personal data in some way that involves fraud or deception.
    a. Identity theft
    b. Advance fee frauds
    c. Phishing
    d. Romance scams

12. Advance fee frauds are most well known as _____.
    a. Nigerian romance scams
    b. Confidence frauds
    c. Nigerian 419 scams
    d. West African confidence fraud

13. The prime target in romance scams has been _____.
    a. older females
    b. younger females

    c. older males

    d. younger males

14. One technique used by romance scammers is to first ask for trivial favors. This is called the _____.

    a. "slippery slope" technique

    b. "triviality" technique

    c. "trapdoor" technique

    d. "foot in the door" technique

15. Countries that have industries that are often the victims of counterfeiting are ____ likely to host counterfeit websites

    a. less

    b. more

16. _____ refers to the illegal acquisition of digital, copyrighted goods.

    a. Digital piracy

    b. Phishing

    c. Confidence frauds

    d. Romance scams

17. When someone takes a good from the original owner, and the owner no longer has access to this good, this can be called a _____ good.

    a. non-rivalrous

    b. rivalrous

18. Rivalrous goods tend to be _____ goods.

    a. material

    b. non-material

19. Why should individuals interested in cybercrime concern themselves with the difference between rivalrous and non-rivalrous goods?

    a. Goods that are non-rivalrous tend to be more susceptible to piracy

    b. Rivalrous goods are protected by governments more

    c. Law enforcement tends to be uninformed about the dynamics of rivalrous goods

    d. Non-rivalrous goods are less common in the digital environment

20. One type of scam where victims are contacted and told they have won a lottery but need to pay a fee in advance to release the funds is called _____.

    a. bogus lottery

    b. career opportunity scam

    c. bogus products

    d. false lottery

21. Why would there need to be a "system" of phishing fraud?

    a. Law enforcement has gotten too good at investigating phishing

    b. Sometimes a successful phishing attempt produces too much PII

    c. Cybersecurity professionals can now prevent an individual from conducting a successful phishing attempt

    d. All of the above

MATCHING

Describe the type of good as rivalrous (a) or non-rivalrous (b):

22. The Java code used to write a cryptocurrency application
23. The mobile phone a student uses to talk to their mother
24. The theories that sociologists and criminologists use to understand cybercrime
25. The music on a hard drive

Critical Thinking Exercise

LONG ISLAND WOMAN CHARGED WITH USING BITCOIN TO LAUNDER MONEY TO SUPPORT ISIS

An excerpt from Laurel Wamsley's article from NPR on December 15, 2017 reads:

Zoobia Shahnaz, 27, is charged with bank fraud, conspiracy to commit money laundering and three counts of money laundering, according to a statement from the Department of Justice. She pleaded not guilty on Thursday in U.S. District Court in Central Islip, N.Y.

Shahnaz is a U.S. citizen born in Pakistan. She lives in the town of Brentwood, N.Y., where she was working as a lab technician in a Manhattan hospital until June, when she quit her job. The government says Shahnaz was detained on July 31 at John F. Kennedy airport as she was headed to Pakistan by way of Istanbul, from where they believe she intended to enter Syria and join ISIS.

"As a health care professional, in 2016, Ms. Shahnaz was a volunteer with the Syrian American Medical Society assisting other health care providers in delivering lifesaving medical care to Syrian refugees," her attorney, Steve Zissou, tells NPR. "She witnessed the suffering of the refugees firsthand. Her humanitarian efforts then and since were motivated by her commitment to helping alleviate the plight of the people in the Middle East."

According to Justice Department court filings, the defendant used more than a dozen credit cards—six of which allegedly were fraudulently obtained—to buy approximately $62,700 in bitcoin and other cryptocurrencies. The government says Shahnaz converted the cryptocurrencies back to U.S. dollars and deposited the funds into a checking account in her name. She also allegedly obtained a $22,500 loan from a Manhattan bank.

The Justice Department says Shahnaz then began transferring money abroad to support ISIS, while taking measures to disguise the nature and purpose of the funds and avoid transaction reporting requirements.

"Cryptocurrencies operate independently of formal banking structures and provide layers of anonymity to their users," the U.S. Attorney's Office writes in its request for a detention order. "Persons engaged in illicit activity such as money laundering and terrorist financing may use cryptocurrencies to avoid detection by law enforcement or intelligence services."

If cryptocurrencies like Bitcoin continue to rise in popularity, do you think activities like the fraud discussed in the above insert are more or less likely to occur? Why/why not?

Further considering the phenomenon of catfishing and romance scamming in general:

1. How might we go about policing such activity? Should such efforts draw from a primarily local or state-level source? Why/why not?
2. Consider what the sanction would/should be for someone convicted of catfishing. What would be a fair sentence? How would you determine "fairness" under such circumstances?
3. Assume for a moment that most catfish scammers are nonviolent offenders. What might be some considerations for sentencing if one were found guilty of catfishing? Would incarceration be an option in your opinion? Why/why not?
4. Now consider if a catfish offense did result in some violent end result (e.g. an instance of stalking, harassment, or a sexual assault)? Would any of your previous responseschange? If so, explain.

NOTES

1 www.ic3.gov
2 www.bjs.gov/content/pub/press/vit14pr.cfm
3 www.bjs.gov/content/pub/pdf/cv14.pdf
4 www.idtheftcenter.org/
5 www.emc.com/collateral/fraud-report/rsa-online-fraud-report-012014.pdf
6 https://assets.publishing.service.gov.uk/government/uploads/system/uploads/attachment_data/file/546223/OCI-tracker-6th-wave-March-May-2016.pdf
7 www.communications.gov.au/sites/g/files/net301/f/online-copyright-infringement-2016-final_report-accessible.pdf
8 www.riaa.com/reports/the-true-cost-of-sound-recording-piracy-to-the-u-s-economy/
9 www.mpaa.org/research-docs/the-dual-impact-of-movie-piracy-on-box-office-revenue-cannibalization-and-promotion/

REFERENCES

Button, M., Nicholls, C. M., Kerr, J., & Owen, R. (2015). Online fraud victims in England and Wales: Victims' views on sentencing and the opportunity for restorative justice? *The Howard Journal of Criminal Justice*, 54(2), 193–211. doi:10.1111/hojo.12123

Heinonen, J. A., Holt, T. J., & Wilson, J. M. (2012). Product counterfeits in the online environment: An empirical assessment of victimization and reporting characteristics. *International Criminal Justice Review*, 22(4), 353–371. doi:10.1177/1057567712465755

Hill, C. W. L. (2007). Digital piracy: Causes, consequences, and strategic responses. *Asia Pacific Journal of Management*, 24(1), 9–25. doi:10.1007/s10490-006-9025-0

Kirk, D. (2014). Identifying identity theft. *The Journal of Criminal Law, 78*(6), 448–450. doi:10.1177/0022018314557418

Konradt, C., Schilling, A., & Werners, B. (2016). Phishing: An economic analysis of cybercrime perpetrators. *Computers & Security, 58*, 39–46. doi:10.1016/j.cose.2015.12.001

Moore, R., & McMullan, E. C. (2009). Neutralizations and rationalizations of digital piracy: A qualitative analysis of university students. *International Journal of Cyber Criminology, 3*(1), 441–451.

Onyebadi, U., & Park, J. (2012). 'I'm Sister Maria. Please help me': A lexical study of 4-1-9 international advance fee fraud email communications. *International Communication Gazette, 74*(2), 181–199. doi:10.1177/1748048511432602

Packard, A. (2013). *Digital media law* (2nd ed.). Malden, MA: Wiley-Blackwell.

Smallridge, J. L., & Roberts, J. R. (2013). Crime specific neutralizations: An empirical examination of four types of digital piracy. *International Journal of Cyber Criminology, 7*(2), 125–140.

Wadleigh, J., Drew, J., & Moore, T. (2015). *The E-commerce market for "lemons": Identification and analysis of websites selling counterfeit goods* (pp. 1188–1197). ACM Press. doi:10.1145/2736277.2741658

Wall, D. (Ed.). (2001). *Crime and the internet*. New York: Routledge.

Wall, D. S., & Large, J. (2010). Jailhouse frocks: Locating the public interest in policing counterfeit luxury fashion goods. *British Journal of Criminology, 50*(6), 1094–1116. doi:10.1093/bjc/azq048

Whitty, M. T. (2013). The scammers persuasive techniques model: Development of a stage model to explain the online dating romance scam. *British Journal of Criminology, 53*(4), 665–684. doi:10.1093/bjc/azt009

Chapter 6

Investigating Cybercrimes

Introduction

In this chapter, we discuss three broad areas of cybercrime investigations. These three areas are not meant to be exhaustive, but they encompass the most common ways in which cybercrimes are investigated. First, we discuss the practice and process of digital forensic analysis. Of the three areas discussed in this chapter, digital forensics may be the most well-known, even if it is the least understood. Many television shows and movies show law enforcement personnel collecting a computer and handing it to a brainy officer in a computer lab who extracts the evidence needed to apprehend the criminal.

There are two other ways of investigating cybercrimes. Investigators also collect data in the form of text, audio, and video that a suspect or victim has left behind—what we describe as "the human presence." We call this investigating data trails. This mode of investigating relies on the ability of the officer to understand how people use applications in the application layer (see Chapter 1)—especially social media. The third type of investigation is a 21st-century form of the stakeout, where investigators follow a suspect online and attempt to collect evidence on that suspect, oftentimes through subterfuge and impersonation. We can call these online undercover operations. All three areas require a high level of awareness and knowledge of the technologies that produce the digital environment.

Digital Forensics

Forensic science is the application of science and scientific principles to criminal investigations and law. Popular television shows like *CSI: Crime Scene Investigation* and *NCIS* consistently depict elements of forensic science in a dramatic fashion. The characters in the program may use high-speed ballistics photography to understand what weapon and type of bullet was used to create a bullet wound. The characters may use DNA profiling to identify a criminal or victim. Digital forensics is a specialization within this larger body of techniques and is focused on digitized evidence. **Digital forensics** is the science of identifying, preserving, verifying, and analyzing digital evidence located on computer storage media and presenting this evidence in a court of law or to a client (Crain, Hopwood, Pacini, & Young, 2017; Furneaux, 2006; Holt, Bossler, & Seigfried-Spellar, 2015).

All data on a computer is stored as binary numbers, including text, video, and audio. For example, the word "Monarch" would be stored as 01001101 01101111 01101110 01100001 01110010 01100011 01101000. Binary notation is cumbersome to display, so most forensic software converts binary notation into hexadecimal notation. And so, "Monarch" can be displayed in hexadecimal notation as 4D6F6E61726368. Figure 6.1 shows a screenshot of the word document "Challenges in Cybercriminology" (the introduction to this text), using the forensic software Autopsy.[1] Autopsy and other forensic software display files in hexadecimal format. A discussion of binary and hexadecimal number systems is beyond the purview of this text. However, readers may use any number of online resources to learn more. One possible online resource is Binary Hex Converter www.binaryhexconverter.com/.

Digital forensic specialists may need to analyze files at this granular level for a number of reasons. They may be able to recover data by piecing together file fragments from a block of deleted data, a process called **file carving**. With file carving, data may have been deleted, but not overwritten by the operating system. A forensic analysis can find the deleted, but not yet overwritten, files and "carve" them out for evidence. Another reason for analyzing files at

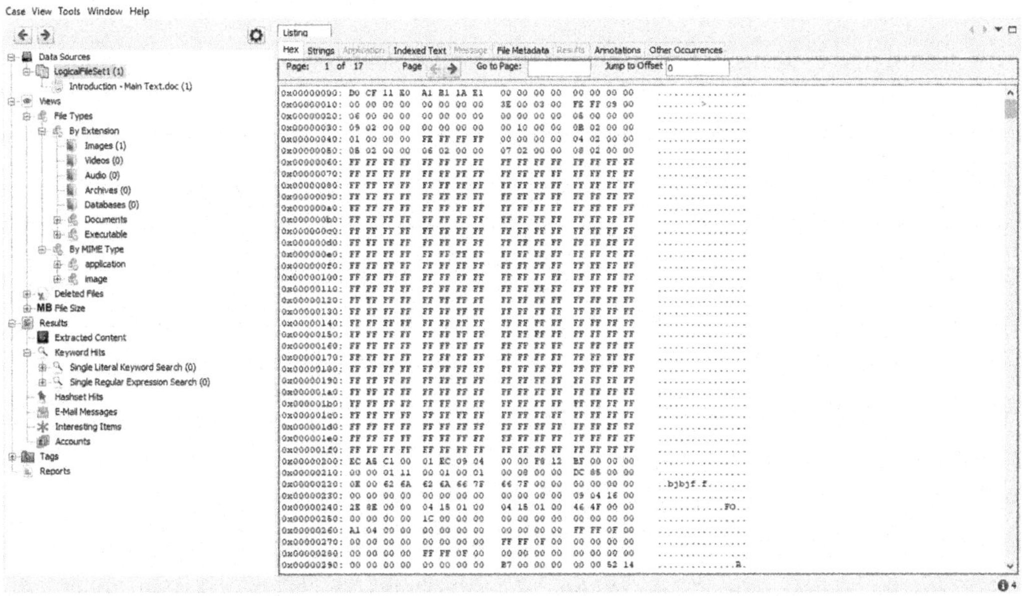

Figure 6.1 Hexadecimal notation example.

the hexadecimal level is to explore hidden contents of a file. As we discussed in Chapter 2 on cybertrespass, there are types of malware that can be embedded in files such as word documents or audio recordings. These documents may appear to be running normally—when infected by a Trojan, for example——but an analysis at the hexadecimal level will show that the malware is present.

There are many types of forensic software that will automate most of the activities necessary for a digital forensic analysis. Forensic software will extract the metadata of a file—the date it was created, modified, and accessed. The software will also detect and recover files that have been deleted, or sift through a collection of files for important keywords. While forensic software can make these tasks easier, the investigator will need to have the requisite training to judge the relevance of the data extracted to a case.

Although one might think of digital forensics as applying primarily to more technologically advanced cases such as hacking or phishing, the reality is that most crimes in the 21st century involve computers in some way. Computer technology and digitized data are found on an ever-wider array of devices. Potential evidence in a case can be found on voice-controlled smart speakers such as Amazon's Echo and Google Home, wearable technologies like Fitbit, and everyday appliances such as televisions and coffeemakers.

THE PROCESS OF DIGITAL FORENSICS

There are five general steps in the process of digital forensics. These steps are sequential, however, and with most there is a considerable amount of back and forth between the steps. These steps are presented visually in Figure 6.2, and we discuss these steps in greater detail next.

1. Identifying Evidence—When law enforcement personnel (LEP) arrive on a scene with computer enabled devices they must decide what machines to collect. In the simplest sense, all data on a machine is considered an **artifact**—data left after the use of a computer. Some artifacts have evidentiary value, and the analyst must make a judgment as to what artifacts they must collect and invest resources in analyzing.

2. Preserving Evidence—In this step, the appropriate evidence is preserved by making a **forensic copy** (also called a forensic image) of the original device's hard drive. A forensic copy is a bit-by-bit copy of the entire hard drive of a device. This is different from, say, copying the contents from a thumb drive to a desktop. A forensic copy also contains the drive space that has not been used or has been used but is now ready to be overwritten (i.e. files that have been deleted by the user). It contains all the files and stored data including passwords, applications, user preferences, log-in files, and more. Often several forensic copies are made. The original is then stored.

3. Verifying Evidence—Once a forensic copy is made, the investigator must verify that the forensic copy is the exact same as the original copy. This is done through a process called hashing. A **hash** is a unique numerical identifier produced by applying a hashing algorithm to a set of data (Konheim, 2010; McKenzie, Harries, & Bell, 1990). The data can be a single file, or an entire hard drive. The common algorithms used are

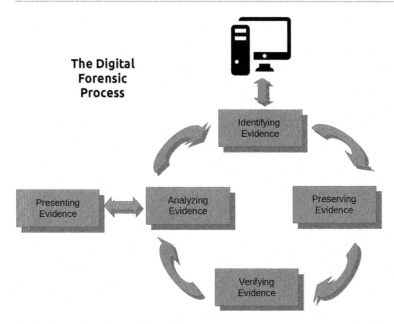

The Digital Forensic Process

Figure 6.2 The process of digital forensics.

called MD5 (Message Digest 5) and SHA256 (Secure Hash Algorithm 256). Like DNA evidence, the value of hashing is in the fact that it is practically impossible for any two files to have the same hash. The investigator can produce a hash of the original evidence and then a hash of the copy, and if the hashes are the same the investigator can conclude that her forensic copy is the same as the original. Online tools can give the student a sense of what a hash looks like. She can then work on the copy and present the evidence confidently to a court or a client. Using the website FileFormat.Info,[2] and inputting this text—"Cybercriminology is for the cool kids"—without the quotations will produce an MD5 hash of "052479b2a7695b330406bef1a8fe6ee9" and a SHA256 hash of "509d4 a94e901534ae649258a6abd22ea36744032b9eedc10e1c952078c333770."

4. Analyzing Evidence—The analysis of evidence requires an understanding of computer technology and an understanding of criminal behavior. For example, an investigator may discover a file with an altered extension. A file that was originally entitled "interesting.jpg" has been modified to "interesting.doc." The investigator will be able to recognize this by looking at the files at the hexadecimal level or using her forensic tool to identify these files. Her training in criminal behavior will alert her to the possibility that people consuming child pornography often hide their images by changing the extension.

5. Presenting Evidence—In court, the computer investigator has at least two challenges. One is to appear credible and knowledgeable when being examined by a defense attorney. The investigator must understand clearly the process by which they have extracted and analyzed their evidence. A second challenge is to explain technical aspects of their analysis to

laymen. A jury or a judge may not understand terminology such as hashing or the purpose of a file extension. The investigator must be able to explain these concepts, or risk their analysis not having the appropriate impact in court. This ability to present technical concepts to a lay audience is also important for investigators who work in the private sector.

These are very general steps in the process of digital forensic analysis. Entire college courses and majors are dedicated to this process. Importantly, however, the steps remain the same even as technology changes.

THE TOOLS USED IN DIGITAL FORENSICS

In carrying out the five-step process described, digital forensics professionals must understand computer fundamentals. They must be able to look at a piece of evidence at the binary or hexadecimal level and make judgments about that evidence. They may, in some cases, need to reconstruct a file that has been deleted using bits and pieces of the file found on the hard drive. They must also be knowledgeable in operating systems—Windows, Linux, Mac OS, and Android—to know how to navigate a piece of hardware and where to look for evidence. The most advanced digital forensics professionals take specialized courses in the discipline and earn certificates and degrees establishing their knowledge of the subject. Table 6.1 lists certificates that signify a digital forensic analyst's expertise. Some of these certificates verify one's ability to work with certain forensic software in forensic analysis and others verify one's competence in the general forensic analysis process. Some certificates are oriented towards a particular occupation such as law enforcement or the military.

Increasingly, tools are available that make digital forensic analysis easier. Both highly specialized professionals and law enforcement with little or no specialized training can conduct

Table 6.1 Digital Forensic Analysis Certifications

- AccessData Certified Examiner (ACE)—certifies that the examiner has proficiency in the Forensic Toolkit software
- Certified Computer Examiner (CCE)—a general certification administered by the International Society of Forensic Computer Examiners
- Certified Forensic Computer Examiner (CFCE)—a general certification administered primarily for local and federal law enforcement administered by the International Association of Computer Investigative Specialists
- Defense Cyber Investigations Training Academy (DCITA)—a general certification primarily for military personnel and administered by the Department of Defense
- Encase Certified Examiner (ENCE)—certifies that the examiner has proficiency in the EnCase forensic software
- Global Information Assurance Certified Forensic Examiner (GCFE)—a general certification administered by the testing company Global Information Assurance Certifications

a forensic analysis using these tools. Several are listed here along with their function in an investigation:

- Write Blocker—When a computer is powered on, the operating system immediately begins writing new information to the hard drive. If a computer is seized in the powered off state, it will need to be powered on for a forensic copy of the hard drive to be made. Any changes to the original state of the hard drive can be used to question the validity of future analyses. A write blocker is used to prevent an operating system, once turned on, from writing new information to its hard drive.
- Disk Imager—Disk imagers create forensic copies to be analyzed by a forensic tool. As mentioned previously, a forensic copy is a bit-by-bit copy of a drive, including unused space and deleted items. There are many tools available for making disk images. These include FTK Imager[3] and Paladin.[4] A free version is Win32 Disk Imager. One of the most common files is the ".e01" or "expert witness" format. Others include "AFF" or advanced forensic format and "dd," or raw evidence format.
- Digital Forensic Analysis Software—Digital forensic analysis software will automate the process of identifying relevant files and will present evidence by producing user-friendly output. Law enforcement agencies that routinely work with digital evidence may purchase forensic analysis software for their officers. Two of the more well-known are EnCase[5] and Forensic Explorer.[6] A well-known free and open source software is Autopsy.

Investigating Data Trails

Investigating cybercrime does not always require the analysis of evidence at the binary level or training in specialized digital forensics. Law enforcement can also investigate crimes by analyzing the "digital footprints" or "digital breadcrumbs" of a suspect (Weaver & Gahegan, 2010). Within a cybercrime context, we prefer to use the term **data trail**, as it connotes following someone or retracing the path of a suspect or victim. By data trail we mean simply the evidence of human presence in the digital environment. This evidence can be interaction with others such as likes and retweets, web searches, text messages, and posts on forums. It can also be the action of signing up for a web service, logging into an account, or completing documentation for a warranty. It can also be the information collected by devices that someone owns such as GPS coordinates.

Consider the case of Andrew Saunders, from Wales, United Kingdom. Saunders, according to *BBC News*, searched for "information on how to make a pipe bomb, how to rig a car so it explodes when started, how to illegally buy a gun, and how to inflict knife injuries."[7] This evidence was used in court to convict Saunders, who stabbed his ex-girlfriend and her new partner outside of a department store.

It is increasingly difficult for people not to leave a data trail. Even individuals who decide to log out of their social media accounts and turn off their mobile phones—go "off the

Table 6.2 Data Trails in the Digital Environment

Type of Layer	Description	Types of Evidentiary Data
Human	The connections and communications between users	Social networks (followers, following)
Content	The information that is produced and shared on the Internet	Information on social media accounts – text, links, likes, photos, etc. Publicly available videos and audio productions
Application	Programs that allow users to perform operations on a computer	The subscription and log-in information for an application (e.g. Skype, Viber, etc.), the content produced on these applications if not shared online.
Operating System	The software that manages the operation of applications on a computer	Warranty Information for Operating Systems
Hardware	The machines that compute and manipulate data	Warranty Information for Hardware and Peripherals
Infrastructure	The technologies that transmit data between machines	Subscription and log-in information

grid"—still may go online to check their bank account or pay a bill or drive their cars to and from work.

Because there is so much data available for law enforcement to collect, we organize data sources by layer of the digital environment (see Table 6.2). The human layer houses the links between people, such as someone's followers on Twitter. Law enforcement can use this information to establish relationships between alleged coconspirators or draw a link between victim and offender. In the content layer, law enforcement can gather information on when and where a person was or where an event happened, and in some cases collect enough contextual clues to establish why something happened (a motive). In the application layer, where most of the human/computer interaction occurs, computer users leave evidence behind when they sign up or log-in to apps, and use apps to produce content. In the next section we will discuss the process by which law enforcement can retrieve data from the companies that own these applications. Below the human, content, and application layers most of the evidence would be stored on hardware, and would therefore require digital forensic analysis.

SEARCH WARRANTS AND INTERMEDIARIES

Data below the content layer—where information is voluntarily made public—is generally considered private and protected by the Fourth Amendment by which American citizens can, in the language of the amendment, "be secure in their persons, houses, papers, and effects, against unreasonable searches and seizures" without probable cause. Once a degree of probable cause is established, law enforcement can request data from the intermediaries that have provided services to the user. **Intermediaries** are companies or organizations that facilitate the communication between users in the digital environment. They usually specialize in a service and produce a profit through the selling of that service or through the advertisements connected to that service. Facebook, Skype, Dropbox, and your local ISP are all intermediaries (Perset, 2010).

These intermediaries collect data on their subscribers, and can provide a detailed account of the when, the where, and in some cases even the why in an investigation. Consider the data that is collected by Pinterest:[8]

- Name
- Email address
- Phone number
- Profile photo
- Pins and Comments
- Location data on Pins and Comments
- Payment information if a purchase is made (what was bought, credit card information, addresses, delivery details)
- Information from Facebook or Google if Pinterest is linked to these accounts
- Internet Protocol address at log-in
- The address of and activity on websites you visit that incorporate Pinterest features
- Web searches
- Browser type and settings
- The date and time of your request
- Cookie data
- Device data
- If you install Pinterest's "save" button, then more information is also collected when this button is used on certain sites

Other social media websites are like Pinterest in what they collect. Much of this data, as mentioned previously, is not publicly available and law enforcement must compel Pinterest to provide this data.

The legislation that governs this process is the **Electronic Communications Privacy Act** (ECPA). The ECPA was passed in 1986 to protect the electronic communications of individuals. It prohibits the interception or attempted interception of an aural, wire, or electronic communication by a device. Wiretapping a phone line, for example, is prohibited by the ECPA. Hacking an Internet connection and intercepting the communications between computers—for example "packet sniffing"—can also be a violation of the ECPA. The ECPA also regulates the type of content that law enforcement can collect on a suspect and can be summarized with three processes that are progressively more invasive and require progressively more justification, shown in Tables 6.3 and 6.4.

The process that requires the least amount of justification is a subpoena, which can be obtained in both civil and criminal cases. A subpoena allows law enforcement to collect specific subscriber info such as the name associated with the account, IP address at time of registration, and time stamps for when a user signs in. This information can be considered **metadata**, as it does not allow law enforcement to read the content of a person's communications, *only the data*

Table 6.3   ECPA Using Google Services as an Example

Legal Process	Description	Gmail
Subpoena (for civil and criminal cases)	Basic subscriber info	Name, account creation information, associated email addresses and phone numbers, time stamp, IP address at registration
Court Order (criminal cases)	Transactional info	Email header information (to and from); IP addresses from where a person is using their account
Warrant (criminal cases)	Content of messages	Email content

Table 6.4   ECPA Using YouTube as an Example

Legal Process	Description	YouTube
Subpoena (for civil and criminal cases)	Basic Subscriber Info	Subscriber registration info; Registration IP addresses and time stamps
Court Order (criminal cases)	Transactional Info	Video upload IP address and time stamp
Warrant (criminal cases)	Content of Messages	Copy of a private video and video info; Private message content

about that data (Baca & Getty Research Institute, 2016; Donohue, 2013; van der Velden, 2015). Examples of metadata include:

- The "tags" associated with a piece of content uploaded to a social media site
- The date that a document was last opened or modified
- The permissions on a document (i.e. can it be modified or is it read only?)
- The geolocation data
- The type of machine that produced the content (e.g. what camera took the picture, what device was used to browse the web)

A court order requires more justification, and specific details about an investigation must be presented and approved by a judge or magistrate. A court order allows the agency to collect transactional info, including the user accounts and IP addresses that have communicated with the account, and places and times where a user has logged in.

A warrant is the most intrusive but requires the most justification from law enforcement. The requesting agency must present to a judge or magistrate "probable cause" that within the content to be searched is evidence relevant to the case at hand. Upon the granting of a warrant, law enforcement can then collect emails or private videos associated with a suspect's account.

The ECPA was written in 1986, at a time before the explosion of internet usage. As a result, many of its provisions are outdated. The provision that is most concerning to civil liberties organizations is that the legal processes discussed earlier are only applicable if the communications are less than 180 days old. Within this six-month period, a user's data is protected.

After the six months law enforcement only needs a subpoena to collect all information from a user's account. In 1986, this was not an issue as most information sent through email was downloaded from computers and removed from the digital environment. Now, however, people store a lifetime's worth of private information in emails, social media accounts, and cloud services. *All* this information can be obtained with little justification after 180 days, and as a result many lawmakers and advocacy groups are working to modify the law.

Online Undercover Investigations

A third way in which cybercrime is investigated is through law enforcement performing undercover or "sting" operations (Grant & Macleod, 2016; Mitchell, Wolak, Finkelhor, & Jones, 2012; Tetzlaff-Bemiller, 2011). These investigations are done to witness someone in the act of committing a crime. Sting investigations are also conducted to collect evidence about an ongoing criminal activity, with the focus being on identifying the network structure of a criminal enterprise and discovering who the most important criminals are. Once the major players are identified, then the operation may use the evidence gathered to request a search warrant of the suspect's hardware or social media accounts.

One type of criminal activity that is routinely investigated through sting operations is online child predation (Grant & Macleod, 2016). Online predators use the anonymity of the digital environment to manipulate children and then exploit them sexually—either through direct sexual contact, for the purposes of producing child pornography, or other activities sexual in nature. The process of manipulation is often called "grooming," where the predator works to gain the trust of a child and prepare them to accept sexual victimization.

A parent may identify the communications their child is having online as being with a child predator and call the police. The police may then take over the account of the child and pose as the child to collect personally identifiable information. Sometimes police are more proactive and pose as a minor on a website or discussion forum where child predators are known to operate. They may also take over the account of a child whose parents have reported that they are being contacted by an adult. The police then collect evidence showing that the adult is making overtures to the minor and ask the adult to meet them in a specific location. If the adult appears at the location, they are apprehended.

A second criminal activity amenable to sting operations is the selling of illegal goods and services on online markets. There are numerous online marketplaces that sell drugs, firearms, malware, and stolen credit card information. Child pornography is also traded on illegal markets. To identify the buyers and sellers on these markers, law enforcement must become buyers or sellers themselves. Many high profile "take downs" of websites on the darknet were aided by information collected in undercover operations. The infamous online drug marketplace Silk Road was busted through an online undercover operation, where the FBI kept tabs on the owner of the website, Ross Ulbricht, until enough evidence was collected to build a strong case.[9]

A case still pending trial at the time of this writing is that of Artem Vaulin of Ukraine. Vaulin allegedly owned and operated Kickass Torrents, or KAT, a commercial website that since

2008 enabled users to illegally reproduce and distribute hundreds of millions of copies of copyrighted motion pictures, video games, television programs, musical recordings, and other electronic media. KAT was collectively valued at more than $1 billion and was the 69th most popular site on the Internet, according to a criminal complaint filed in U.S. District Court in Chicago. Vaulin is charged with:

- One count of conspiracy to commit criminal copyright infringement
- One count of conspiracy to commit money laundering
- Two counts of criminal copyright infringement

This case is instructive for the cybercrime student because of the several ways in which officers collected evidence to charge Vaulin:

- Investigators used the "Wayback Machine" website at www.archive.org to view the historical content of the website (Murphy, Hashim, & O'Connor, 2007). The domain had been moved several times because the website had been seized or blocked by authorities in each country. Using the Wayback Machine, investigators could chart and document the movement of KAT (see Table 6.5). As per court documents:
- To establish that Vaulin was indeed making money from copyright infringement, on about November 13, 2015, an undercover IRS Special Agent sent a request to the email address pr@kat.cr (an email account listed on KAT's website for "press"), inquiring about advertising. In a later correspondence, a KAT representative agreed to provide advertising at $300 per day. The agents bought advertising on KAT on two separate occasions.
- In order to pay for advertising, undercover agents were given two bank account numbers. One of which was to a bank in Latvia under the Mutual Legal Assistance Treaty. Law enforcement was able to establish some sense of the scale of the operation, with the account showing a total of approximately €28,411,357 in deposits between on or about August 28, 2015, and on or about March 10, 2016. This is quite a large sum, and this was only one of the banks used.

Undercover sting operations are necessary for investigating cybercrime. Many cases require investigators to "follow the breadcrumbs" or to link several offenders and organizations together. This requires time and a degree of subterfuge.

Table 6.5   The Domain History of KickAss Torrents

Date Range	Domain
November 2008 through April 2011	kickasstorrents.com
April 2011 through June 2013	kat.ph
June 2013 through December 2014	kickass.to
December 2014 through February 2015	kickass.so
February 2015 through June 2015	kickass.to

However, there are concerns with undercover sting operations. The Center for Problem Oriented Policing identifies several.[10] We list some here:

- They do not reduce or prevent recurring crime problems—If the criminal activity is a repeated one, such as human trafficking or drug selling, then a sting operation may not reduce overall rates of crime. An individual offender may be apprehended, but the root causes remain.
- They may increase crime—Baits and decoys provide new opportunities for criminal behavior. For example, to establish trust or evade suspicion, an undercover officer may need to participate in the criminal enterprise—such as the buying or selling of malware on an online market.
- The government may overreach—To apprehend criminals, law enforcement may be creating conditions for the behavior. As the center writes, "Is it the government's role to construct enticements and situations that encourage all citizens to commit a crime?"
- There are entrapment issues—Offenders can argue that law enforcement tricked them into committing the crime. Courts have standards for determining entrapment; however, often a jury must decide if the offender was entrapped.
- They are expensive—Undercover operations often require the use of props. For example, an undercover officer may need to have in his possession drugs to be sold online. Alternatively, the officer may need money to purchase goods on the illegal market. More importantly, a considerable amount of time may need to be invested in an undercover operation. Operations can take months or years.

Pluralized Policing in the Digital Environment

Policing in the digital environment is characterized by **pluralized policing**, where several non-state actors aid formal law enforcement in the investigation of crime (Loader, 2000; McCahill, 2008; O'Neill & Fyfe, 2017). By non-state actors we mean businesses, nonprofit organizations, advocacy groups, and even private individuals. These non-state actors have an interest in reducing crime, and help law enforcement by collecting data, identifying potential criminals or criminal spaces, crafting legislation, and publicizing cybercrimes.

Pluralized policing is a common characteristic of modern societies. However, non-state actors can have a greater influence on cybercrime investigations. First, many cybercrimes are technologically sophisticated, and their investigation requires a degree of expertise that may not be present in many law enforcement agencies. Second, cybercrimes as a class of crimes are considered less serious than street crimes. Law enforcement, especially at the local level, orient manpower and material resources towards preventing street crimes. Cybercrime investigations, then, are outsourced to non-state actors.

One prominent non-state actor is the Internet Watch Foundation, or IWF.[11] The IWF's mission is to remove "child sexual abuse content hosted anywhere in the world," and "non-photographic [fantasy] child sexual abuse images hosted in the UK." The IWF provides a host of services to law enforcement and content providers. Among other things, they compile a hash list of images that content providers can use to quickly identify illegal images. They also operate a hotline, where computer users can report instances of child pornography. In this way, the IWF performs many of the functions that have been traditionally associated with state law enforcement agencies.

Another example is Romancescams.org. Romance scams are the type of cybercrimes that are difficult to investigate and receive less priority than other types of crimes. Romancescams.org performs the function of informing the public in the way that a local police precinct may hold community meetings about street crime. The website is organized by dating site genre, and lists articles by genre.

Law Enforcement Challenges

Law enforcement has developed many techniques for investigating crime in the digital environment. However, there are unique challenges that make these investigations difficult. One problem is the lack of education for law enforcement. This is a problem primarily at the local levels, where police departments may be small or lack adequate funding for training. Police and detectives do not receive adequate training in cybercrime investigations. Although there are numerous "out of the box" tools for performing digital forensic analyses, personnel must still be trained on those tools. Even less technical investigations, such as following a data trail or performing online investigations, will require training. Law enforcement may need training on the writing of warrants or the possible types of data that can be used as evidence in a case. There are numerous training programs available, however law enforcement may need to pay for this training or allocate precious time to attending the training.

A second challenge is the international nature of many cybercrimes. The Internet Watch Foundation—the non-state actor discussed earlier—claims on its website that "In 1996, the UK hosted 18% of the world's known online child sexual abuse material. Today, it hosts just 0.2%." This may be true, but consumers of child pornography can simply find material in another country. It is only through a coordinated effort that law enforcement can truly tackle the crime. As such, the IWF must work with other international organizations including the European Financial Coalition (EFC) against Commercial Sexual Exploitation of Children Online and the Internet Governance Forum (IGF) Dynamic Coalition on Child Online Protection. Cybercriminals may live in one country, route their Internet activity through a second, and then victimize a user in a third. The international nature of cybercrimes means that coordination is needed between non-state, local, and federal agencies and national agencies in different countries.

Conclusion

In this chapter we explored aspects of policing in the digital environment. We focused on three broad areas—digital forensics, exploring data trails, and online undercover investigations.

These three separate areas are mainly for teaching purposes. The reality of investigations is that these three areas comingle, and many cases require a combination of forensic analysis, collecting information from intermediaries, and doing undercover work to collect more evidence.

National trends suggest that the number of crimes in the physical environment is decreasing. Indeed, aside from some minor deviations, the number of street and property crimes has been steadily decreasing since the late 1980s–early 1990s. Meanwhile, because so many human activities are occurring in the digital environment, the number of cybercrimes is increasing. Given these trends, it is imperative that current and future professionals be trained in cybercrime investigations.

Vocabulary

1. **Artifact**—Data left after the use of a computer.
2. **Data Trail**—The evidence of human presence in the digital environment.
3. **Digital Forensics**—The science of identifying, preserving, verifying, and analyzing digital evidence located on computer storage media and presenting this evidence in a court of law or to a client.
4. **The Electronic Communications Privacy Act (ECPA)**—A federal statute that prohibits the interception or attempted interception of an aural, wire, or electronic communication by a device.
5. **File Carving**—The process of recovering data by piecing together file fragments from a hard drive.
6. **Forensic Copy**—A bit-by-bit copy of the entire hard drive of a device, including the files, the deleted files, and the unallocated space.
7. **Hash**—A unique numerical identifier produced by applying a hashing algorithm to a set of data.
8. **Intermediaries**—Companies or organizations that facilitate the communication between users in the digital environment.
9. **Metadata**—Data that describes another set of data.
10. **Pluralized Policing**—A method of policing in which several non-state actors aid formal law enforcement in the investigation of crime.

Study Questions

TRUE OR FALSE

1. Most forensic software represents computer information in hexadecimal notation.
   a. True
   b. False

2. A disk imager is used to prevent an operating system, once turned on, from writing new information to its hard drive.
   a. True
   b. False

3. Digital forensic analysis does not usually apply to non-technological crimes like stalking and murder.
   a. True
   b. False

4. The IP address from where a YouTube video was uploaded is an example of metadata.
   a. True
   b. False

5. In the human layer, where most of the human/computer interaction occurs, computer users leave evidence behind when they sign up or log-in to apps, and use apps to produce content.
   a. True
   b. False

6. Law enforcement can collect information about who you emailed with a court order.
   a. True
   b. False

7. One drawback of undercover investigations is that they may increase crime.
   a. True
   b. False

MULTIPLE CHOICE

8. Select all the ways of investigating cybercrimes as discussed in the text.
   a. Investigating data trails
   b. Surveying techniques of offenders
   c. Undercover sting operations
   d. Digital forensic analysis
   e. Crime analytics

9. What is one of the main reasons that undercover investigations are undertaken?
   a. To uncover the personal connections of those involved in a complex criminal activity
   b. To investigate a crime using the minimal amount of resources
   c. To involve officers who are both experienced and new
   d. To incorporate the suggestions of politicians and academics

10. What type of criminal activity from the list below is best suited for an undercover criminal investigation?
    a. The use of social engineering to gain PII
    b. A mass murder in a school

    c. The growth of hate speech online

    d. Activities on an online drug marketplace

11. Which of these are problems with undercover investigations?

    a. Law enforcement may be charged with deceiving a criminal into committing the crime

    b. Officers may be biased towards people they come to know during an operation

    c. It may not decrease overall rates of crime

    d. Operations can be very expensive

12. All data in a computer is stored as _____.

    a. fractions

    b. binary numbers

    c. exponents

    d. text

13. _____ are businesses, nonprofit organizations, advocacy groups, and even private individuals.

    a. Non-state actors

    b. Public actors

    c. Private actors

    d. Pluralized actors

14. _____ create bit-by-bit copies of a drive to be examined using forensic software.

    a. Disk imagers

    b. Write blockers

    c. Transponders

    d. Anti-virus software

15. The term _____ refers to the evidence of human presence in the digital environment.

    a. intermediaries

    b. warrant trail

    c. data trail

    d. forensic evidence

16. Which of these are examples of intermediaries?

    a. Facebook

    b. Netflix

    c. Cox Cable

    d. All of the above

17. What is one function of the ECPA?

    a. It identifies when law enforcement can enter into a person's home and search for evidence

    b. It regulates the distribution of adult content online

    c. It regulates the circumstances in which law enforcement can request private data from a citizen

    d. It identifies the occasions when law enforcement can arrest a citizen for suspicious online activity

MATCHING

Match the data with the layer it is found in.

18. The playlist in a person's YouTube channel
19. Your log-in activity from your Internet Service Provider
20. A person has bought a subscription to the online dating service Ashley Madison
21. The serial number on a laptop
    a) human
    b) content
    c) application
    d) operating system
    e) hardware
    f) infrastructure

ORDERING

22–26. There is an agreed-upon process of analyzing and presenting digital forensic evidence to a court. Place this process in order from beginning (1) to end (5):
    a) presenting evidence
    b) identifying evidence
    c) verifying evidence
    d) preserving evidence
    e) analyzing evidence

Critical Thinking Exercise

Have students in the class consider the coursework and training required to become a police officer with cybercrime/cyberdeviance distinction.

- What do you envision such a distinction would entail? What skills/abilities would you envision are part of such a distinction?
- What are some policing questions and/or issues that would need to be addressed specifically by an officer carrying such a distinction?
- What might be some challenges facing police officers specializing in cybercrime or cyberdeviance offenses?

Referring back to Wall's typology of cybercrime and cyberdeviance (see Chapter 1), discuss some policing challenges unique to each category: cybertrespass, cyberpornography, cyberviolence, and cyberdeception.

Have students consider and discuss the various types of digital forensic evidence, data trails, and online undercover investigative practices unique to each of Wall's categories. Further, have students note where there is overlap between categories for the respective policing aspects.

NOTES

1 www.sleuthkit.org/autopsy/
2 www.fileformat.info/tool/hash.htm
3 http://marketing.accessdata.com/ftkimager3.4.2
4 https://sumuri.com/software/paladin/
5 www.guidancesoftware.com/
6 www.forensicexplorer.com/
7 www.bbc.com/news/uk-wales-south-east-wales-39100854
8 https://policy.pinterest.com/en-gb/privacy-policy
9 http://theconversation.com/end-of-the-silk-road-how-did-dread-pirate-roberts-get-busted-18886
10 www.popcenter.org/
11 www.iwf.org.uk/

REFERENCES

Baca, M., & Getty Research Institute (Eds.). (2016). *Introduction to metadata* (3rd ed.). Los Angeles, CA: Getty Research Institute.

Crain, M. A., Hopwood, W. S., Pacini, C., & Young, G. R. (Eds.). (2017). Digital forensics. In *Essentials of forensic accounting* (pp. 301–339). New York: American Institute of Certified Public Accountants, Inc. doi:10.1002/9781119449423.ch11

Donohue, L. (2013). Bulk metadata collection: Statutory and constitutional considerations. *Harvard Journal of Law and Public Policy, 37*(3), 757–900.doi:10.2139/ssrn.2344774

Furneaux, N. (2006). An introduction to computer forensics. *Medicine, Science and the Law, 46*(3), 213–218. doi:10.1258/rsmmsl.46.3.213

Grant, T., & Macleod, N. (2016). Assuming identities online: Experimental linguistics applied to the policing of online paedophile activity. *Applied Linguistics, 37*(1), 50–70. doi:10.1093/applin/amv079

Holt, T. J., Bossler, A. M., & Seigfried-Spellar, K. C. (2015). *Cybercrime and digital forensics: An introduction.* London; New York: Routledge.

Konheim, A. G. (2010). *Hashing in computer science: Fifty years of slicing and dicing.* Hoboken, NJ: John Wiley & Sons, Inc. doi:10.1002/9780470630617

Loader, I. (2000). Plural policing and democratic governance. *Social & Legal Studies, 9*(3), 323–345. doi:10.1177/09646639000900301

McCahill, M. (2008). Plural policing and CCTV surveillance. In M. Deflem & J. T. Ulmer (Eds.), *Sociology of crime law and deviance* (Vol. 10, pp. 199–219). Bingley: Emerald (MCB UP). doi:10.1016/S1521-6136(07)00209-6

McKenzie, B. J., Harries, R., & Bell, T. (1990). Selecting a hashing algorithm. *Software: Practice and Experience, 20*(2), 209–224. doi:10.1002/spe.4380200207

Mitchell, K. J., Wolak, J., Finkelhor, D., & Jones, L. (2012). Investigators using the Internet to apprehend sex offenders: Findings from the Second National Juvenile Online Victimization Study. *Police Practice and Research, 13*(3), 267–281. doi:10.1080/15614263.2011.627746

Murphy, J., Hashim, N. H., & O'Connor, P. (2007). Take me back: Validating the wayback machine. *Journal of Computer-Mediated Communication, 13*(1), 60–75. doi:10.1111/j.1083-6101.2007.00386.x

O'Neill, M., & Fyfe, N. R. (2017). Plural policing in Europe: Relationships and governance in contemporary security systems. *Policing and Society, 27*(1), 1–5. doi:10.1080/10439463.2016.1220554

Perset, K. (2010). *The Economic and Social Role of Internet Intermediaries* (OECD Digital Economy Papers No. 171). doi:10.1787/5kmh79zzs8vb-en

Tetzlaff-Bemiller, M. J. (2011). Undercover online: An extension of traditional policing in the United States. *International Journal of Cyber Criminology, 5*(2), 813–824.

van der Velden, L. (2015). Forensic devices for activism: Metadata tracking and public proof. *Big Data & Society, 2*(2), 1–14. doi:10.1177/2053951715612823

Weaver, S. D., & Gahegan, M. (2010). Constructing, visualizing, and analyzing a digital footprint. *Geographical Review, 97*(3), 324–350. doi:10.1111/j.1931-0846.2007.tb00509.x

Chapter 7

Organized Cybercrime

Introduction

Organized crime has captivated the American public for decades. We can see this in the movies and television shows that act as a mirror of society. The mafia has historically attracted the most attention with high-profile figures such as Al Capone and John Gotti becoming a part of our national imagination and cultural products such as *The Godfather* and *The Sopranos* being landmarks in American cinema. Beginning in the 1980s, increased rates of street crime and the explosion of the crack epidemic placed attention on drug gangs. Like the Italian Mafia in the mid-20th century, these street gangs, primarily black and Latino, operated through a combination of violence and corruption. The HBO series *The Wire* provides an example of this.

In the 21st century, organized crime is poised to take on a new look. On the one hand, you have more traditional organized crime groups migrating some of their activities into the digital environment. Again, we can think about movies and television shows in which organized crime groups that traffic in drugs or prostitution have one or more technically sophisticated hackers assisting them in their exploits. On the other hand, wholly new organized crime groups are working entirely online. These groups, because of the lack of fisticuffs, provide less fodder for action, and may never be a common subject of movies. However, academic research suggests that these groups are plentiful and will continue to proliferate.

This chapter explores organized crime in the digital environment. First, we define and describe traditional organized crime and then import these understandings into the digital environment. We then explore the forms that organized crime takes in the digital environment. Like comparisons made in previous chapters, we find both similarities and differences between the physical and digital. In short, organized crime online is just as sophisticated as traditional organized crime, however the structure of groups is less hierarchical and more networked. We next discuss some of the criminal activities of organized crime groups. These crimes are the same as those covered in previous chapters—cybertrespass, cyberpornography, cyberviolence, and cyberdeception. However, they are done on a larger scale and with more sophistication. We use as example the activities of the Carbanak/Cobalt Group. Finally, we discuss the key legislation used to prosecute organized cybercrime and raise questions as to the appropriateness of these laws.

Defining and Describing Organized Crime

There has been a debate within the social sciences about how to conceptualize organized crime. The debate revolves around the term "organized" (Finckenauer, 2005, 64). Almost any crime can be committed by a group of people working together as coconspirators. For example, individual juveniles may make temporary alliances to commit an armed robbery. Or, disgruntled associates in a retail business may work together to embezzle money. These are certainly crimes that are organized. The offenders must coordinate their activities to attain their goals. They will have some type of rudimentary leadership structure and assigned roles. However, their lack of sophistication and lack of permanence constrains the scale of their activities. Once the "crime that is organized" has been committed, the group may not attempt to build on their success or further develop their infrastructure to commit more sophisticated crimes. They are not as serious or as disruptive to society, and do not require the type of resource-intensive investigations by federal agencies that the Italian Mafia or MS-13 have historically called for.

In order to distinguish between crimes committed by temporary groups, and crimes committed by stable, sophisticated organizations, Hagan (2006) designates the latter as a proper noun. We do the same here. Groups like the Italian Mafia and drug cartels are participating in Organized Crime.

Social scientists have explored what makes a collection of individual criminals an Organized Crime group. Finckenauer writes that a criminal organization is a social network of individuals who vary along several dimensions (2005, 75–76). These dimensions are good starting points for identifying Organized Crime:

- *Criminal sophistication—The degree of planning used in carrying out a crime, how long does the commission of a criminal act take, and how much skill and knowledge is required to carry out the crime.* Consider drug trafficking, which may require coordinating the negotiation and acquisition of contraband from entities that may be outside of the country, securing safe passage of that contraband, distributing it to sellers in the most advantageous locations, and monitoring the sales of the sellers, all while evading law enforcement. They can also be sophisticated in the amount of technical skill required.
- *Structure—The degree to which a division of labor defines authority and leadership, and to which the structure maintains itself over time and across crimes.* As with all large groups, a stable group structure is needed for individuals to work together efficiently. Organized Crime groups tend to have relatively large group structures with several levels of authority. Consider the well-known organization of the Italian American Mafia crime

families. Each family begins with a "Boss" or "Don" at the top who leads the organization, followed by a second in command or "Underboss." The Don is advised by a counselor, or consiglieri, who is usually third in command. Under these leaders are "Capos" who lead a crew of "Soldiers." At the bottom of the organization are "Associates" who may not be official members of the family but assist in criminal activity.

- *Self-identification—The degree to which individuals in the network see themselves as being a part of an organization: there are examples of group connections such as use of colors, special clothing, special language, and tattoos.* The individuals in Organized Crime groups self-identify as being members of a group. In street gangs, drug cartels, and the mafia an erstwhile member may need to undergo some type of initiation, often involving committing a crime of some kind. In some cases, the crime could be as serious as committing murder. There will also be certain customs, beliefs, and **argot** unique to the group that a person who identifies with this group will adopt. The colors chosen by a gang—red for Bloods and blue for Crips—is an instance of this.

- *Authority of reputation—The degree to which the organization has the capacity to force others to do what it dictates through fear and intimidation, without resorting to violence.* Organized Crime groups can intimidate civilians and law enforcement and defend their zone of criminal activity through their reputation. Previous acts of violence precede Organized Crime groups, such that potential rivals, concerned citizens, and even law enforcement are less likely to interfere with current or future crimes. This reputation develops over time and speaks to a permanence and stability that Organized Crime groups have, that individuals committing crimes that are organized do not.

These dimensions are good theoretical tools for analyzing a group and determining if it can be sufficiently categorized as an Organized Crime group. However, it is important to note that these dimensions are only guideposts, and groups will vary in the degree to which they fall on any given dimension. Ultimately labeling a group as an Organized Crime group is a matter of informed judgment.

For our purposes, we will use these dimensions to construct a working definition of Organized Crime for this chapter. Organized Crime groups are defined as hierarchical and structured organizations conducting sophisticated criminal activities in which the members develop their own inner culture and the group develops a reputation for criminality. Our next task is to import this definition into the digital environment and explore the ways Organized Crime is conducted online.

The Activities of Organized Crime in the Digital Environment

Organized Crime can entail any of the crimes discussed within the four categories of cybertrespass, cyberpornography, cyberviolence, and cyberdeception. However, certain crimes are more effectively done using the infrastructure and resources of Organized Crime groups. Grabosky (2007) discusses several of these crimes, and we highlight four of these here—digital piracy, forging official documents, money laundering, and cyberterrorism. We also add a fifth—**wide-stroke attacks**.

- Digital piracy—Digital piracy, as discussed in a previous chapter, is commonplace in society. Most computer users who illegally download or share material do not consider their activities criminal. Indeed, there is little incentive for content creators, content distributors, or law enforcement to pursue digital piracy cases because an individual person's copyright infringement has little impact on the industry. However, Organized Crime groups pirate content on a large scale and cost industries millions of dollars. They have the financial resources to purchase the hardware to copy digitized content on compact discs. They also have the connections and infrastructure to deliver the pirated materials to marketplaces.
- Forging Official Documents—Organized Crime groups participate in the digital reproduction of official documents, especially passports. The forging of official documents is itself a crime. But as Grabosky argues, it is also a crime facilitator. Fraudsters use driver's licenses to open bank accounts for the depositing of stolen money. Criminals of all stripes may wish to cross borders to evade law enforcement and can use false passports to do so.
- Money Laundering—Governments monitor cash transactions, making it difficult for criminals to conceal the origins of their cash. However, the infrastructure of Organized Crime makes it possible for money to be "cleaned." For example, the Organized Crime group may have built a ledger of accounts in a number of countries and can route monies across many jurisdictions making it difficult for funds to be traced. Another strategy is to use people as mules to deposit cash below the threshold of surveillance. Yet another strategy is to coordinate a phantom sale on an online auction website, where stolen cash is deposited in an account disguised as monies from a sale. What is important here is that these types of activities require a level of coordination and depth of infrastructure most likely found in stable Organized Crime groups.
- Cyberterrorism—Terrorist activities, primarily seen as ideologically or politically motivated, are not usually labeled as the work of Organized Crime groups. But as Grabosky (2007) writes, "Most terrorist activity is certainly organized. And it is usually, if not always, criminal. Moreover, one sees examples of terrorist organizations engaging in more traditional criminal activity in order to raise revenue" (153). Cyberterrorists use the digital environment for psychological warfare by making webcasts of executions and bombings. They may also use the digital environment to disseminate instructional materials on how to commit terrorist acts.
- Wide-stroke attacks—In addition to the crimes already listed, Organized Crime Groups supervise the mass deployment of malware, or what can be called wide-stroke attacks. These attacks include the collection of personally identifiable information (PII) sometimes needed to deploy the malware, the extraction of money or information, and the laundering of that money. Individual hackers or temporary groups can also perform

these activities; however, Organized Crime groups can better organize the collection of monetizable data and the laundering of money stolen. Moreover, because many examples of cybertrespass require social engineering, Organized Crime groups can better deploy individuals over a variety of locations to steal PII to circumvent two-factor authentication.

AN EXAMPLE OF ORGANIZED CRIME IN THE DIGITAL ENVIRONMENT—THE CARBANAK/COBALT GROUP

One example is the Russian Organized Crime group called Carbanak/Cobalt. The group has been in operation since 2013, and the name derives from the two pieces of malware—Carbanak and Cobalt—used to steal over 1.3 billion dollars during that time frame (see Figure 7.1). Carbanak was the name of the first penetration tool used, and Cobalt followed. The group has attacked over

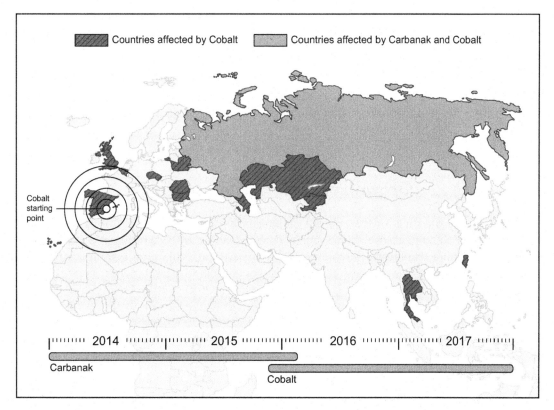

Figure 7.1   The countries affected by the Carbanak and Cobalt malware (Adapted from: www.europol.europa.eu/newsroom/news/mastermind-behind-eur-1-billion-cyber-bank-robbery-arrested-in-spain).

100 financial institutions across 14 European countries, including Britain, Russia, Spain, and the Netherlands.

The attacks follow a general pattern. First, the group deploys the malware through a spear phishing attack. Emails are sent to company employees, asking them to click on a link. Once one computer is infected, the malware spreads throughout the financial institution's network, eventually infecting the servers and ATMs. Next, criminals use money mules to extract cash. One way this is done is by inflating the balance of bank accounts and then having a money mule withdraw cash. Another is for the money mule to be at a specified ATM at a time when cash is automatically ejected. Next, the money is laundered by purchasing goods on black markets or converting the cash into cryptocurrencies.

The Carbanak/Cobalt gang has many of the characteristics of an Organized Crime group. The crimes are complex and sophisticated, with the production of specialized malware deployed across a range of countries, and the need for a variety of coconspirators working together. The organization exhibits a structure, with hackers and money mules being the two known roles. There is also a recognized leader. In 2018, the leader of Carbanak/Cobalt, called "Denis K" was arrested along with three other members of the group.[1]

The two other characteristics of Organized Crime we introduced—self-identification and authority of reputation—are likely present. One indirect way of assessing reputation is to look at how much resources are dedicated to investigating and stopping the crime. The arrest of "Denis K" required the work of the Spanish National Police, Europol, the FBI, the Romanian, Moldovan, Belarussian, and Taiwanese authorities, and private cyber-security companies.

Arresting the leaders of mafias and street gangs will slow down and destabilize an Organized Crime group. However, these groups can often reorganize after a shuffle of roles and responsibilities within the group structure. After the arrest of "Denis K," the Carbanak/Cobalt group is still active.

Organized Cybercrime Myths

Many scholars are critical of the public's understanding of Organized Crime. They believe that the media sometimes over-hypes an instance of crime by describing it as organized, and therefore more dangerous. Lavorgna (2018) argues that explaining instances of activities that are organized as organized crime is a rhetorical tool to attract more resources to law enforcement agencies. In a study of UK news reports from 2010 to 2016, Lavorgna found consistent evidence that reports linking cybercrime with organized crime were "moral panics." Stories painted hyperbolic and exaggerated pictures of the prevalence and threat of organized cybercrime. Similarly, Leukfeldt and colleagues (2017) argue that many countries, such as the United Kingdom, link the seriousness of a crime to organized crime. A hacking activity that creates a large data breach, like the ones discussed in Chapter 2, may be considered an instance of Organized Crime simply because of the amount of money stolen. These crimes may indeed be sophisticated. But their lack of structure, lack of self-identification amongst those who participated in the crime, and the lack of reputation suggests that these crimes were committed by a collection of temporary co-conspirators, and not a stable group of organized criminals.

Caution is required because the digital environment makes it easy for collections of individuals to come together and commit crime. However, the labeling of these networks as Organized Crime may be premature. Because organized crime investigations are challenging and time-consuming, much-needed resources in time, money, and intellectual energy may be wasted on the wrong criminal activities.

The Unique Form of Organized Crime Online: Networks

The unique qualities of the digital environment have changed the way individuals work together to commit crimes. One change is that crimes can be coordinated over greater distances and greater time spans. For example, communication between leaders and subordinates can occur via emails and instant messages, with one party being in North America sending an email or text message, to be read by a subordinate in Estonia. Another change is that this coordination can occur amongst a greater number of people. In the research for his famous ethnography *Gang Leader for a Day* (2008), Dr. Sudhir Venkatesh comments on how the gang leader J.T. had to find places for his gang to meet. As the leader, he had to identify and secure places large enough and secret enough for upwards of 100 gang members to meet. This is no small task when law enforcement is attempting to monitor the movements of most of those individuals. The digital environment greatly reduces this difficulty as one need not meet physically to communicate in real time.

Thus, Organized Crime in the digital environment is characterized by networks—the ties between individuals via their computer technology. And so, while sophistication, structure, self-identification, and reputation are still important characteristics of Organized Crime, scholars have worked to describe the new forms Organized Crime has taken in the digital environment. We discuss two scholars' attempts to categorize these new forms next.

MCGUIRE'S ORGANIZED CRIME TYPOLOGY

One typology, developed by McGuire (2012) posits three major types of organized cybercrime networks (see Table 7.1). These major types are first organized by the amount of criminal activity in the digital environment, and then divided into sub-types according to their level of cohesion.

Type I groups operate solely in the digital environment, meaning that the crimes they commit are committed online and their interactions with each other are online. These groups can be either loosely organized **swarms** or more organized **hubs**. Swarms are quite common when committing acts that are considered as deviant but not necessarily criminal. For example, groups of people may decide to harass someone on social media that they do not like because of a comment

Table 7.1   McGuire's Organized Crime Typology

Major Type	Weaker Associations	Stronger Associations
Type 1 Operate solely in the digital environment	**Swarms** Collections of individuals who are minimally organized (e.g. hate speech groups, Anonymous)	**Hubs** Networks characterized by a smaller, stable leadership "core," and many peripheral and transient associates (e.g. various "markets," including carding markets and the distribution of child pornography)
Type 2 Hybrids that operate in both the physical and digital environments	**Clustered Hybrid** A small group of individuals with numerous peripheral associates— similar in composition to hubs (e.g. hackers working with individuals who place credit card skimmers in stores)	**Extended Hybrid** More complex than clustered hybrids, with numerous associates and groups that carry out a wider range of criminal activities (e.g. a group may skim and sell credit card data, and operate an online site soliciting prostitution)
Type 3 Operate in the physical environment, but use Internet technologies to help perpetrate crimes	**Hierarchies** Traditional organized crime groups such as the mafia that use online technologies to aid in their activities (e.g. drug smuggling, gambling)	**Aggregate Groups** Less organized collections of people who may only temporarily work together and use technology to commit crimes (e.g. flash robs)

they have made or stance they have taken. This behavior in most contexts does not require any true coordination. Individuals can see one person they follow or admire flame someone online, and then emulate them. In this manner, a few people with a large following can create a swarming effect. This same dynamic may underlie political resistance efforts such as BlackLivesMatter and MeToo, where influential users of Twitter rally their followers to speak out about a cause. Hubs are like swarms in that the activity occurs entirely online. However, there is a more well-defined leadership core. It is possible that within this core one can see more clearly the elements of an organized crime unit—sophistication, structure, self-identification, and reputation. Around this core are people who may not maintain long connections with the core, but temporarily work with the core to commit crimes.

Types 2 and 3 are not exclusively digital in their interactions and orientation. Type 2 organized crime networks commit crimes both online and off. An example of this would be a group that installs credit card skimmers in the physical environment, and then attempts to sell the card data or make purchases in the digital environment. Type 2 networks are also divided by their sophistication, clustered **hybrids** being less sophisticated than extended hybrids. Type 3 networks are primarily traditional offline organized crime groups that are now conducting activities online. For example, mafia groups have traditionally operated illegal gambling spaces in the physical environment. They have now migrated online and have organized illegal gambling operations in the digital environment.

LEUKFELD'S TYPOLOGY

Leukfeldt and colleagues (2017) have provided a second typology, derived from a study of 18 phishing criminal investigations in Denmark. According to these scholars, organized cyber-crime networks can be divided into three types based upon the sophistication of technology used and the degree of victim–attacker interaction:

- Type 1: Low-tech attacks with a high degree of victim–attacker interaction—The attacker sends a phishing email to a victim stating that their account is not secure. The victim supplies banking information when clicking on the link. An attacker then contacts the victim by phone and gains more information that can be used to steal monies from the victim's account.
- Type 2: Low-tech attacks with a low degree of victim–attacker interaction—These attacks are more sophisticated and find ways of extracting necessary information without the use of a phone call. A phishing email may be designed such that a victim inputs all the necessary information via the email.
- Type 3: High-tech attacks with a low degree of victim–attacker interaction—These attacks are the most sophisticated and rely on various types of malware to infect and control a computer. Once this occurs, the criminal network can manipulate the bank transfers of the victim.

THE IMPORTANCE OF TYPOLOGIES

A typology can aid one in understanding how to investigate a criminal network. For example, using McGuire's typology, a hierarchical group will require a different approach than a swarm. The former is likely to be more serious in the types of criminal activities it can undertake and will require more long-term investigation techniques. Meanwhile, swarms may not require as much long-term investment, however law enforcement may need to develop online strategies that can be deployed quickly to deal with the types of offenses associated with this type.

For the social scientist, questions can be asked as to what kind of offenders are more likely to associate with a given organized network. For example, using Leukfeldt's typology, it is likely that the low-tech, high-interaction network is populated with offenders of different profiles than those in the high-tech, low-interaction network. Those offenders who migrate to low-tech, high-interaction crime networks are comfortable with human interaction in the physical environment and may branch off to other traditional types of con-artistry. Meanwhile, offenders operating in high-tech, low-interaction networks may be classic "black hat hackers" who write malware for crimes solely in the digital environment.

Division of Labor in Organized Cybercrime Networks

Broadhurst et al. (2014) summarizes the ten roles in organized cybercrime networks, as outlined in a speech given by Steven R. Chabinsky, Deputy Assistant Director, Cyber Division, Federal Bureau of Investigation:[2]

1. Coders or programmers—They create the malware and exploits. The creation of malware and exploits is not in itself criminal.
2. Technicians—They maintain the supporting technologies, such as servers, ISPs, and encryption.
3. Distributors or vendors—They trade and sell stolen data in carding markets.
4. Hackers—They search for vulnerabilities in applications, systems, and networks.
5. Fraud specialists—They develop and employ non-technical social engineering schemes.
6. Hosts—They provide facilities—servers and sites—for the storing and sharing of illicit content.
7. Cashers—They control drop accounts and provide those names and accounts to other criminals for a fee; they also manage individual cash couriers, or "money mules."
8. Money mules—They transfer the proceeds of frauds to a third party for further transfer.
9. Tellers—They assist in transferring and laundering illicit proceeds through digital currencies and national currencies.
10. Executives—They select the targets, and recruit and assign members to the above tasks. They also manage the distribution of criminal proceeds.

These roles speak to the complexity of organized cybercrime networks. They can grow quite large and sophisticated. Not all networks will have a person or persons that fulfill each of these roles. However, as an organized cybercrime network grows larger and undertakes a wider range of activities it will need individuals to take on these roles. It is also the case that one person can fulfill several of these roles. For example, one person may perform the roles of coder, technician, and hacker as they require a similar skill set. Meanwhile, another person may handle the "human contact" skills such as being a distributor or fraud specialist.

Prosecuting Organized Crime in the Digital Environment

United States law enforcement agencies can use at least two statutes to prosecute organized crimes. One is the **Racketeer Influenced and Corrupt Organizations (RICO) Act**. Individuals who are members of a criminal enterprise and who have committed two acts of racketeering activity within the previous 10 years can be sentenced to up to 20 years in prison per racketeering account. There are several forms of racketeering, including:

- Bribery
- Counterfeiting
- Money Laundering
- Murder for Hire
- Drug Trafficking
- Prostitution
- Sexual Exploitation of Children
- Alien Smuggling
- Murder
- Kidnapping
- Gambling
- Arson
- Robbery
- Extortion

The second is the **Continuing Criminal Enterprise (CCE) Statute**. This statute is narrower in its scope and is used to prosecute leaders of criminal enterprises associated with drug trafficking. CCE is often referred to as the "Kingpin" statute for this reason. A conviction under CCE results in a minimum 20 years in prison and a maximum fine of $2 million.

The term "enterprise" is important for both of these laws, as Organized Crime is equated to a type of criminal enterprise. An enterprise, according to the RICO act, is defined as "any individual, partnership, corporation, association, or other legal entity, and any union or group of individuals associated in fact although not a legal entity." A *criminal* enterprise according to RICO, then, is:

> any group of six or more people, where one of the six occupies a position of organizer, a supervisory position, or any other position of management with respect to the other five, and which generates substantial income or resources, and is engaged in a continuing series of violations.[3]

DAVID RAY CAMEZ

In 2013, David Ray Camez became the first person convicted of a cybercrime under the Racketeer Influenced and Corrupt Organizations (RICO) Act. Camez, operating out of Phoenix, Arizona, participated in criminal activities on Carder.su. Carder.su was a website on which fraudsters bought and sold a variety of goods and services including stolen credit card data and malware. The website cost, according to prosecutors, about $51 million in losses for individuals and businesses. Camez was caught during an undercover online sting operation. Camez paid an undercover agent money for a fake Arizona driver's license under an alias. At a press conference, Assistant Attorney General for Arizona David O'Neill said of the case:

> Camez was a member of a vast criminal organization that facilitated rampant cyber fraud throughout the world ... This organization is the new face of organized crime—a highly structured cyber network operated like a business to commit fraud on a global scale. Members, like Camez, paid to tap into the network and gain control of highly sensitive information, like compromised credit card numbers and stolen identities. Thanks to sophisticated law enforcement efforts, Camez will now pay for his crimes with decades in prison.[4]

Camez was convicted of one count of participating in a racketeer-influenced corrupt organization and one count of conspiracy to participate in a racketeer-influenced corrupt organization. His penalty is 20 years in prison, three years supervised release, and he must pay $20 million in restitution.

The prosecutors in the case were able to convince the jury that Camez was a "member of a vast criminal organization," and therefore could be prosecuted under RICO. However, social scientists may question if a person who buys and sells illegal goods and services from a website is being prosecuted under the spirit of the law, in which the aim is to address members of criminal organizations. By way of contrast, Roman Olegovich Zolotarev was an administrator of Carder.su. He was a more permanent and instrumental node in the criminal network. However, Zolotarev, a Russian citizen, is as of this writing at-large.

The conviction has wide-ranging implications. This suggests to future prosecutors that other individuals who participate in online markets can be prosecuted under RICO and face similar penalties. It is possible, for example, that individuals who upload and download data bit-torrent websites that make money from advertisements can be "members of criminal organizations" and prosecuted under RICO.

ROSS ULBRICHT

It would not be wholly inaccurate to call Ross Ulbricht the face of cybercrime. Ulbricht was the creator of the original Silk Road, an online marketplace where drugs, weapons, and illegal goods were sold. Silk Road was one of the more successful online black markets and gained a large amount of media attention when several magazines published articles about the site in 2011. It was the first time that many casual Internet users had heard of the "dark web" or "Tor," the software application used to access the marketplace.

Ulbricht, who went by the alias "Dread Pirate Roberts," was arrested in 2013 and charged with several offenses including aiding and abetting distribution of drugs, conspiracy to commit computer hacking, and continuing a criminal enterprise. Ulbricht was charged under the Continuing Criminal Enterprise (CCE) Act because Silk Road trafficked in narcotics. As such, Ulbricht was identified by prosecutors as the leader of a criminal organization. In essence, he was understood to be a drug "kingpin." In 2015, Roberts was sentenced to life in prison with no possibility of parole.

Manhattan U.S. Attorney Preet Bharara said of the case:

> Make no mistake: Ulbricht was a drug dealer and criminal profiteer who exploited people's addictions and contributed to the deaths of at least six young people. Ulbricht went from hiding his cybercrime identity to becoming the face of cybercrime and as today's sentence proves, no one is above the law.[5]

Like Camez's conviction, the Ulbricht conviction raises questions about how we understand organized crime in the digital environment. Ulbricht was indeed the owner of Silk Road, and in this sense the "leader." However, it does not appear as if he gave orders to subordinates who were then engaged in drug trafficking. So, one must ask, are the activities of Ulbricht similar in function to those of "El Chapo"? Currently, federal prosecutors have agreed that the activities of these two people, while different in form, are indeed similar in function.

Conclusion

In this chapter we explored Organized Crime as it operates in the digital environment. We discussed some of the difficulties in defining and describing what makes Organized Crime different than "crimes that are organized." While acknowledging that there are other ways of defining the phenomena, we settled on a definition that incorporates the elements of sophistication, structure, self-identification, and reputation. Organized Crime in the digital environment is characterized more by network connections, and we discussed two typologies developed by social scientists. We suggest that as life becomes more digital, Organized Crime, like street and property crimes, will continue to migrate into the digital environment. We see this already with traditional mafia groups moving their operations online.

Although crime has changed form, the United States still applies RICO and CCE to prosecute Organized Crime, with David Camez and Ross Ulbricht being notable examples. As we point out in this chapter, these laws may be misapplied. While it is accurate to say that there is Organized Crime online, the structure of Organized Crime groups in the digital environment is much different than the structure of traditional Organized Crime groups. Lawmakers may need to fashion laws that are more applicable to networked groups.

We suggest that investigating Organized Crime will be increasingly difficult for law enforcement agencies. The borderless digital environment makes it easier for networked criminals to elude law enforcement agencies that are bound by geography. Even cross-national agencies like Europol—the police agency for countries in the European Union—will encounter difficulties. The agency must still negotiate with non-European Union countries such as Russia and the United States. Moreover, as an international agency they may lack the local, on the ground knowledge of local police forces. One way forward is a United Nations or ICANN type of law enforcement agency invested with special jurisdiction over organized cybercrime. This agency can coordinate investigations across a wider range of nations and more effectively investigate and prosecute Organized Crime.

Vocabulary

1. **Argot**—The unique language used by members of a subculture or counterculture
2. **Continuing Criminal Enterprise [CCE] Statute**—Federal statute used to prosecute leaders of criminal enterprises associated with drug trafficking
3. **Hub**—A network of individuals with a defined leadership structure connected solely in the digital environment
4. **Racketeer Influenced and Corrupt Organizations [RICO] Act**—Federal statute targeting individuals who are members of a criminal enterprise and have committed two acts of racketeering activity within the previous ten years
5. **Swarm**—A collection of individuals with a loose leadership structure connected solely in the digital environment
6. **Wide-Stroke Attack**—The mass deployment of malware across a range of targets

Study Questions

TRUE OR FALSE

1. One difference between Organized Crime offline and online is that Organized Crime groups online can coordinate their activities over greater distances.
   a. True
   b. False
2. One difference between Organized Crime offline and online is that Organized Crime groups online have a more hierarchical group structure.
   a. True
   b. False
3. Hubs are more likely to conduct more serious criminal activities than swarms.
   a. True
   b. False
4. Ross Ulbricht went by the alias "Dread Pirate Roberts."
   a. True
   b. False
5. Within organized crime groups, technicians trade and sell stolen data in carding markets.
   a. True
   b. False
6. A hacking activity that creates a large data breach is often considered an instance of Organized Crime because of the amount of money stolen.
   a. True
   b. False

MULTIPLE CHOICE

7. One of the dimensions scholars use to identify cybercrime is _____, which means the degree to which the organization has the capacity to force others to do what it dictates through fear and intimidation.
   a. criminal sophistication
   b. structure
   c. self-identification
   d. authority of reputation

8. One of the dimensions scholars use to identify cybercrime is _____, which means the degree to which individuals in the network see themselves as being a part of an organization.
   a. criminal sophistication
   b. structure
   c. self-identification
   d. authority of reputation

9. The characteristic of organized crime groups having defined roles and responsibilities is an indicator of _____.
   a. criminal sophistication
   b. structure
   c. self-identification
   d. authority of reputation

10. _____ might prevent law enforcement from investigating Organized Crime groups because they fear reprisals.
   a. Criminal sophistication
   b. Structure
   c. Self-identification
   d. Authority of reputation

11. Which crime is *least* likely to be committed by cyber-Organized Crime groups?
   a. Voter fraud
   b. Money laundering
   c. Wide stroke attack
   d. The reproduction of government documents

12. When committing _____, organized crime groups use mules to deposit cash below the threshold of surveillance.
   a. voter fraud
   b. money laundering
   c. wide-stroke attack
   d. the reproduction of government documents

13. The Carbanak/Cobalt group has focused its operations in _____.
   a. Europe
   b. Asia
   c. Canada
   d. Africa

14. Which of these are Organized Crime groups?
    a. Carbanak/Cobalt
    b. Crackas with an Attitude
    c. Flash robs
    d. All of the above
15. One reason why typologies of Organized Crime groups are needed is because _____.
    a. different types of groups require different types of investigative strategies
    b. academics achieve tenure through the analysis of different groups
    c. typologies make it possible for policy-makers to devise unique strategies for each group
    d. all of the above
16. _____ described several roles within Organized Crime networks while with the FBI.
    a. Steven R. Chabinsky
    b. Homer Simpson
    c. Chadwick Arington
    d. Joseph Willingham
17. Ross Ulbricht was the owner of _____.
    a. Silk Road
    b. Honey Pleasures
    c. Backpage
    d. None of the above
18. Ross Ulbricht was prosecuted by federal authorities under the _____.
    a. Continuing Criminal Enterprise Act
    b. Racketeer Influenced and Corrupt Organizations Act
    c. Electronic Communications and Privacy Activities Act
    d. Idiot's Act of 2010
19. Ross Ulbricht was sentenced to _____ in prison.
    a. 5 years
    b. 10 years
    c. 20 years
    d. Life

MATCHING

Match the description of McGuire's Organized Crime Typology with the definition.

    a. Swarms
    b. Hubs
    c. Clustered hybrid
    d. Extended hybrid
    e. Hierarchies
    f. Aggregate groups

20. Hackers working with individuals who place credit card skimmers in stores.
21. An online market that sells methamphetamine.
22. A group of people who come together to hack into a school database and change their grades.
23. Individuals who are unhappy about a person's actions and send negative or hateful communications to that person.

Critical Thinking Exercise

NOTE TO INSTRUCTOR: You might consider having students gather some basic statistical data from a reputable mass data source on cybercrime activity (e.g. the FBI Internet Crime Complaint Center) prior to conducting this exercise. Alternatively, you may see fit to provide the material yourself.

Have students form an *organized crime syndicate*! In doing so, have them consider and address the following:

- What type of crime would you set out to commit? Note the four general categories—cybertrespass, cyberpornography, cyberviolence, and cyberdeception—discussed in the preceding chapters. In your selection, be careful to consider the rationale for committing the crime (e.g. Is it rewarding? Are victims comparatively easy to target?) and the argument for why an organized group is needed to carry it out vis-à-vis a more individualized effort.
- How would/should the organization be structured? Noting the discussion of various roles within a syndicate in this chapter, which roles would be required in your hypothetical crime syndicate and why? HINT: think *very carefully* about the nature of the crime and what skill sets are needed to carry it out successfully.
- How would you go about establishing/maintaining order within the organization? Consider what this chapter reveals about the nature of organizational structure within digital crime syndicates.

NOTES

1 www.reuters.com/article/us-cyber-banks-spain/spanish-police-arrest-suspected-mastermind-of-bank-cyber-attacks-idUSKBN1H21H3
2 https://archives.fbi.gov/archives/news/speeches/the-cyber-threat-whos-doing-what-to-whom
3 www.fbi.gov/investigate/organized-crime#Glossary-of%20Terms
4 www.justice.gov/opa/pr/member-organization-operated-online-marketplace-stolen-personal-information-sentenced-20
5 www.fbi.gov/contact-us/field-offices/newyork/news/press-releases/ross-ulbricht-aka-dread-pirate-roberts-sentenced-in-manhattan-federal-court-to-life-in-prison

REFERENCES

Broadhurst, R., Grabosky, P., Alazab, M., & Chon, S. (2014). Organizations and cyber crime: An analysis of the nature of groups engaged in cyber crime. *International Journal of Cyber Criminology, 8*(1), 20.

Finckenauer, J. O. (2005). Problems of definition: What is organized crime? *Trends in Organized Crime, 8*(3), 63–83. doi:10.1007/s12117-005-1038-4

Grabosky, P. (2007). The internet, technology, and organized crime. *Asian Journal of Criminology, 2*(2), 145–161. doi:10.1007/s11417-007-9034-z

Hagan, F. E. (2006). "Organized crime" and "organized crime": Indeterminate problems of definition. *Trends in Organized Crime, 9*(4), 127–137. doi:10.1007/s12117-006-1017-4

Lavorgna, A. (2018). Cyber-organised crime. A case of moral panic? *Trends in Organized Crime,* 1–18. doi:10.1007/s12117-018-9342-y

Leukfeldt, E. R., Kleemans, E. R., & Stol, W. P. (2017). A typology of cybercriminal networks: From low-tech all-rounders to high-tech specialists. *Crime, Law and Social Change, 67*(1), 21–37. doi:10.1007/s10611-016-9662-2

Leukfeldt, E. R., Lavorgna, A., & Kleemans, E. R. (2017). Organised cybercrime or cybercrime that is organised? An assessment of the conceptualisation of financial cybercrime as organised crime. *European Journal on Criminal Policy and Research, 23*(3), 287–300. doi:10.1007/s10610-016-9332-z

McGuire, M. (2012). *Organised crime in the digital age.* John Grieve Centre for Policing and Security and BAE Systems Detica.

Venkatesh, S. A. (2008). *Gang leader for a day: A rogue sociologist takes to the streets.* New York: Penguin Press.

Chapter 8

Algorithms, Big Data, and Policing

In this chapter, we turn our attention away from the cybercrimes committed by individuals. Instead, we look at how the criminal justice system is using algorithms and Big Data to investigate and prosecute crimes. Algorithms have been embraced by the police, the courts, and correctional institutions as they promise a more effective means of accomplishing the goals of these respective branches of the criminal justice system. However, these new technologies are not beyond criticism. Many advocacy groups question the use of algorithms and allege that they are violating civil liberties and can be biased towards minority groups.

This chapter proceeds as follows. First, we define and describe the two foundational concepts of this chapter—algorithms and Big Data. We look at these two concepts through a social science lens and how they can be applied to issues within the criminal justice system. We also link these two concepts together, as it is when these two concepts are connected that they have consequences for criminal justice. We then discuss how these concepts are impacting the processes of policing, sentencing, and surveillance. Throughout this chapter, we take a critical approach to the use of algorithms and attempt to highlight their benefits and drawbacks.

Understanding Algorithms

In general, an **algorithm** is a sequence of instructions used to solve a problem. The algorithm takes input in the form of data, performs a set of instructions, and produces an output. In her book *Hello World: Being Human in the Age of Algorithms*, Dr. Hannah Fry (2018) organizes the real-world tasks of algorithms into four categories:

- *Prioritization—The ordering of data regarding importance.* The selection-sort algorithm described here is an example of prioritization, as it orders a list of numbers regarding their absolute numerical value. Other examples of prioritization are the ordered search results on a webpage. The list of results presented by Google is produced by prioritization. Real estate applications such as Zillow may also use prioritization algorithms to list the homes a user is likely to buy or rent.

- *Classification—Placing data into meaningful categories.* Companies or organizations want to place users into categories they deem important so that they can make decisions about what content to provide or what actions they should take. The fictional risk assessment algorithm classifies offenders into "high risk" and "low risk." When inappropriate content is removed from YouTube, it is through a classification algorithm that scans videos and places them into "appropriate" and "inappropriate."
- *Association—Finding relationships between data.* When someone sees "You might like this" on a software application, an association algorithm may be at the core of the suggestion. An association algorithm connects two or more pieces of data from databases in the past and assumes that similar pieces of data will be connected in the future. And so, because so many users who bought a pair of sneakers in the past also bought an activity tracker, a person buying a new pair of running shoes will get a suggestion for Fitbit models.
- *Filtering—Removing data deemed unimportant.* Software applications that aggregate content for users, such as Facebook or Twitter, use algorithms that filter out unimportant news stories, tweets, and posts. Filtering algorithms present a more pleasant experience for the user, as content that he or she may find boring or unpleasant is removed. However, some scholars have found fault with these algorithms when used to filter out news stories.

Most computer applications and institutions need to accomplish all four of these tasks to produce their products or services. Fry writes:

Take UberPool, for instance, which matches prospective passengers with others heading in the same direction. Given your start point and end point, it has to filter through the possible routes that could get you home, look for connections with other users headed in the same direction, and pick one group to assign you to—all while prioritizing routes with the fewest turns for the driver, to make the ride as efficient as possible.

(2018, 10)

ALGORITHMS IN PROGRAMMING

Algorithms power much of the software applications we use in our daily lives. A common algorithm is a "selection-sort" algorithm (using Fry's schema previous, a selection-sort algorithm prioritizes data). This algorithm can be described with these general steps:

1. Given a set of numbers—"50," "40," "8," "33," "1," and "10," create two lists, A and B.
    - List A is the unsorted list. List B is an empty list that will contain the sorted numbers.

2. Call the input slot for list B, where a number will be placed, X.
3. Let X = 0.
4. Search for the minimum value in list A and transfer it to list B at X.
   - Now, the lists are "50," "40," "8," "33," and "10" for list A, and "1" for List B.
5. Set X to X + 1
   - This will allow the next sorted number to be placed in the subsequent empty slot.
6. Repeat steps 4 and 5 until no numbers remain in List A.

These steps would be written in a computer language such as Java, Python, or C++. For people who write algorithms in programming languages, a measure of quality is how fast the algorithm performs its task, called **execution time**. Each step, or operation, requires an amount of time for a computer to process it. In most cases, this execution time appears almost instantaneous to a computer user—a computer can sort a list of 100 or so numbers in milliseconds.

But consider a list with one million entries or more. This will take considerably more time. Even if the time to complete it is in minutes, these could be precious minutes. Or consider a sorting algorithm that must decide on where a person ranks in terms of "most dangerous," and the algorithm sorts based on the number of days a person has spent in prison. Now imagine that this sorting algorithm takes two minutes *each time* a law enforcement officer wishes to evaluate a person. An officer who wishes to sift through the profiles of 100 suspects will need over three hours (200 minutes) of wait time for this evaluation. This would be a poor algorithm.

ALGORITHMS IN SOCIAL SCIENCE

For social scientists, algorithms are often experienced as formulas that take socially relevant data and produce outputs to be interpreted. These algorithms are based on mathematical formulas that have been informed by theory and prior research.

As an example, a sociologist studying addiction may have access to 1,000 prior patients of a drug treatment facility. The sociologist has collected data on the patient, their family, and whether they relapsed five months after leaving the facility. Using standard statistical techniques, the sociologist can generate a formula that predicts the likelihood that future patients will relapse after release. This formula is a type of algorithm:

1. Set the value of a first-time patient to the facility = 1, and a patient with multiple visits = 2
2. Set the value of being male = 1, and being female = 0
3. Set the value of having a parent who has used drugs = 1, and not having a parent who has used drugs = 0
4. Add the values
5. If the value is 3 or greater, then label the patient "likely" to relapse; otherwise, label the patient "not likely" to relapse

ALGORITHMIC OUTPUTS AS SOCIAL CONSTRUCTIONS

There may be a tendency to assume that the values produced by an algorithm are objective, neutral, and can be trusted (Lee, 2018; O'Neil, 2016). Indeed, in most professions, the data produced through computer applications are rarely questioned by those who use them. One reason for this is that algorithms appear to have a sense of objectivity because the decisions are made by a computer. If a computer says that a black offender is more likely to recidivate, then this is seen as being more trustworthy than if a judge makes the same claim based on her experience. People may view the judge as being biased because of stereotypes, but not the computer. Another reason is that those who are using the data produced by algorithms are not aware of how the data is produced (Burrell, 2016). If police are told to patrol in a certain area because it is a high crime area, they may not be aware of what inputs were used to produce the output of "high crime area."

But algorithms and their outputs are socially constructed just like crime, deviance, victimization, and policy. Individuals make decisions as to what phenomena are important. They determine what data are used as inputs. They make decisions as to what procedures or formulas are used to produce outputs. And, they make decisions about how those outputs are used. All those decisions are contingent upon what individuals and groups have decision-making power. This understanding necessitates a constant critique of the use of algorithms in society (Mittelstadt, Allo, Taddeo, Wachter, & Floridi, 2016).

Big Data

In the simplest sense, **Big Data** refers to the presence of large quantities of information produced by and stored on computers (Kitchin & McArdle, 2016). The amount of discussions surrounding Big Data lends support to the notion that modern societies are in the "age of Big Data." Organizations and governments are developing ways of collecting and organizing massive amounts of data generated by computers. "Data analytics" has become a profession and a college major. "Chief Data Scientist" or "Chief Information Officer" are executive positions that are well paid and hold a high degree of status. A question one can ask is, why has Big Data become so important? There are several reasons.

First, computer hardware has become more powerful. As computer hardware is only ever an information producing machine—taking inputs and producing outputs—more powerful machines mean potentially more data produced. An oft-cited example of this is the fact that a modern smartphone is more powerful than the computers used in the original Apollo space mission.

Second, software applications, and the algorithms powering those applications, have become more sophisticated. As we will discuss later, computer programmers and mathematicians have developed algorithms that can read handwriting, recognize speech patterns, and learn the language.

Third, more of life's activities have migrated into the digital environment. This means that more data can be collected. In *Everybody Lies: Big Data, New Data, and What the Internet Can Tell Us About Who We Really Are*, data scientist Seth Stephens-Davidowitz (2017) uses Google search data to answer questions about racism, abortion, and pornography among other things. Google collects the searches of users (even if someone is not logged in with their Google account) and makes this data available publicly. Stephens-Davidowitz uses this data to show, for example, that a large proportion of young men are attracted to elderly women, and men search for ways to perform oral sex on themselves as often as they search for pleasuring the opposite sex.[1] He also found that areas of the United States that showed the most support for Donald Trump made the most Google searches for the racial epithet "n-----." These types of insights would be unavailable if people chose not to conduct these activities online.

While we can talk about Big Data in shorthand as large quantities of information, scholars and writers have identified specific characteristics that identity data as "Big":

- *Volume—The sheer amount of information.* Organizations are often manipulating data that are many terabytes or petabytes in size. For comparison, many students carry a flash drive that stores 10 gigabytes (GB) of data, or their personal computers store 500 GBs of data. For most students and families, this is enough storage for all their videos, music, and files. A terabyte (TB) is approximately 1,000 gigabytes, and mid to large size organizations have databases and servers housing several terabytes of data. A petabyte is even larger and is applicable mainly to government databases or the largest organizations. One petabyte is 1,000 terabytes or 1,000,000 gigabytes. Some organizations like the United States military and social media companies have several petabytes (PB) of data stored on their machines.
- *Velocity—The speed at which new data is produced.* Some databases are relatively static, meaning that once data is collected, it remains relevant for months and even years. An example would be the US Census, which can be downloaded via an Excel file. One can make changes to their copy, but the original information is meant to remain a permanent record to be of value for generations to come. As such, the analysis of the data can occur at a slower speed and will remain relevant to the organization for a longer period. However, with Big Data new information is being added to databases and necessitates a much quicker data analysis. Organizations that analyze data from social media applications to gauge public opinion are constantly revising their conclusions based upon new information.
- *Variety—The number of sources and formats in which data is retrieved.* Organizations must analyze data in the form of raw numbers, video, audio, and text. Moreover, this information can come from a variety of sources. For example, facial recognition technology uses at least two streams of data—the video feed from CCTV along with the images, text, and numerical data from a state license database. The technology must extract meaningful information from both streams to match an image with a license, and then present this information to law enforcement.

It is important to note that there are degrees of Big Data. Any particular use of information will vary on levels of volume, velocity, and variety. For example, the data used in law enforcement for predictive policing is likely lower in volume, less dynamic, and has less variety than the data used by large technology companies. However, it is still "Big" relative to the types of data historically used in policing.

There are other characteristics of Big Data. Many scholars include **veracity**—the accuracy of the data collected—as an important characteristic. Veracity can be important, as conclusions cannot be drawn if the data collected is not accurate. Consider the problems that can be caused if police reports did not record actual events or biased events in favor of officers. This would mean that any algorithms applied to the data will produce erroneous conclusions.

Some scholars also include **volatility**. This is similar to velocity. However, velocity refers to the speed at which new data is produced and collected, while volatility refers to the relevance of that data over time to the organization. Consider a rapid response team during a hurricane using an application that places help requests on a map and plots the most efficient rescue path. This information is highly volatile, as the number of people needing rescue and their locations will change by the hour.

Linking Algorithms and Big Data

Previously, we described algorithms and Big Data separately. However, the goal of this chapter is to discuss the criminological consequences of these two phenomena when they are paired together. This is because, as Andrew Ferguson (2017) in *The Rise of Big Data Policing* writes, "Big data becomes intelligible because of algorithms and the large-scale computer processing now available" (2017, 18). By "intelligible," Ferguson is referring to what is usually termed **smart data**, or outputs that are actionable and can be used by individuals or organizations (see Figure 8.1).

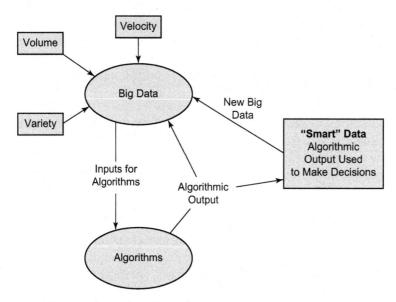

Figure 8.1   The relationship between Big Data, algorithms, and smart data.

The relationship between Big Data and algorithms is reciprocal. On the one hand, algorithms make sense of Big Data and turn Big Data into Smart Data. An algorithm can be designed to collect and sift through terabytes of data (high volume), that change frequently (high velocity), from different databases (variety). The output of that algorithm can then be used by businesses and governments. At the same time, algorithms are used to produce new data streams that become the forms of Big Data.

Thinking About the Impact of Algorithms and Big Data

In 2016, Georgetown University's Center on Privacy & Technology Law produced a report entitled *The Perpetual Line-up: Unregulated Police Face Recognition in America* (Garvie et al., 2016). The report stated that:

> 16 states let the FBI use face recognition technology to compare the faces of suspected criminals to their driver's license and ID photos, creating a virtual line-up of their state residents. In this line-up, it's not a human that points to the suspect—it's an algorithm.

Along with the FBI, at least 26 states allow their law enforcement personnel to use facial recognition technology, and over 117 million American adults are affected.

Facial recognition matches images from an established database holding personal information, such as a driver's license database, with images collected from the web, from public cameras, or even from law enforcement taking pictures on the spot. The technology sifts through the collected images and matches them with the established database. The algorithm provides a probabilistic answer based upon certain characteristics, including the distance between the eyes, the width of the nose, and geometric proportions of the face. Because a person's facial image can be collected anywhere and everywhere as they walk or drive through a town and post images of themselves online, it is possible to identify and monitor a person without them knowing it.

The report highlighted several aspects of facial recognition technology that threaten civil liberties. Agencies do not need a warrant to search a database of images. It can be argued that this violates citizens' Fourth Amendment protection from illegal search and seizure. People can be searched without their consent, and this monitoring can be done without reasonable suspicion. The use of the technology can also threaten a citizen's First Amendment rights to free speech and freedom of assembly. Because the right to anonymity is the backbone of this amendment, facial recognition technology threatens this fundamental civil liberty. Individuals may hesitate to join protests, and law enforcement may target an individual simply because they attended a protest.

Another problem is that the algorithm used may be better at detecting some phenotypes than others. According to the report:

> algorithms developed in East Asia performed better on East Asians, while algorithms developed in Western Europe and the U.S. performed better on Caucasians. This result suggests

that algorithms may be most accurate on the populations who developed them—a concerning effect given that software engineers in the United States are predominately Caucasian males.

Because algorithms are probabilistic, a collected image can fit many possible matches in a database. If the algorithm is more inaccurate for racial minorities, then a greater proportion of innocent non-white people may be approached by law enforcement.

The use and misuse of facial recognition software illustrate the importance of understanding the impacts of Big Data and algorithms. The outputs of algorithms are used by individuals and institutions to make important, sometimes life-altering decisions. The decision by law enforcement to approach and question a person could set off a series of life-changing events. If these algorithms are consistently inaccurate, it can negatively affect an entire group of people. This logic can be extended to other domains of life. One's credit score is based on an algorithm. The tests given to potential new hires are also algorithmic in nature. Insurance companies decide premiums based upon algorithms, and so on. Because Big Data and algorithms impact people's life chances, they need to be studied systematically by social scientists. There are also legal implications to algorithms. As the Center on Privacy & Technology Law argues, both the First Amendment (free speech) and Fourth Amendment (protection from illegal search and seizure) are threatened by facial recognition technology.

Algorithms and Big Data in Policing

One way in which algorithms have become a part of law enforcement practices is through predictive policing (Bennett Moses & Chan, 2016; Chan & Bennett Moses, 2016; Hunt, Saunders, & Hollywood, 2014; Mantello, 2016). **Predictive policing** can be defined as "the application of statistical methods to identify likely targets for police intervention (the predictions) to prevent crimes or solve past crimes, followed by conducting interventions against those targets" (Hunt et al., 2014). Data and statistical analysis are at the heart of predictive policing. However there is much more involved. As Chan and Bennett Moses (2016) write, predictive policing is a process, "which consists of a cycle of activities and decision points: data collection, analysis, police operations, criminal response, and back to data collection" (2). We describe this process below using Chan and Bennett Moses's cycle of activities (see Figure 8.2) to order our discussion.

DATA COLLECTION

The first decision point in the cycle of predictive policing is the collection of data. Data has been collected on crime rates by local and federal law enforcement since the early 20th century. For example, the Federal Bureau of Investigation has administered the Uniform Crime Reports program since 1929. The Uniform Crime Report is a compilation of crime statistics reported by local agencies. These crimes include murder, rape, robbery, arson, and more.

Figure 8.2   The predictive policing process.

In the era of predictive policing local agencies have become more purposeful in their data collection and often collect a wider range of data specific to their locality. Most police precincts input data into a **records management system** (RMS). Police RMSs are relatively standardized in that they are databases which can be manipulated using Structured Query Language (SQL). A crime analyst can then retrieve relevant data using SQL and present crime data to police or management. Placing data into a standardized RMS also facilitates the extraction of that data by third-party software for crime mapping or predicting future high crime areas (forecasting).

The collection of data is not an objective process where crimes happen and are then recorded. The values that end up in a database depend on people. As such, it is fraught with human-related issues. For example, if police have historically policed one area of a city, then they will have more data on that area. Similarly, if police are more likely to take notice of a person of color, they are more likely to stop that person (the infamous "driving while black" phenomenon) and are more likely to find and record some type of infraction.

ANALYZING DATA

At this stage of the cycle, some type of algorithm is applied to the collected data. As mentioned above, law enforcement agencies use third-party computer software to draw conclusions about the data they have collected. One well-known example is Predpol predictive software.

Predpol uses three data points to make predictions about crime—the type of crime, the location of the crime, and the date/time of the crime.[2] These data points are retrieved from the law enforcement agency's database. Predictions for high-risk areas are visualized on a map. One of the more interesting aspects of Predpol is the algorithm used to make these predictions. The software's designers theorized that crimes might emanate from an initial crime in the same way that aftershocks occur after an initial earthquake. Predpol applies a formula that is used to model earthquake aftershocks to predict these future crimes.

The software and algorithms applied in the process of predictive policing have been questioned by scholars and activities organizations. One reason is that the algorithms used are not oriented towards the underlying causes of crime. With the Predpol software, police will be able to anticipate and arrest the "aftershocks" from initial crimes. However, this does not mean that they will be in any better position to address the underlying causes of crimes.

POLICE OPERATIONS

Police use the outputs from algorithms to inform how they use their resources. Algorithms are used to inform who is targeted, where, and when. For example, the Chicago police department uses a "heat list" (Ferguson, 2017). As described by Ferguson:

> the heat list uses 11 variables to create risk scores from 1 to 500. The higher the score means the greater risk of being a victim or perpetrator of gun violence. Who gets shot? The algorithm knows … Using the heat list, police have prioritized youth violence to intervene in the lives of the most at-risk men.
>
> (2017, 37)

Person-based policing allows law enforcement to be more proactive by identifying potential victims and perpetrators. They can monitor those who are "at-risk" and possibly prevent crimes.

This same rationale underlies the use of algorithms to determine where to police. Place-based policing, also called hot-spot policing, makes it possible to place units in the areas where crime is likely to occur. Predpol, as discussed, is an example of an algorithm that helps police anticipate the places where crime is likely to occur.

A third way that algorithms affect police operations is by altering decisions in real time. An example of this would be law enforcement using facial recognition technology on a suspect while on the scene. The response from the technology—"likely a match," "not likely a match," will determine the next actions of the officer. Another way in which real-time decisions are made is with **automated license plate readers** (ALPRs). These devices can be mounted on police cars or at strategic locations in a city. The ALPRs then scan license plates and match them to the records associated with those license plates such as the owner of the vehicle, traffic or parking violations, the number of times the vehicle has been seen in the area, and more. This information can then be sent in real time to law enforcement.

For all these algorithmically informed operations, law enforcement must balance the efficiency of these operations with the potential harms they may cause in communities. For example, place-based policing can lead to an increase in police shootings and animosity from citizens. "In the targeted areas, police may feel additional license to investigate more aggressively. Because the areas have been designated as more dangerous, police may respond in a more aggressively protective posture" (Ferguson, 2017, 79). Similarly, if police officers are more likely to investigate marginalized communities or communities of color, they are more likely to collect license plate data and facial images from the people in those communities. This may help with their investigations, but it also means that the people in those communities are more likely to have their civil liberties violated.

CRIMINAL RESPONSE AND NEW DATA COLLECTION

The predictive policing process is an iterative cycle. The operations adopted by the police will be successful and criminal patterns will change in response to these operations. Potential offenders learn from past experiences or others about who is being targeted, where, and when. If, for example, police learn of an open-air drug market and deploy units in those spaces, drug dealers will migrate to another space. This will then require new data and then a new response.

Even if criminals are not aware of the technologies brought to bear on their behavior, the effectiveness of predictive policing as a general practice must be repeatedly evaluated. Does predictive policing lead to a reduction in the number of crimes committed in the locality in which it is applied? There is some debate as to the effectiveness of predictive policing. This debate is complicated by several factors. All types of predictive policing are not the same. When evaluating effectiveness, distinctions need to be made between place-based policing, person-based policing, and real-time policing. Moreover, even when comparing the same type of predictive policing, the context and culture of a locality may matter. Place-based policing may have a different impact in a dense urban metropolis like Chicago than in a less dense, mid-sized city like Virginia Beach, Virginia. Another factor that must be considered is the perceptions of the community. If people feel that their rights are being violated, then even if crime is reduced, they may want police practices to change. Police may need to balance the objective decreases in crime with a more subjective but no less real increase in public animosity.

Algorithms and Big Data in Sentencing

The application of data in sentencing has long been an aspect of criminal justice. The use of data and algorithms during this phase of the criminal justice process is primarily about assessing risk.

Court judges and professionals in corrections must estimate the likelihood that an individual will commit future crimes and base their decisions accordingly. The individual may need to be detained before trial because he or she is likely to be violent or not return to trial, given more severe penalties. Algorithms may also be used to determine more appropriate interventions such as drug treatment. Sentencing algorithms fall into two broad groups—algorithms for assessing pretrial detention or release, and algorithms used for assessing sentencing.

PRETRIAL DETENTION AND RELEASE

There has been a recent push by states to use algorithms to determine if an accused person should be released before trial or put in jail. A primary reason for using an algorithm during pretrial is to save the state money. At a pretrial court appearance, a judge must determine if an accused individual is a flight risk—not returning for trial, a risk to the community—and thus needs to be jailed until their trial, or are nonviolent and low risk—and can be released. On some rare occasions, people can be released on the good faith that they will attend trial, what is called "personal recognizance." On most occasions, however, people must post bail money to ensure they will return for their court date. Unfortunately, many defendants are not able to post bail, and therefore must stay in jail awaiting trial. The housing of people in jails awaiting the trial costs the state money. There is also a human cost of housing people before a trial, often for months, for minor offenses. An algorithm that can determine risk may allow courts to be confident that individuals will return for their court date without requiring them to post bail.

The state of New Jersey has eliminated traditional bail proceedings and now relies heavily on the use of an algorithm that determines flight risk. An article written in *The Economist* (2017) states:

> Defenders of New Jersey's experiment [pretrial algorithms] point to a dramatic decline in the state's jail population, driven by a reduction in the number of poor, non-dangerous offenders who are incarcerated while awaiting trial for no other reason than their inability to pay bail. In September 2017 New Jersey's jails held 36% fewer people than they did in September 2015.

Other states are also considering or have adopted some form of pretrial algorithms, including Arizona, Kentucky, and Alaska.

In 2013, former Attorney General for the State of New Jersey Anne Milgram gave a talk on using data in the criminal justice system.[3] "We weren't using data-driven policing. We were essentially trying to fight crime with yellow Post-it notes," Milgram said in her talk. Milgram went on to describe the project she led to introduce algorithms and Big Data into an important decision—should a person who has been arrested be detained and put into jail before trial or released on bail. People who are likely to not return for trial, or more importantly commit another violent act while awaiting trial, need to be detained. On the other hand, it is costly to taxpayers to detain someone who is not violent or a flight risk. According to Milgram, 50% of people currently in jail and awaiting trial are non-violent and low risk. To address the issue, Milgram and her team of researchers developed an assessment tool to judge pre-trial risk. Using data from 1.5 million cases across the United States, Milgram and her team developed a universal risk assessment tool based on nine factors. The tool gives a judge a score, based on an algorithm, that shows (1) the likelihood of committing a new crime, (2) if the person will commit an act of violence if not put in jail, and (3) if the person will appear in court for trial if released.

Although algorithms like the one explained by Milgram appear to be a fairer approach to pretrial sentencing, some groups may be unhappy with their use. If New Jersey is indicative of other states, then states that use pretrial algorithms may have more people released pretrial. Citizens in those localities may feel unsafe, and there is a real possibility that although an algorithm may label a person "low risk," it does not mean that the person will not commit a crime while awaiting trial. And so, the savings gained by local and state governments may be matched by the emotional costs of people who now feel less safe.

SENTENCING

Sentencing involves deciding what punishment, or penalty, to levy on a convicted offender. The penalties are usually prison time, a fine, or community service. The next decision is the intensity of the penalty. There are often wide ranges in the amount of prison time or fines for any given guilty sentence. For example, under the Computer Fraud and Abuse Act, the penalty for giving an unauthorized person a password to a computer network ranges from a minimum of one year to a maximum of ten years.

The primary function of algorithms during the sentencing process is predicting the risk of recidivism. A high risk of recidivism means that a judge may wish to imprison that offender for longer periods of time. There are many companies that provide risk assessments for courts. One major company is COMPAS (Correctional Offender Management Profiling for Alternative Sanctions).

A notable case with regards to algorithmic sentencing and COMPAS is *State v. Loomis* in 2016. Eric Loomis was arrested for driving the vehicle during a drive-by shooting and pleaded guilty to the charges. The court requested and received a risk score report from COMPAS. COMPAS classified Loomis as high risk for recidivism. Taking this score into account, the presiding judge sentenced Loomis to six years in prison and cited his COMPAS score as one of the factors in determining the sentence.

Loomis challenged the sentence. He argued that the algorithm violated his Sixth Amendment right to a fair trial. Specifically, the algorithm is proprietary, and the formula used to generate the risk scores is hidden. Loomis could not, then, confront his accuser or the evidence presented against him publicly. The supreme court of Wisconsin rejected Loomis's argument and ruled that proprietary algorithms could be used as supplemental information in sentencing but could not be the only criterion.

Big Data and Surveillance

Some scholars have argued that we live in a "surveillance society," meaning that we now live in an age when governments and corporations routinely identify and monitor individuals. Surveillance scholar David Lyon calls surveillance a process of "social sorting" (2007). People are sorted, for example, into "high-risk" and "low-risk" parolees, as mentioned earlier. Or, as Lyon (2007) writes, "People from suspect countries of origin or with suspect ethnicities can expect different treatment from others."

In the past, an individual or a group needed to be suspected of criminal activity to justify any resources devoted to their surveillance. However, two factors have reduced the barriers to surveillance. First, people live online, and it is easier to gather information in the digital environment. All Internet traffic must travel through a series of intermediaries such as an ISP or social media company's server. These intermediaries make it possible to collect information on a range of people at one source. Second, it has become much easier to store information—both in terms of space and money. It is possible to store all the possible information collected on a person on a thumb drive that costs less than $10. Moreover, that information is stored on a microchip the size of an adult fingernail. Contrast this with an analog world, where reams of paper, rows of bookshelves, and thousands of square feet could be dedicated to one person.

In an article published in the *Yale Law Journal*, Bankston and Soltani (2014) show in stark detail the investments that an agency like the Federal Bureau of Investigations must make to monitor a suspect (see Figure 8.3). Their analysis shows that surveilling someone through digital

Method	1 day		1 week		28 days	
	Estimated cost	Cost per hour	Estimated cost	Cost per hour	Estimated cost	Cost per hour
Foot Pursuit	$1,200.00	$50.00	$8,400.00	$50.00	$33,600.00	$50.00
Car Pursuit	$2,520.00	$105.00	$17,640.00	$105.00	$70,560.00	$105.00
Covert Foot Pursuit	$6,000.00	$250.00	$42,000.00	$250.00	$168,000.00	$250.00
Covert Car Pursuit	$6,600.00	$275.00	$46,200.00	$275.00	$184,800.00	$275.00
Beeper	$2,720.00	$113.33	$17,840.00	$106.19	$70,760.00	$105.30
IMSI Catcher or "Stingray"	$2,520.00	$105.00	$17,640.00	$105.00	$70,560.00	$105.30
GPS	$240.00	$10.00	$240.00	$1.43	$240.00	$0.36
Cell Phone (AT&T)	$125.00	$5.21	$275.00	$1.64	$800.00	$1.19
Cell Phone (T - Mobile)	$100.00	$4.17	$700.00	$4.17	$2,800.00	$4.17
Cell Phone (Sprint)	$30.00	$1.25	$30.00	$0.18	$30.00	$0.04

Figure 8.3 Average costs of different surveillance methods (from Bankston & Soltani, 2014).

means is much less costly. Therefore, agencies can be much less discriminating and careful in whom they monitor. They could, if they so wish, participate in "dragnets," where they monitor a wide range of people without sufficient probable cause.

For example, the cost of surveilling someone through foot pursuit would cost the agency approximately $1,200, with the average agent costing the agency $50 per hour, and surveillance being for the entire 24-hour period. The cost of foot pursuit becomes quite costly, with 28 days costing the agency over $33,000 to follow *1* person. The costs are even more in a covert car pursuit—where four cars (four agents) must work together to surveil a suspect. A covert car pursuit costs the agency approximately $6,000 for one day and $184,800 for 1 month. Now contrast these costs with following someone using the GPS on their phone. The FBI must pay an intermediary, for example, Sprint at $30 per person, for the capability of collecting the suspect's data. The costs for a 28-day period do not increase. In fact, the costs *decrease* to 4 cents per day. This low cost provides a powerful incentive for agencies to surveil someone digitally, even if there is not yet a strong case supporting the surveillance (see Figure 8.3).

DATAVEILLANCE

We have already discussed how suspected criminals are monitored. In this section, we focus on surveillance as it relates to non-offenders. Van Dijk (2014) has called this type of surveillance **dataveillance**, "a form of continuous surveillance through the use of (meta)data." Metadata refers to data about data. Metadata could be, for example, the GPS coordinates embedded in a picture taken with a digital camera and uploaded to a social media site. It could also be the time stamp on an email or the last modified date on a word processing document. Another form of metadata would be the people that you have friended on a social media account or the people you have text messaged or emailed.

Unlike the more focused surveillance via predictive policing, dataveillance is more diffuse but more pervasive. Almost *every* citizen in some form or other has metadata attached to them that can be collected by governments and businesses. Our rationale for highlighting these types of surveillance is that many scholars and activist organizations have argued that law enforcement and corporations have overstepped their bounds in the collection and use of metadata, and they must be tightly regulated to preserve civil liberties. In other words, these organizations assert that governments and corporations have committed transgressions against individuals and violate the social contract between government and citizen.

Conclusion

In the early 1990s New York City policeman Jack Maple purchased a computer from Radio Shack to help the department map crime. This one idea slowly developed into a system of mapping and analyzing crime statistics called alternatively Compare Statistics or Computer Statistics, or more commonly known as CompStat. Maple and his fellow officers were unaware that they were at the cusp of a revolution in policing. Since the 1990s, computers have become more ubiquitous and powerful, producing massive quantities of data—Big Data. Computer programmers, mathematicians, and social scientists have developed more efficient and accurate ways of producing actionable intelligence from this data—algorithms. We now live in an age where computers are essential to an effective criminal justice system.

As we have discussed, relying solely on data collection and mathematical formulas for processes that often require nuanced human judgment can be problematic. The indiscriminate use of algorithms can lead to bias towards racial minorities and violations of civil liberties. Thus, it is important that social scientists explore the societal implications of the use of algorithms and Big Data in the criminal justice system. On the other hand, a wealth of social science research, along with a glance at national headlines, shows that individual police and the criminal justice system was dealing with race and class biases before the advent of algorithms. Moreover, predictive policing and algorithmic sentencing have been shown to make elements of the criminal justice system more effective. Big Data and algorithms are here to stay in policing, the courts, and correctional institutions.

Vocabulary

1. **Algorithm**—A sequence of instructions used to solve a problem.
2. **Automated License Plate Readers**—Devices that scan license plates and match the plate values to government records associated with those license plates.
3. **Big Data**—The presence of large quantities of information produced by and stored on computers.
4. **Dataveillance**—Continuous surveillance of people by governments and corporations using data.
5. **Execution Time**—The time it takes for an algorithm to complete a task.
6. **Predictive Policing**—The application of statistical methods to identify likely targets for police intervention and for conducting interventions against those targets.
7. **Records Management System**—A database software application used in law enforcement for maintaining data on crime patterns.
8. **Smart Data**—Outputs from algorithms that can be used by individuals or organizations to complete tasks.
9. **Velocity (Big Data)**—Within a big data context, refers to the speed at which new data is generated.
10. **Veracity (Big Data)**—Within a big data context, refers to the accuracy of data.
11. **Volatility (Big Data)**—Within a big data context, refers to the length of time a set of data is relevant to an organization.
12. **Volume (Big Data)**—Within a big data context, refers to the total amount of data in a given situation.

Study Questions

TRUE OR FALSE

1. A list of search results for the search query "Boxing" by the DuckDuckGo web browser is an example of a classification algorithm.
    a. True
    b. False
2. The function of algorithms during the sentencing process is predicting the risk of recidivism.
    a. True
    b. False
3. Criminals change their patterns of offending after police have been using predictive policing.
    a. True
    b. False
4. Algorithms with lower execution times are higher quality algorithms.
    a. True
    b. False
5. The use of facial recognition technology may violate US citizens's Fourth Amendment protections.
    a. True
    b. False
6. Algorithms and their outputs are subjective products of interactions between individuals and groups.
    a. True
    b. False

STUDY QUESTIONS

7. An algorithm is best defined as _____.
    a. a set of policies used to govern the digital environment
    b. a computer program designed for individual use
    c. cybersecurity policies designed to prevent hacking
    d. citizens' Fourth Amendment protection
8. One measure of quality in algorithms is _____.
    a. how fast they are at completing a task
    b. how inexpensive they are for consumers
    c. the number of individuals who wrote them
    d. none of the above

9. _____ algorithms produce the Facebook information you see (that is different from another person's Facebook feed).
   a. Prioritization
   b. Classification
   c. Filtering
   d. Association

10. Real estate applications such as Zillow may use _____ algorithms to list the homes a user is likely to buy or rent.
    a. prioritization
    b. classification
    c. filtering
    d. association

11. _____ refers to the presence of large quantities of information produced by and stored on computers.
    a. Algorithms
    b. Hexadecimals
    c. Digital forensics
    d. Big Data

12. Big Data has become increasingly important in modern society. Why?
    a. Software applications, and the algorithms powering those applications have become more sophisticated
    b. Computer hardware has become more powerful
    c. People are doing more activities online
    d. All of the above

13. What is an incentive for a state to use algorithms during pretrial detention?
    a. It can save the state money by only sending the least dangerous people to jail
    b. It can save the state money by only sending the most dangerous people to jail
    c. It can save the state time by reducing the number of patrol hearings
    d. It reduces the amount of racial bias in detention sentencing

14. Another way of describing smart data is as _____.
    a. actionable outputs
    b. algorithmic inputs
    c. detestable bastards
    d. outputs from applications

15. _____ is defined as "the application of statistical methods to identify likely targets for police intervention to prevent crimes or solve past crimes, followed by conducting interventions against those targets."
    a. Preventative policing
    b. Proactive policing
    c. Predictive policing
    d. Person-based policing

16. One of the problems with predictive policing is that the data collected is _____.
    a. subject to human error or biases

    b. not enough (low volume)

    c. too much (high volume)

    d. depends on the number of criminologists in the area

17. _____ allows law enforcement to be more proactive by identifying potential victims and perpetrators.

    a. Preventative policing

    b. Predictive policing

    c. Practical policing

    d. Person-based policing

18. Ann Milgram led a project that designed an algorithm for _____.

    a. the death penalty

    b. organized crime

    c. person-based policing

    d. pretrial detention

19. The research by Bankston and Soltani showed that surveillance in the digital environment costs ____ for law enforcement agencies than surveillance in the physical environment.

    a. less

    b. more

    c. the same

20. According to Bankston and Soltani, the cost of a covert foot pursuit by the FBI for a month would cost about _____.

    a. $70,000

    b. $100,000

    c. $170,000

    d. $1 million

Critical Thinking Exercise

Concerning algorithmic sentencing—specifically, the use of big data mining and algorithmic models in court sentencing—each state currently chooses if and how they use algorithms in court sentencing. Under this decentralized model, some states use algorithms and some do not. Additionally, the states that use algorithms may choose different algorithmic tools. An alternative would be for a federal, centralized approach towards algorithms where each state uses the same policy and tools during sentencing.

- What are some of the potential advantages of a centralized model of algorithmic sentencing?
- What are some possible disadvantages of such a centralized model?
- Based upon your responses to the preceding questions, do you think it makes more sense to develop a centralized system for algorithmic sentencing or remain decentralized as it currently stands? Provide supporting evidence for your position.

INSTRUCTOR: For this exercise, you may want to consider an additional activity where students research the use of precursors to big data mining and algorithms in sentencing (e.g. mandatory minimums, in/out guidelines, truth-in-sentencing laws, the 1994 Violent Crime Control and Law Enforcement Act).

In the use of big data and algorithms for deriving court sentences, a major consideration is the factors that are implemented into the technology. Consider and discuss the factors that would be essential to an algorithmic sentencing protocol for the following offenses:

- Sexual assault of a minor (*INSTRUCTOR: assume either under 18 or model the designation of "minor" by the standards of a specific state*)
- Homicide of a spouse
- Illegal narcotics distribution
- Public intoxication/disturbing the peace
- Vandalism of private property
- Auto theft (consider both with and without the use of a firearm)

INSTRUCTOR: Feel free to be creative with such an exercise. There are literally countless offense scenarios for which students could be asked to consider relevant algorithmic factors.

NOTES

1 www.theguardian.com/books/2017/aug/17/everybody-lies-seth-stephens-davidowitz-review
2 www.predpol.com/how-predictive-policing-works/
3 www.youtube.com/watch?v=ZJNESMhIxQo

REFERENCES

Bankston, K. S., & Soltani, A. (2014). Tiny constables and the cost of surveillance: Making cents out of *United States v. Jones*. Retrieved January 27, 2019, from https://www.yalelawjournal.org/forum/tiny-constables-and-the-cost-of-surveillance-making-cents-out-of-united-states-v-jones

Bennett Moses, L., & Chan, J. (2016). Algorithmic prediction in policing: assumptions, evaluation, and accountability. *Policing and Society*, 28(7), 806–822. doi:10.1080/10439463.2016.1253695

Burrell, J. (2016). How the machine 'thinks': Understanding opacity in machine learning algorithms. *Big Data & Society*, 3(1), 1–12. doi:10.1177/2053951715622512

Chan, J., & Bennett Moses, L. (2016). Is big data challenging criminology? *Theoretical Criminology*, 20(1), 21–39. doi:10.1177/1362480615586614

Ferguson, A. G. (2017). *The rise of big data policing: Surveillance, race, and the future of law enforcement*. New York: New York University Press.

Fry, H. (2018). *Hello world: Being human in the age of algorithms* (1st ed.). New York: W.W. Norton & Company.

Garvie, C., Bedoya, A. M., Frankle, J., Daugherty, M., Evans, K., George, E. J., ... Singleton, K. (2016). The perpetual line-up unregulated police face recognition in America. www.perpetuallineup.org/.

Hunt, P., Saunders, J. M., & Hollywood, J. S. (2014). *Evaluation of the Shreveport predictive policing experiment.* Santa Monica, CA: RAND Corporation.

Kitchin, R., & McArdle, G. (2016). What makes big data, big data? Exploring the ontological characteristics of 26 datasets. *Big Data & Society, 3*(1), 1–10. doi:10.1177/2053951716631130

Lee, M. K. (2018). Understanding perception of algorithmic decisions: Fairness, trust, and emotion in response to algorithmic management. *Big Data & Society, 5*(1), 1–16. doi:10.1177/2053951718756684

Lyon, D. (2007). Surveillance, security and social sorting: Emerging research priorities. *International Criminal Justice Review, 17*(3), 161–170. doi:10.1177/1057567707306643

Mantello, P. (2016). The machine that ate bad people: The ontopolitics of the precrime assemblage. *Big Data & Society, 3*(2), 1–11. doi:10.1177/2053951716682538

Mittelstadt, B. D., Allo, P., Taddeo, M., Wachter, S., & Floridi, L. (2016). The ethics of algorithms: Mapping the debate. *Big Data & Society, 3*(2), 1–21. doi:10.1177/2053951716679679

O'Neil, C. (2016). *Weapons of math destruction: How big data increases inequality and threatens democracy* (1st ed.). New York: Crown.

Replacing bail with an algorithm. (2017, November 23). *The Economist.* Retrieved from https://www.economist.com /united-states/2017/11/23/replacing-bail-with-an-algorithm

Stephens-Davidowitz, S. (2017). *Everybody lies: Big data, new data, and what the Internet can tell us about who we really are* (1st ed.). New York, NY: Dey St., an imprint of William Morrow.

van Dijck, J. (2014). Datafication, dataism and dataveillance: Big data between scientific paradigm and ideology. *Surveillance and Society, 12*(2), 197–208. doi:10.24908/ss.v12i2.4776

Chapter 9

Cybervictimization

Introduction

Building from the previous chapter, we narrow our focus in this chapter to the discussion of victimization within the digital environment. Cybercrime victimization or **cybervictimization** has been tracked consistently in the United States since the early 2000s. Law enforcement entities like the FBI's **Internet Crime Complaint Center** have played a pivotal role in illustrating the general scope of victimization activity upon which scholarly studies of the phenomenon have developed. The prevailing data and discourse from such agencies notes the vast range of such victimization (see Table 9.1), and illustrates many of the themes and concepts discussed in the preceding chapters:

In 2013, the Internet Crime Complaint Center recorded approximately 262,000 victims and $780 million in financial losses due to cybercrime (Federal Bureau of Investigation, 2017). Within just half a decade, the number of victims reporting skyrocketed to five times that amount, and total losses increased sevenfold.

Yet, as rates and damage continue to climb, there is still much to answer concerning what cybervictimization entails, the types of harms resulting from cybercrime offenses, and the results of such harms. This chapter aims to introduce these topics, as well as provide some clarity on the relevance of traditional victimization theory in contemporary consideration of harmful experiences in digital settings.

The Concept of Cybervictimization

In many ways, the digital world is best thought of as an extension of the physical world within which we interact. One might say the Internet "augments real-world social life rather than

Table 9.1 Number of Victims Reporting Nationwide by Cybercrime Type (2017)

By Victim Count

Crime Type	Victims	Crime Type	Victims
Non-Payment/Non-Delivery	84,079	Misrepresentation	5,437
Personal Data Breach	30,904	Corporate Data Breach	3,785
Phishing/Vishing/Smishing/Pharming	25,344	Investment	3,089
Overpayment	23,135	Malware/Scareware/Virus	3,089
No Lead Value	20,241	Lottery/Sweepstakes	3,012
Identity Theft	17,636	IPR/Copyright and Counterfeit	2,644
Advanced Fee	16,368	Ransomware	1,783
Harassment/Threats of Violence	16,194	Crimes Against Children	1,300
Employment	15,784	Denial of Service/TDoS	1,201
BEC/EAC	15,690	Civil Matter	1,057
Confidence Fraud/Romance	15,372	Re-shipping	1,025
Credit Card Fraud	15,220	Charity	436
Extortion	14,938	Health Care Related	406
Other	14,023	Gambling	203
Tech Support	10,949	Terrorism	177
Real Estate/Rental	9,645	Hacktivist	158
Government Impersonation	9,149		

providing an alternative to it" (Shirkey, 2008). With respect to victimization in both the cyber- and terrestrial world, some scholars contend the two phenomena need not be regarded as totally exclusive of one another since cybercrime and physical, conventional crime are not so distant from one another conceptually (Yu, 2014). Thus, to better understand cybervictimization, it stands to reason an understanding of the general concept of victimization is necessary.

In theory, every crime has a victim (Quinney, 1972). The core definition of a crime entails that a deviation from prevailing social construction—which laws have been created to pre-serve—has occurred that brings about some type of harm. For harm to be determined, there must be at least one entity within the social landscape that can encompass the end result of the deviant act in such a way that a general understanding of inflicted harm can be reached. Even within the scope of so-called **victimless crimes** (e.g. software piracy, prostitution), social insti-tutions that ban such activities would argue that the victims are not so much absent as they are unknown and/or inconsistently acknowledged. Furthermore, dating back to some of the earliest developments in victimology, victimization can be understood from at least three perspectives: 1) the formal identification/definition of the victimization act, 2) the events or circumstances that cause one to experience the victimization act, and 3) the outcomes resulting from such victimization.

Formally defining an act of victimization comprises several ponderings. First, what "wrong-ful" act was committed? For victimization to manifest and therefore be studied, there needs to be a firm understanding that something wrong occurred. Importantly, this may or may not constitute an actual crime—an act for which there is specific legal identification and precedence for sanction—for we know that formal legal systems do not always align with what is actually deemed a wrongful act in the broader social context. Rather, if the act is determined to have produced a harm, and especially if that determination has originated and/or is supported by the ruling class(es) of said context (Quinney, 1972), then indeed a wrongful act has occurred.

Presuming that a wrongful act has been determined, the next consideration is the target. Specifically, who is/was the target upon which the wrongful act was inflicted? In order for there to be victimization, it stands to reason there must be an entity upon which a wrongful act was committed. Granted, the extent of victim identification can and does vary, and it is certainly possible to conceive of a victimization event where victim identification is problematic (e.g. crimes like sexual assault, for which the victim(s) are reluctant to come forward and identify themselves). Nonetheless, identification of at least one victim—versus none—goes a long way to cementing whether or not victimization has occurred and the nature of it.

Upon establishing a wrongful act and a target, we arrive at the issue of identifying harm done and the extent of damage caused. Any firm determination of victimization must clearly state how and to what extent the identified target was harmed. Ideally, this harm would be measurable, but criminology often teaches that many harms are not so. For instance, in the Bernie Madoff fraud scandal, the amount of money Mr. Madoff embezzled and the number of investors connected to those sums has been calculated to within a fair degree of accuracy; thus, the quantitative harm was measurable. However, the psychological and emotional trauma Madoff's scheme wrought upon said victims would be more difficult to calculate.

Finally, what precursory elements led to the victimization event? What factors influenced the likelihood of the victimization event taking shape? Numerous demographic, behavioral, and status triggers impact victimization. Prominent among these factors are age, gender, race/ethnicity, family dynamics, relationship statuses, wealth, and extracurricular activities. Coincidentally, many of these same factors—notably, age and gender—are preconditions for cybervictimization experiences as well.

For example, we know that cybervictimization is especially prevalent and pernicious among those on the polar ends of the age spectrum. On one hand, and to little surprise given the comparatively higher concentration of Internet usage among audiences aged 34 and under (Dutton, Blank, & Groselj, 2013), many online victims skew on the young side (Campbell & Moore, 2011; Bernat & Godlove, 2012). Some rationale for this points to online victims demonstrating too little experience with notions of criminal behavior, unawareness of their own legal rights when navigating digital space, or lack of agency to advocate for themselves if they do become aware of their own victimization.

On the senior end of the spectrum, some scholars have found older Internet users become more susceptible to online information theft and fraud when such victimization targeting centers upon higher incomes and/or financial activity, and in combination with greater online shopping activity or inexperience with the threats associated with such activities (Reyns, 2013; Jorna, 2016; Williams, 2016). Ironically and unfortunately, as illustrated in Campbell and Moore's study of cyberstalking (2011), it is often these naïve and vulnerable population segments —as opposed to formal law enforcement —that carry the burden of initially diagnosing if they have fallen victim to some manner of cybercrime.

On the subject of gender, being male or female has warranted some concern (Popovic-Citic, Djuric, & Cvetkovic, 2011; Henson, Reyns, & Fisher, 2011) in light of varying observations on the propensity between men and women to fall prey to certain online attacks. Despite indications of nearly identical amounts of Internet usage (Popovic-Citic et al., 2011; Pew Research

Center, 2017), males seem more susceptible to cyberbullying (Popovic-Citic et al., 2011; Zhou et al., 2013; Festl & Quandt, 2016), violent threats (Nasi, Oksanen, Keipi, & Rasanen, 2015), and online identity theft (Reyns, 2013), while female users are more prone to mobile-phone bullying (Holt, Fitzgerald, Bossler, Chee, & Ng, 2016), sexual harassment/solicitation online (Holt, Bossler, Malinski, & May, 2016; Khurana, Bleakley, Jordan, & Romer, 2015; Saha & Srivastava, 2014; Nasi et al., 2015), romance scams (Saha & Srivastava, 2014), and other online offenses centered upon intimacy and/or deep, emotional interaction (Marganski & Fauth, 2013; Saha & Srivastava, 2014).

Clarity on the influence of other demographic factors aside from age and gender becomes more problematic in light of current empirical evidence. Consider cybervictimization by race or ethnic classification. Compared to the relative consistency in measured effects for the aforementioned age and gender categories, accounting for one's racial classification tends to vary greatly in producing evidence of correlation with cybervictimization. Demonstrative of the conflicting findings, while some studies report non-white audiences experience higher rates of cyberbullying (Hinduja & Patchin, 2010) and computer crime involving financial loss (Choi, 2010), others contend race is not a significant factor in cyberbullying (Hinduja & Patchin, 2007, 2008) or overall online harassment (Holt & Bossler, 2009).

In line with a recent proposition from Sobba, Paez, and Bensel (2017), such shortcomings in the confirmation of variables like race and ethnicity as cybervictimization correlates may simply be a matter of inconsistencies in operationalization, low sample sizes, differing sample sources, or a host of other issues related to the nature, method, and history of data captured. Alternatively, as much as demographic traits matter in traditional victimization models, the actual online behavior of users may speak more to victimization risk when considering relative models in the digital world. Compared to terrestrial settings, victimization in digital settings appears to be more dependent upon *what* one does online rather than the demographic category one falls into. This idea is precisely captured throughout the multitude of studies applying *routine activities theory* to cybervictimization models, and is likely one of the reasons why the theory has gained much notoriety as a popular framework for victimization research among scholars of digital phenomena ( ).)

The Routine Activities Perspective of Cybervictimization

Among the preeminent theories available to explain victimization in digital settings,[1] the general sentiment behind routine activities theory (Cohen & Felson, 1979) is that the interaction between *motivated offenders*, *suitable targets*, and *available guardianship* explains much of the victimization one could experience in such settings (Dodel & Mesch, 2017; Kirwan, Fullwood, & Rooney, 2018; Holt & Bossler, 2009):

1. *A **suitable target**—A target can be a person or thing that has value. In the language of the theory, the target needs to be "suitable" for victimization. A new Mercedes is probably

a more suitable target than a new Chevrolet because the Mercedes has more monetary value. Value can also be symbolic and contextual. Brand new, high profile sneakers in urban neighborhoods have greater symbolic value and are suitable targets. Within a cybercrime context, computers that house the most information are the most suitable targets (Graham & Triplett, 2017). For this reason, when a new exploit is found—what are called zero-day exploits—it is often reserved for computers that could yield the highest returns.

2. *The lack of a **capable guardian***—A guardian is something or someone that can protect the target, and the theory dictates it must be "capable" of such protection. Bodyguards are capable guardians for celebrities. Car alarms are capable guardians for cars. In the digital environment, there are several ways of guarding a computer and the information it houses (e.g. firewalls, virus protection software, fingerprint scanners).

3. *A **motivated offender***—Motivated offenders are assumed to always be present in routine activities theory. There will always be someone in a space or environment willing to commit crimes. This is especially so in the digital environment because time and space are so collapsed. A motivated offender in Scotland can victimize someone in their home country or much further away with the same ease.

Whether in a terrestrial or digital environment, the theory maintains victimization will be influenced by these three factors (see Figures 9.1 & 9.2).

Routine activities studies of cybercrime victimization focus on the various interactions between **motivated offenders**, **target suitability**, and **capable guardianship** that influence victimization risk. Successes in empirical applications of the theory have contributed much to its popularity throughout recent scholarly discourse, and offer an important pathway to

Figure 9.1   Conventional routine activities model of victimization.

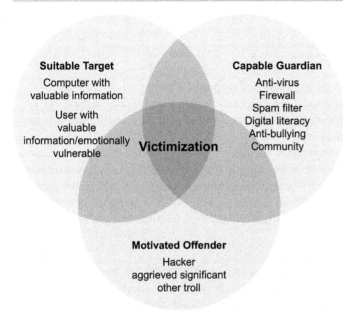

Figure 9.2   Routine activities theory and victimization in the digital environment. (Cohen and Felson, 1979.)

understanding victimization paradigms in the digital world such that even the term ***cyber-RAT*** has begun to appear.

Featured most notably in the works of Majid Yar (2005), and Kyung-shick Choi (2008, 2010) not long after, cyber-RAT theory maintains that cyberspace serves as host to scores of suitable targets—online users connecting to the Internet with little to no concern for data precaution or computer security—and motivated offenders. When combined with a lack of capable guardianship, victimization in digital environments tends to increase. Pivotal to the theory is an understanding that the nature of Internet access is such that the typical user transmits personal and valuable information from their computer throughout the vast expanse of cyberspace, where prospective offenders (equipped with sufficient hardware and/or software for targeting such individuals) are drawn to seek out potential victims (Yar, 2005; Choi 2008, 2010). Further empowered by the anonymity and range of worldwide access offered to offenders, particularly when employing higher-end technology, the Internet then becomes characterized by a constant presence of targets and offenders occupying the same space. Consider the first concept in the triumvirate: *motivation*.

MOTIVATION

What motivates the cybercrime offender to seek the intended target? What compels one to target entities in an online setting? One reason is fairly obvious: *the potential for financial gain*.

More specifically, the digitization of money, and general reconceptualization of wealth into a digital form compels would-be thieves to the digital world. Today's Internet is inundated with countless financial activities. Online auction bidding, wire transfers, bill payments, transactions within bank accounts, stock trading—there is virtually no manner of financial transaction or aspect of finance itself that cannot and is not managed through some digital avenue in the post-industrial 21st century. The advent of cryptocurrency (see Chapter 5) marks the dawning of a new reality where the digital concept of money has become synonymous with, and arguably more relevant than, its physical counterpart.

It is increasingly less likely in the present that one would opt to access financial assets exclusively from physical resources (i.e. walking into a bank and making a withdrawal), and more likely that asset exchanges both routine and atypical will occur digitally (i.e. pulling money from an ATM, making payments through online accounts). Thus, the prospective thief no longer perceives their potential prospects for targets as merely physical entities. Rather, as money has become an increasingly digital concept, so too has shifted the direction and efforts of those who would seek to illegally acquire it through predatory behavior.

Another motivation for targeting victims online is the aforementioned benefit of *anonymity*. Much like the bank robber who covers his/her face and disguises their voice to avoid having their identity revealed, the cyber-offender is often motivated by the fact that they could pull off a criminal act without being detected. The probability of avoiding detection is a compelling motivation to criminal offending online. As covered in several areas of book, there are numerous means in which one can mask one's identity online.

Internet trollers, flamers, and stalkers alike can create false profiles to use in targeting their victims. Ransomware attackers use highly sophisticated software to mask IP addresses. Cyberpornographers often keep their illicit materials in encrypted folders and/or hard drives—sometimes offline in physically secured facilities; this has also been true of purveyors of black market goods on the darknet. Indeed, the reduction of detection is quite compelling to many cyber-offenders.

Still others may be compelled by a *sense of attraction* (however misguided) towards their victims. As in the case of the cyberstalker, catfisher, and cyberpornographer, the offender is often drawn by their sensual urges to act in an illicit manner. Whereas the physical world would present the risk of increased attention, likelihood of detection, rejection from the target of their affections, and other considerable obstacles to act on these urges, digital environments provide the aforementioned anonymity and safety in distance that emboldens the offender to engage in their deviant behavior.

Then there is the possible motivation of *ego*. The sheer sense of superiority one might feel in accomplishing a particularly dastardly and technologically complex type of victimization cannot be overlooked. A hacker might find it deeply gratifying to invade a highly structured and encrypted network such as Google's servers or Facebook's user database. Such feats could serve to boost such an offender's sense of self-confidence, as well as their reputation amongst their offending peers, and on their own serve as stimuli for the cyberoffender.

Last but not least, there is the potential motivation provided by the pursuit of an *emotional vendetta* or *revenge*; a cyberoffender could simply have an axe to grind against an individual or group of individuals in a personal sense. The college student failing at a particular institution might see fit to exact their frustration by hacking into the records of the institution and disrupting important information such as grade records or financial aid data. Perhaps a group of disgruntled employees at a large corporation might initiate a flaming campaign against one or more of the corporation's senior executives or the company as a whole. Either way, the personal satisfaction to be gained from seeking revenge is a palpable motivation.

TARGET SUITABILITY

Turning to the victims' side, what makes one more or less suitable to being targeted by cyber-offenders? What makes one a more likely "victim" of a cybercrime or act of digital deviance? For starters, being visible online—often synonymous with being heavily active—is a mainstay among risk factors for being targeted. Frequent social media usage, texting activity, and general web browsing is often cited among those experiencing digital victimization. Belonging to a demographic group deemed highly vulnerable and/or susceptible to particular types of offending is another strong risk element. For instance, as mentioned at the outset of this chapter, those residing towards the respective tail ends of the age spectrum among Internet audiences are highly coveted targets.

Recalling also that female audiences online are likely targets for certain digital offenders, some scholars have found that romance scammers and other "relationship-oriented" cyber-offenders have been comparatively more successful with female targets when the sociocultural setting is more patriarchal and women are generally socialized to be more emotionally available and expressive (Saha & Srivastava, 2014; Halder & Jaishankar, 2011; Parkins, 2012). This phenomenon is enhanced by the ease with which offenders can obscure their true identity in committing such acts in comparison to similar offending in the physical world.

Demographic and behavioral evidence notwithstanding, perhaps the most consistent finding concerning target suitability in the digital world is that viable targets are nigh infinite. Suitable targets in the digital world can range from machines housing valuable data (e.g. healthcare records, corporate trade secrets, government intelligence, financial information) to individuals possessing precious information (e.g. passwords leading to banking information or access to a company's networks). A computer user who is emotionally or psychologically vulnerable can also be considered a suitable target. By design, the Internet connects all machines and users; those accessing the online world are not inherently isolated from digital presences at large. Thus, there are limitless convergences online between suitable targets and motivated offenders.

GUARDIANSHIP

With respect to guardianship, the topic of digital victimization confronts the matter in two distinct ways. In one respect, guardianship is squarely a matter of what the end user does to safeguard his/her online experience. As Internet usage tends to be a highly personalized affair, the public at large are expected to pursue a reasonable amount of precaution against the potential threats available online. Keeping important user credentials securely hidden, maintaining hardware and software integrity on one's devices (e.g. updating operating systems, antivirus software), and being aware of strangers in one's vicinity during online activity are just a few habits expected of the end user in the age of post-industrial awareness.

On the other hand, to the extent that guardianship is held as a responsibility of individual users, there is also an expectation that the architects and custodians of Internet content will practice due diligence in ensuring that the content made available online will minimize opportunities for victimization. Commercial and political entities alike have a vested interest and responsibility in providing adequate security measures for their online patrons. Financial institutions and social media entities are expected to provide a safe and secure environment for those individuals visiting their online spaces. Government organizations and political representatives are tasked with providing and enforcing guidelines in accordance with healthy online experiences.

A core precept of the routine activities perspective is that we are creatures of functional habit. We often are driven by predetermined tasks as essential to our daily routines and consume ourselves with carrying out those tasks. Usually, we structure our interactions with others around these routines and the acts themselves take on a certain predictability due to repetition. The extent to which we expose ourselves to positive and negative experiences is also rooted in these routines.

For example, consider the process we might engage in to start our work day. We wake up at certain times, dress a certain way based upon particular external factors (e.g. weather, type of occupation, expected duties for the day), prepare children for school (if they are present), eat certain things generally considered as "breakfast-fare," and depart our respective domiciles at certain times … all within a predictable pattern that can be carried out almost without thought. With respect to victimization risk, such pre-work routines might catch the attention of prospective thieves seeking easy targets to rob (i.e. homes where a physical presence is less likely during certain times), and thus increase our likelihood of victimization via burglary. Yet, that same predictability might also catch the attention of neighbors and/or local law enforcement aware that our home is vacant by a certain time every day. Thus, the presence of another individual near such a home during work hours might be more likely to raise suspicion and consequently decrease the risk of victimization. Either way, the routine becomes a critical correlate of victimization risk under the theory.

As our routines in terrestrial settings fall within certain bounds of predictability, so too have we become prone to routines in our digital lives. How we text and to whom is often consistent. Our browser histories are often saturated with multiple visits to a relatively narrow list of locations. We often use and reuse passwords for the various digital destinations we frequent, and we often conduct our digital affairs from the same IP addresses and accounts. Accordingly, under routine activities theory (see Table 9.2), our predictable digital behaviors contribute greatly to varying types and levels of potential harm.

Though our focus in this chapter, and generally this book, is the cybercrime investigative community, cybersecurity professionals may also find the insights from digital applications of routine activities theory of practical use. In effect, what cybersecurity professionals attempt to do is increase guardianship over computers, networks, and data, or reduce the suitability of those targets. Indeed, cybersecurity practices are based on the premise that there is something worth guarding (most commonly data), that there is a continuous supply of hackers attempting to access

Table 9.2 Routine Activities: Terrestrial vs. Digital Settings

EXAMPLES OF ...	... TERRESTRIAL SETTINGS	... DIGITAL SETTINGS
MOTIVATED OFFENDERS IN ...	Home burglars, car thieves, pickpockets, kidnappers, sex traffickers, stalkers	Catfishers, cyberbullies, online phishing consortiums, credit card scammers, trollers, cyberstalkers
SUITABLE TARGETS IN ...	Any individual careless in securing their personal belongings (e.g. home, car, wallet, pocketbook)	Any individual careless in securing their digital belongings (e.g. email address, browser history, user credentials on websites, laptops, mobile phones)
GUARDIANSHIP IN ...	Home security systems, anti-theft automobile devices, local law enforcement, neighbors, friends/family, security officers, electronic screening devices (e.g. metal detectors)	Parents, IT security professionals, federal/government-level watchdogs (i.e. FBI), friends/family, anti-virus software, password sophistication, Wi-Fi firewalls, dual-factor authentication
POTENTIAL HARMS IN ...	Emotional distress, financial loss, physical damage	Emotional distress, financial loss, physical harm (in response to the digital victimization experience)

the data (motivated offender), and that their only option is to develop methods and technologies to protect the data (guardianship).

Cybervictimization Types

Long before applications to the digital world, early crime scholars have pondered the various groups crime victims might fall into. Among the originating theorists on this subject, criminologist Hans Von Hentig proposed thirteen victim types—six general demographic classes, six grounded in one's psychological state, and one transitional label (where the victim becomes the offender)—during the early development of victimology. Several decades later, attorney and "founding father of victimology" Benjamin Mendelsohn held that victims generally fall into one of six distinct types: *the Completely Innocent Victim, the Victim with Minor Guilt, the Victim Who Is as Guilty as the Offender, the Victim More Guilty Than the Offender, the Most Guilty Victim,* and *the Imaginary Victim.* However, a slightly more simplified model proposed by Abdel Fattah offers perhaps the most ideal framework from traditional victimology for delineating contemporary cybervictimization types (1967).

Fattah summarized in *Towards a Criminological Classification of Victims* (1967) five victim types: non-participating, latent/predisposed, provocative, participating, and false. For the **non-participating victim**, there are two distinguishing characteristics—an attitude of denial or repulsion toward the offense and the offender, and no contribution to the origin of the offense. Unfortunately, the prevailing literature and data on cybervictimization tells us that, while many victims would be inclined to deny or abhor being victimized in a digital environment, most fall short in avoiding contributing to their own victimization. Rather, we find cybercrime victims often knowingly or unknowingly contribute to victimization in a number of ways.

Beginning with the notion of a **latent or predisposed victim**—people who, because of peculiar predispositions or traits of character, are more liable than others to be victims of certain types of offenses—these victims are squarely covered under routine activities considerations of cybervictimization. An example could be the individual that regularly leaves their phone unlocked or tends to access sensitive, personal data in public settings; such an individual exposes him/herself to a higher risk of identity-related offenses. As long as the contributing precondition remains unaddressed, so too does the increased risk (perhaps even repeated targeting from the same or similar offenders). Again, such explanations have gained much traction in cybervictimization scholarship; thus, we can conclude that the latent/predisposed typology of cybervictimization is among the more popular at present.

Those victims that play a role by either inciting the criminal to commit a crime, or by creating or fostering a situation likely to lead to crime—the **provocative victim**—are not uncommon in spaces where certain acts of cyberviolence or cyberharassment thrive. For instance, consider the online gaming community and the act of *swatting*—calling in a false report of an emergency situation (e.g. bomb threat, hostage taking, gunshot victim) with the intent of inciting an aggressive response from public safety and/or law enforcement agencies. An increasingly common scenario is for the swatting offender/s to call in the false threat following either some negative exchange between themselves and the intended target in an online gaming environment, or in a practical joke attempt against an individual live-streaming to a large audience.

Such was the case when Joshua Peters of St. Cloud, Minnesota was swatted by an unknown prankster following a live-stream of his gaming efforts in the online fantasy role-playing game, *Runescape*. During the stream, Peters paused the game to answer his front door while the webcam video of the stream continued running. The next series of events captured entailed the aggressive response from St. Cloud authorities raiding Peters's home under the false report of a shooting involving Peters and his roommate. In this instance, the provocation was nothing more than the live-stream itself and the volume of audience members actively watching Peters's progress in the game. Unfortunately, the provocative victim may not have to engage in an act that is willfully antagonistic in order to become victimized. In Peters' case, the mere act of creating access to a large audience was all that was needed to incite the would-be offender.

A **participating victim** would be any such targeted individual that plays an active role in their victimization either by adopting a passive attitude towards their own security (thus making the crime possible or easier) or else by assisting the criminal. Note that for the former defining quality—a passive attitude—this might already present itself under the latent victim category. The distinction, however, is if such an attitude exists *prior* to the victimization attempt. For instance, one who willfully engages in online bank transactions while logged into a public Wi-Fi hotspot, and especially while in an establishment of high-volume activity (e.g. a Starbucks cafe) presents a number of risk opportunities and as such could be construed as playing a role in their victimization experience (participating victim). However, an argument could be made for labeling this victim as latent if their passive attitude towards data security predates the offenders' efforts.

Nonetheless, ignoring such risks and willfully failing to engage in proper security measures in such instances (e.g. using a personal, encrypted hotspot, shielding one's screen from potential shoulder-surfing) would be characteristic of the participating victim. Similarly, giving out one's user credentials to personal websites for whatever reason opens one up to potential identity theft and cybertrespass attempts. Any ensuing victimization from sharing such credentials would be a failure associated with participating victimization.

Under the final category, the **false victim**, we would find those individuals that are not really victims at all of a crime committed by another person. They also include those who become victims of their own actions. As cybercrime becomes more ubiquitous and included among the general range of victimizations one could experience, we should expect to find fewer instances of false victimization. However, given the rapid pace at which technological innovations occur, it remains conceivable that user inexperience with emerging technology could result in negative experiences attributable solely to user errors. For similar reasons, it is also an ever-present challenge for the criminal justice community to keep crime definitions and legal statutes relevant with the various new deviance opportunities that emerge from new technology. An offense like cryptocurrency fraud might literally have been defined as false victimization barely ten years ago, for there would have been no specific legal code addressing fraud of that particular nature.

Outcomes of Cybervictimization

Few would contest that cybervictimization is a harmful experience. Victimization in the digital world is just as damaging as that which one could experience in a non-digital setting, and in some respects more so. Illustrating the range of such harm, Cross, Richards, and Smith (2016) noted in a study of online fraud victims:

> Consistent with prior research … the overwhelming majority of participants in this study reported profound emotional and psychological impacts following their victimization. Participants described the fraud as 'devastating', 'soul-destroying', or as an event that 'changed [their] attitude to life'. One admitted having 'a bit of a nervous breakdown' following the fraud, and another claimed the impacts were such that 'it was the first thing I thought about when I woke up and the last thing I thought of before I went to sleep'. Participants described a number of (often interconnected) emotional responses following the fraud. The most common were shame or embarrassment, distress, sadness and anger. Others described stress, worry, shock and loneliness.
>
> (Cross et al., 2016, 4)

Compounding such qualitative damage, recent data on the financial impact and nationwide expanse of cybervictimization (see Figures 9.3 & 9.4) underscore the reality of harm experienced (Cross et al., 2016) .

Between 2010 and 2015, the U.S. Federal Bureau of Investigation (2015) averaged just over 288,000 complaints of Internet scams and recorded over one billion dollars in total loss in 2015 alone (Dutton et al., 2013). In 2017, these trends remained virtually the same, and as illustrated in Figures 9.2 and 9.3, the damage wrought stretches across the national landscape.

Cybervictimization results in a variety of direct negative impacts on digital identity, digital assets, software/hardware integrity, and device performance (Dodel & Mesch, 2017). Subsequent indirect effects may take shape as well via stress induced from tracking down victimization culprits, closing down personal accounts, and managing financial losses suffered (Dodel & Mesch, 2017). Broader economic impacts such as decreased consumer confidence and spending activity in e-commerce destinations, which can have especially pernicious impacts in light of the postindustrial age of paperless spending, have also been recorded (Dodel & Mesch, 2017).

Online harassment has been proven to produce high levels of fear and distress, and notably among female audiences when the harassment stems from a relationship of intimacy (Lindsay, Booth, Messing, & Thaller, 2016). Within the context of dating, Schenk and Fremouw (2012) even note a differentiated set of responses to cybervictimization by gender; whereas males tended to resort to substance abuse as a coping mechanism, female victims were more likely to avoid the technology altogether. Furthermore, while men tend to experience more instances of space violations online, female victims more often report feelings of distress and physical threat during such experiences (Lindsay et al., 2016; Schenk & Fremouw, 2012).

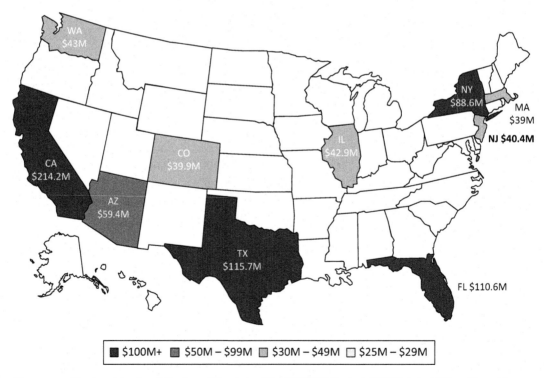

Figure 9.3   Top ten states by victim loss. (Courtesy of the FBI ICC Center's 2017 Internet Crime Report.)

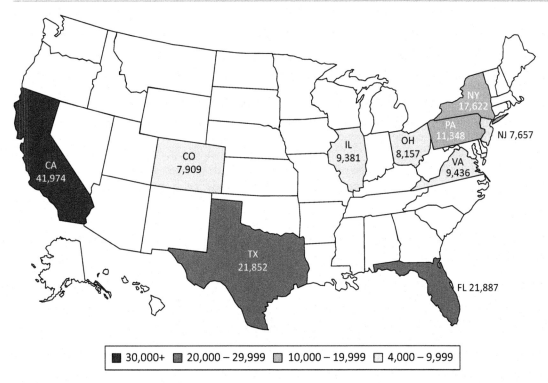

Figure 9.4 Top ten states by number of victims. (Courtesy of the FBI ICC Center's 2017 Internet Crime Report.)

Perhaps nowhere are the vast and substantial damages associated with cybervictimization displayed more vividly than among the targets of cyberbullying. School-aged victims of cyberbullying experience a gamut of emotional and cognitive trauma, including depression, low self-esteem, fear, and powerlessness (Kota, Schoohs, Benson, & Moreno, 2014; Wood Jr. & Graham, 2018). Suicidal thoughts and struggles with concentration are also common among cyberbullying victims (Schenk & Fremouw, 2012; Lindsay et al., 2016), as are lower grades and other signs of academic maladjustment (Kota et al., 2014).

Outwardly, the cyberbullied demonstrate greater hostility and proclivity towards delinquent—sometimes violent—behavior (e.g. school avoidance, weapon brandishing, alcohol consumption, sexual frequency) both in- and outside of school grounds (Kota et al., 2014; Hinduja & Patchin, 2007; Wood Jr. & Graham, 2018). The cyberbullied individual often expresses greater generalized fear of being victimized in digital environments, alongside those who've suffered from computer virus attacks, online scams, and digital piracy infractions (Yu, 2014).

These insights notwithstanding, conclusions on the scope of cybervictimization outcomes must also be taken with some level of skepticism as the full reality of such victimization is not necessarily captured. Again, considering the example of cyberbullying, Sobba and colleagues (2017) found that while over 40% of teens in the United States reported experiencing some form of cyberbullying, only 25% tell their parents about their victimization. Their example illustrates the broader point that cybervictimization is difficult to track in some respects given that many cybercrimes go unreported, and victims of cybercrime tend to be reluctant to come forward for a variety of reasons.

Common among them include trivialization of the full impact of the crime itself by victims and law enforcement officials alike, and victims' own feelings of shame for falling victim to the offense committed against them (Halder & Jaishankar, 2011; Cross et al., 2016). This apprehension, along with an ever-fluctuating list of cybercrime definitions, and the general ease with which offenders can conceal themselves behind a variety of identity-masking conventions, are key reasons victimization in the digital world tends to go underreported. This, in turn, leads to inaccuracies in the documentation of such crimes and causes greater difficulty in implementing proper safeguards since the full scope of the trends can rarely be ascertained.

Cybervictimization Restitution

"WHO IS THE VICTIM?"

From Richard Quinney's "Who Is the Victim," published in *Criminology* (Volume 10, Issue 3, 1972):

The modern movement for compensation of victims also has its own conventional wisdom regarding the victim. The numerous proposals for victim compensation contain their own conceptions as to who is the victim. Moreover, these proposals are addressed to specific points regarding the victim, including ideas about the offender–victim relationship, responsibility, human nature, governmental functions, and the nature of society. "Who is the victim?" is not an innocent question.

Recognition of the need to compensate victims ... is grounded on the notion that modern criminal law has evolved away from the victim's right to private redress. And since the state has taken upon itself the function of maintaining law and order, it is liable for the personal injuries of the victims of some forms of crime.

There are, of course, disclaimers to this notion of the victim and his right to be compensated. Some [writers] stress more emphatically the role of individual responsibility and question welfare programs by the government.

Those who argue against victim compensation or for extremely limited programs conceive of the victim as being responsible for his own victimization.

Another proposal ... suggests the "functional responsibility" of both the victim and the offender ... that the offender should compensate the victim when possible. Restitution to victims by offenders, it is suggested, would serve to rehabilitate the offender. Further, the victim is to prevent his own victimization and the offender is to account for his violation.

On the general matter of victim restitution, the preceding excerpt from Richard Quinney's "Who Is the Victim?" sets forth some key talking points to frame the discussion. What role should the state play in compensating victims of crime? To what extent should victims seek to address their recompense, particularly in light of the possibility that they may have contributed to their own victimization risk? And for that matter, what role should the offender have in compensating his her/victim? Albeit over 40 years removed from any notion of the cybervictimization concept we are confronted with today, questions and ideas Quinney proposed are no less relevant.

At least one piece of landmark legislation, the **Identity Theft Enforcement and Restitution (ITER) Act** of 2008, sets a position on such questions in establishing the US government's role in cybercrime victim compensation, as well as the respective responsibilities of victims and offenders alike. In essence, the ITER Act states that victims have the right to use the US federal court system to the fullest extent possible in seeking restitution from entities associated with the theft and subsequent misuse of the victim's identity. Particularly, the ITER Act states:

- the victim may seek compensation for the time spent fixing problems ensuing from the theft. Specifically, the victim is allowed to receive a sum "equal to the value of the time reasonably spent by the victim in an attempt to remediate the intended or actual harm incurred by the victim from the offense."
- prosecutors may pursue offenders who threaten to take or release information from computers with the intent of cyberextortion
- prosecutors may pursue charges against cybercriminals with conspiracy to commit a cybercrime

The ITER Act further removes a previous restriction of having to show at least $5,000 in damages before filing charges associated with unauthorized computer access, and allows for federal prosecution even when parties reside within the same state (Doyle, 2014).

Since its inception, there has been one major federal ruling specifically invoking the ITER Act. The case, *United States of America v. Janosko (2011)*, ruled in favor of the plaintiff and subsequently ordered the defendant, Mr. Francis G. Janosko (Mass.) to pay restitution resulting from illegally accessing secured computer equipment and files housed within the Plymouth County Correctional Facility (where he was an inmate). Restitution was ordered as follows: $4,309 for the cost of purchasing elements of the system needed to replace those damaged by Mr. Janosko and retained as evidence, and $6,600 for the cost of monitoring credit records of the individuals who suffered the privacy violations and consequent risk of identity theft (United States v. Janosko, 2011).

Aside from the aforementioned ruling against Janosko, numerous other decisions in cybercrime court cases offer precedents for the awarding of compensation to cybercrime victims. The vast majority fall within the realm of infractions of cyberpornography, cybertrespass, or cyberdeception, and especially when a specific quantifiable amount of loss can be determined:

A SNAPSHOT OF FEDERAL CYBERCRIME COURT RULINGS RESULTING IN RESTITUTION

United States v. Watt (2010)

In 2010, Stephen Watt pled guilty to conspiracy, in violation of 18 U.S.C.S. § 371, based on his adaptation of software that enabled the principals of the conspiracy to steal credit and debit card information from certain companies. He was sentenced to 24 months incarceration, three years of supervised release, and ordered to pay **restitution of \$171.5 million**.

United States v. Green (2010)

In 2010, Benjamin Green pled guilty to six counts of aggravated identity theft in violation of 18 U.S.C. §§ 1028 (a)(1) and (a)(4), six counts of fraud with an access device in violation of 18 U.S.C. § 1029(a)(2), and one count of bank fraud in violation of 18 U.S.C. § 1344. He was sentenced 84 months' imprisonment, five years of supervised release, and ordered to pay **restitution of \$95,522.64,** along with a special assessment of \$1,300.

United States v. Kearney (2012)

Patrick Kearney pled guilty (and later appealed) to 17 counts of transportation, distribution, and possession of child pornography, which he did through use of the Internet. As his appeal was denied, the original ruling that he pay **\$3,800 in restitution** to the subject, "Vicky," depicted throughout the pornographic materials under 18 U.S.C.S. § 2259 was upheld. In the ruling, it was noted that restitution was calculated based upon Vicky's status as a minor during the time period of the offending behavior, as well as the expectation that she would require mental-health treatment following Mr. Kearney's conduct.

U.S. v. Benoit (2013)

In 2013, Joseph Benoit was convicted of receipt of child pornography in violation of 18 U.S.C.S. § 2252(a)(2) and (b)(1), and possession of child pornography in violation of 18 U.S.C.S. § 2252(a)(4)(B) and (b)(2). He was sentenced to concurrent terms of 125 and 120 months' imprisonment and **ordered to pay \$11,466 in restitution.**

U.S. v. Gammon (2013)

William Gammon pled guilty to one count of possession of child pornography, in violation of 18 U.S.C.S. § 2252A(a)(5)(B) and (b)(2). Pursuant to 18 U.S.C.S. § 2259, the United States District Court for the Southern District of Texas ordered **restitution in the amount of \$125,000 to each of three victims.**

Given what is now known about the variety of damage wrought from cybercrime offenses, few would argue that cybercrime victims are deserving of some recompense in cases such as the aforementioned. Yet, reconciliation of the harm committed against a target in the digital world may be the most troubling aspect of cybervictimization, and thus is still a matter of limited precedent at this time. Prominent among contributing factors to the complexity in awarding victim compensations for cybercrime offenses are: 1) dubious and/or unreliable methods for calculating proper compensation, 2) similarly questionable means of determining the total scope of victims/

victimization resulting from the offense(s) considered, and 3) inability of convicted defendants to produce victim compensation associated with their sentence.

Conclusion

In this chapter, we have discussed and considered the ramifications associated with cybervictimization. Clearly, the subject has warranted and been paid much attention in recent scholarship and criminal justice legislation. By and large, the extant literature firmly settles on the notion that victimization in the digital world can be and usually is profoundly damaging. Accordingly, via such benchmark policy developments as the CFAA (see Chapter 2) and the ITER Act, federal court rulings, and some reinvention of the agency infrastructure in place to address victimization, the criminal justice community has responded in acknowledgment of the various pains endured by those targeted in the cyberworld.

Yet, it is important to also remember that the discourse and treatment of victimization in the digital world is still developing and much remains to be explored and resolved. Paramount among such gray areas is the unawareness of and apathy towards the extent of potential damage from cybercrime still defining many academics, criminal justice practitioners, and the public at large. The extent of underreporting from victims, along with conflicting notions concerning the very concept of what victimization means in a digital sense, remain confounding obstacles hampering progress in research and policy development on this subject.

Vocabulary

1. **Capable guardian/guardianship**—Something or someone that can protect a target from being victimized.
2. **Cyber-RAT** *(short for Cyber-Routine Activities Theory)*—Maintains that cyberspace serves as host to scores of suitable targets and motivated offenders. Alongside these factors, risk of victimization in digital environments increases when capable guardianship is lacking.
3. **Cybervictimization**—Victimization within a digital environment (e.g. the Internet, mobile devices, encrypted computer networks).
4. **False Victim**—Victims who are not really victims of a crime committed by another person; may be victims solely of their own actions.
5. **Internet Crime Complaint Center**—The FBI's central hub for investigating cyber-attacks by criminals, overseas adversaries, and terrorists; a nationwide depository and reporting service for information on both suspected and confirmed Internet-facilitated criminal activity.
6. **Latent Victim**—A victim prone to offense targeting due to peculiar predispositions or traits of character; often includes the behavioral tendencies theorized under routine activities models of victimization.
7. **Motivated Offender**—An individual with a desire to commit criminal behavior.

8. **Nonparticipating Victim**—A victim who is uncooperative in the offending act for which they have suffered due either to a repulsion toward the offense or a lack of contribution to the origin of the offense.

9. **Participating Victims**—A victim who is complicit in the offending act for which they have suffered due to their active role in the act—either by adopting a passive attitude towards their own security or else by assisting the criminal.

10. **Predisposed Victim**—*See Latent Victim.*

11. **Provocative Victim**—The victim that plays a role in the offending act for which they have suffered by either inciting the criminal to commit the criminal act, or by creating or fostering a situation likely to lead to the criminal act.

12. **Target suitability**—A person or thing of value that can potentially be a target for victimization or crime.

13. **Victimless Crime(s)**—Criminal acts for which there is either no true victim, or for which one has not been or cannot be determined.

Study Questions

TRUE OR FALSE

1. Much of cybervictimization can be understood from traditional notions and studies of victimization.
   a. True
   b. False

2. Cybervictimization has been tracked consistently in the United States since the early 2000s.
   a. True
   b. False

3. Online harassment has been proven to produce high levels of fear and distress among female audiences when the harassment stems from a relationship of intimacy.
   a. True
   b. False

4. Andrew spends a great deal of time leaving negative comments on the YouTube pages of video content owners. One such owner decides to seek revenge on Andrew by cyberstalking his social media pages and flaming him by leaving slanderous messages over a period of several weeks. In this case, we would say Andrew's actions <u>did not</u> contribute to the cyberstalking victimization he ultimately experienced.
   a. True
   b. False

5. Under the Identity Theft Enforcement and Restitution Act of 2008, the victim of a cyber-theft may seek compensation for the time spent fixing problems ensuing from the theft.
   a. True
   b. False

6. School-aged victims of cyberbullying experience a range of emotional and cognitive trauma. Low self-esteem is *not* one of those trauma.
   a. True
   b. False
7. Hans Von Hentig proposed a simplified model of victimology wherein the victimization experience could be summarized within just five categories.
   a. True
   b. False

MULTIPLE CHOICE

1. Dana is talking about the latest episode of American hit TV-show *Game of Thrones* with several of her work colleagues. After explaining that she hasn't caught up with the latest season, one of her co-workers offers to give her an access code to a torrent website where pirated copies of the latest episodes can be downloaded for free. Even though Dana has misgivings about using the code, she ultimately concludes that it is okay since the producers of the show aren't really losing any money and she is a big fan of the show. In this way, Dana is resting upon the perception that downloading pirated entertainment content is a/an _____.
   a. victimless crime
   b. example of cyberbullying
   c. activity justifiable under routine activities perspective on victimization
   d. crime only if the content originates
2. Each of the following represents one of Abdel Fattah's five victimization categories EXCEPT:
   a. Participating
   b. False
   c. Latent
   d. Transitional
3. The _____ victim tends to contribute to his/her own victimization by inciting the criminal to commit a crime, or by creating or fostering a situation likely to lead to crime.
   a. Provocative
   b. Latent
   c. Participating
   d. False
4. The first federal case to invoke the Identity Theft Enforcement and Restitution Act of 2008 was _____.
   a. United States of America v. Gammon
   b. United States of America v. Janosko
   c. United States of America v. Kearney
   d. United States of America v. Green

5. Which of the following would be reasonable to conclude concerning cybervictimization in the United States of America?
   a. Cybervictimization is solely a problem experienced by Americans in the easternmost United States.
   b. Cybervictimization is a nationwide phenomenon threatening the financial, cognitive, and emotional well-being of millions of Americans each year.
   c. Cybervictimization is a problem mainly experienced by the rich and famous segments of society.
   d. Social disorganization theory is a popular perspective for understanding cybervictimization.

MATCHING EXERCISE—ROUTINE ACTIVITIES PERSPECTIVE

Accounting for the routine activities perspective to cybervictimization, match the following component with whether you would likely observe it in a terrestrial setting (T), a digital setting (D) or both (B):

1. Home burglars
2. Emotional distress
3. Loss of financial security
4. Individuals leaving their laptops open in a public setting (e.g. a coffee shop) while they go use nearby bathroom
5. Credit card scammers
6. Bullies
7. Home security systems
8. Parents
9. Anti-virus software

Critical Thinking Exercise

Consider the notion of "victimless" crimes (crimes where the identity of a victim is either unknown or ignored). How might certain aspects of the digital world precipitate the notion of a victimless crime? What characteristics of the digital world could contribute to a victim going unidentified or unrecognized?

Consider what a cybervictimization "bill of rights"—a document that would establish what rights and protections should be afforded to Internet users against victimization—would look like. Given what you've read in this chapter, what should such a document entail in terms of standards for safeguarding Internet visitors from victimization attacks?

NOTE

1 *For a more comprehensive discussion of cybercrime theories, see Chapter 10 – Cybercriminology.*

REFERENCES

Bernat, F., & Godlove, N. (2012). Understanding 21st century cybercrime for the "common" victim. *89*, 2. Retrieved from www.crimeandjustice.org.uk/publications/cjm/article/understanding-21st-century-cybercrime-%E2%80%98common%E2%80%99-victim.

Campbell, J., & Moore, R. (2011). Self-perceptions of stalking victimization and impacts on victim reporting. *Police Practice and Research, 12*, 13.

Choi, K.-S. (2008). Computer crime victimization and integrated theory: An empirical assessment. *International Journal of Cyber Criminology, 2*, 27.

Choi, K.-S. (2010). *Risk factors in computer-crime victimization.* El Paso, TX: LFB Scholarly Publishing LLC.

Cohen, L. E., & Felson, M. (1979). Social change and crime rate trends: A routine activity approach. *American Sociological Review, 44*, 588–608.

Cross, C., Richards, K., & Smith, R. G. (2016). The reporting experiences and support needs of victims of online fraud. In R.Brown (Ed.), *Trends and issues in crime and criminal justice.* Canberra, ACT: Australian Institute of Criminology. Retrieved from https://aic.gov.au/publications/tandi/tandi518.

Dodel, M., & Mesch, G. (2017). Cyber-victimization preventive behavior: A health belief model approach. *Computers in Human Behavior, 68*, 359–367.

Doyle, C. (2014). *Cybercrime: An overview of the federal computer fraud and abuse statute and related federal criminal laws.* Washington, DC: Congressional Research Service.

Dutton, W. H., Blank, G., & Groselj, D. (2013). Culture of the Internet: The Internet in Britain. *Oxford Internet Survey 2013.* Oxford, UK: Oxford Internet Institute.

Fattah, A. (1967). Towards a criminological classification of victims. *The International Journal of Criminal Police, 209*, 162–169.

Federal Bureau of Investigations (2017). Internet Crime Report. Washington, DC: Federal Bureau of Investigations: Internet Crime Complaint Center.

Festl, R., & Quandt, T. (2016). The role of online communication in long-term cyberbullying involvement among girls and boys. *Journal of Youth Adolescence, 45*, 14.

Graham, R., & Triplett, R. (2017). Capable guardians in the digital environment: The role of digital literacy in reducing phishing victimization. *Deviant Behavior, 38*, 1371–1382.

Halder, D., & Jaishankar, K. (2011). Cyber gender harassment and secondary victimization: A comparative analysis of the United States, the UK, and India. *Victims and Offenders, 4*, 13.

Henson, B., Reyns, B. W., & Fisher, B. S. (2011). Security in the 21st century: Examining the link between online social network activity, privacy, and interpersonal victimization. *Criminal Justice Review, 36*, 16.

Hinduja, S., & Patchin, J. W. (2007). Offline consequences of online victimization: school violence and delinquency. *Journal of School Violence, 6*, 89–112.

Hinduja, S., & Patchin, J. W. (2008). Personal information of adolescents on the Internet: A quantitative content analysis of Myspace. *Journal of Adolescence, 31*, 125–146.

Hinduja, S., & Patchin, J. W. (2010). Cyberbullying and self-esteem. *Journal of School Health, 80*, 614–621.

Holt, T. J., & Bossler, A. M. (2009). Examining the applicability of lifestyle-routine activities theory for cybercrime victimization. *Deviant Behavior, 30*, 1–25.

Holt, T. J., Bossler, A. M., Malinski, R., & May, D. C. (2016). Identifying predictors of unwanted online sexual conversations among youth using a low self-control and routine activity framework. *Journal of Contemporary Criminal Justice, 32*, 20.

Holt, T. J., Fitzgerald, S., Bossler, A., Chee, G., & Ng, E. (2016). Assessing the risk factors of cyber and mobile phone bullying victimization in a nationally representative sample of Singapore youth. *International Journal of Offender Therapy and Comparative Criminology, 60*, 598–615.

Jorna, P. (2016). The relationship between age and consumer fraud victimisation. *Trends & Issues in Crime and Criminal Justice, 17*. Retrieved from https://aic.gov.au/publications/tandi/tandi519.

Khurana, A., Bleakley, A., Jordan, A. B., & Romer, D. (2015). The protective effects of parental monitoring and internet restriction on adolescents' risk of online harassment. *Journal of Youth Adolescence, 44*, 8.

Kirwan, G. H., Fullwood, C., & Rooney, B. (2018). Risk factors for social networking site scam victimization among malaysian students. *Cyberpsychology, Behavior, and Social Networking, 21*, 123–128.

Kota, R., Schoohs, S., Benson, M., & Moreno, M. A. (2014). Characterizing cyberbullying among college students: Hacking, dirty laundry, and mocking. *Societies, 4*, 549–560.

Lindsay, M., Booth, J. M., Messing, J. T., & Thaller, J. (2016). Experiences of online harassment among emerging adults: Emotional reactions and the mediating role of fear. *Journal of Interpersonal Violence, 31*, 3174–3195.

Marganski, A., & Fauth, K. (2013). Socially interactive technology and contemporary dating: A cross-cultural exploration of deviant behaviors among young adults in the modern, evolving technological world. *International Criminal Justice Review, 23*, 20.

Nasi, M., Oksanen, A., Keipi, T., & Rasanen, P. (2015). Cybercrime victimization among young people: A multination study. *Journal of Scandinavian Studies in Criminology and Crime Prevention, 16*, 8.

Parkins, R. (2012). Gender and emotional expressiveness: An analysis of prosodic features in emotional expression. *Griffith Working Papers in Pragmatics and Intercultural Communication* [Online], *5*. Retrieved from https://cms-uat.itc.griffith.edu.au/__data/assets/pdf_file/0006/456459/Paper-6-Parkins-Gender-and-Emotional-Expressiveness_final.pdf [Accessed June 6, 2017].

Pew Research Center (2017). *Internet and Broadband Fact Sheet* [Online]. Retrieved from http://www.pewinternet.org/fact-sheet/internet-broadband/ [Accessed]

Popovic-Citic, B., Djuric, S., & Cvetkovic, V. (2011). The prevalence of cyberbullying among adolescents: A case study of middle schools in Serbia. *School Psychology International, 32*, 12.

Quinney, R. (1972). Who is the victim? *Criminology, 10*, 314–323.

Reyns, B. W. (2013). Online routines and identity theft victimization: Further expanding routine activity theory beyond direct-contact offenses. *Journal of Research in Crime and Delinquency, 50*, 23.

Saha, T., & Srivastava, A. (2014). Indian women at risk in the cyber space: A conceptual model of reasons of victimization. *International Journal of Cyber Criminology, 8*, 12.

Schenk, A., & Fremouw, W. (2012). Prevalence, psychological impact, and coping of cyberbully victims among college students. *Journal of School Violence, 11*, 21–37.

Shirkey, C. (2008). *Here comes everybody: The power of organizing without organizations.* New York, NY: The Penguin Press.

Sobba, K. N., Paez, R. A., & Bensel, T. T. (2017). Perceptions of cyberbullying: An assessment of perceived severity among college students. *Tech Trends, 61*, 570–579.

United States of America, Appellee, v. Francis G. Janosko, Defendant, Appellant., 642 F.3d 40 (2011). U.S. App. LEXIS 7433 (United States Court of Appeals for the First Circuit April 12, 2011, Decided). Retrieved from https://advance-lexis-com.proxy.lib.odu.edu/api/document?collection=cases&id=urn:contentItem:52KX-FJY1-JCNH-T00W-00000-00&context=1516831

United States of America, Plaintiff—Appellee, v. Joseph Eddy Benoit, Defendant—Appellant. VICKY, Amicus Curiae., 713 F.3d 1 (2013). U.S. App. LEXIS 6645, 2013 WL 1298154 (United States Court of Appeals for the Tenth CircuitApril 2, 2013, Filed). Retrieved from https://advance-lexis-com.proxy.lib.odu.edu/api/document?collection=cases&id=urn:contentItem:583N-JV71-F04K-W0M4-00000-00&context=1516831

United States of America, Plaintiff-Appellee v. William George Gammon, Defendant-Appellant, 533 Fed. Appx. 437 (2013). U.S. App. LEXIS 8668, 2013 WL 3238722 (United States Court of Appeals for the Fifth CircuitApril 29, 2013, Filed). Retrieved from https://advance-lexis-com.proxy.lib.odu.edu/api/document?collection=cases&id=urn:contentItem:589F-YYG1-F04K-N075-00000-00&context=1516831

United States of America v. Benjamin Green, Appellant, 389 Fed. Appx. 146 (2010). U.S. App. LEXIS 15673 (United States Court of Appeals for the Third CircuitJuly 29, 2010, Filed). Retrieved from https://advance-lexis-com.proxy.lib.odu.edu/api/document?collection=cases&id=urn:contentItem:8025-1MF0-YB0V-F02W-00000-00&context=1516831

United States of America, v. Stephen Watt, Defendant., 707 F. Supp. 2d 149 (2010). U.S. Dist. LEXIS 41070 (United States District Court for the District of Massachusetts April 27, 2010, Decided). Retrieved from https://advance-lexis-com.proxy.lib.odu.edu/api/document?collection=cases&id=urn:contentItem:7YBG-MKD0-YB0N-800T-00000-00&context=1516831

Williams, M. (2016). Guardians upon high: An application of routine activities theory to online identity theft in Europe at the country and individual level. *British Journal of Criminology*, 56, 29.

Wood, F. R., Jr., & Graham, R. (2018). "Safe" and "at-risk": Cyberbullying victimization and deviant health risk behaviors in youth. *Youth & Society*, 1–20.

Yar, M. (2005). The novelty of 'cybercrime': An assessment in light of routine activity theory. *European Journal of Criminology*, 2, 407–427.

Yu, S. (2014). Fear of cyber crime among college students in the United States: An exploratory study. *International Journal of Cyber Criminology*, 8, 36–46.

Zhou, Z., Tang, H., Tian, Y., Wei, H., Zhang, F., & Morrison, C. (2013). Cyberbullying and its risk factors Chinese high school students. *School Psychology International*, 34, 17.

Chapter 10

Cybercriminology

Introduction

People are often dismissive of theory. The law enforcement professional, the business executive, and the policy-maker assume that decisions are made based upon the facts as they are in the real world. Meanwhile, students see theory as simply a course they need to take or block of ideas within a course, but not information that can be of use once they begin their lives in a world of work. But the importance of theory is not in how applicable it is in specific everyday situations but in its ability to explain in general terms how and why phenomena are connected and hopefully predict what will happen in the future. A law enforcement officer may find in her specific situation a need to think about a wide array of variables when trying to prevent a rash of assaults along a dark path near a college campus. The idea from such theories as routine activities (see Chapter 9)—that one needs a "capable guardian" to prevent crime—may seem far too simplistic for her immediate purposes. However, that officer can use the ideas of routine activities theory as a starting point upon which to build her own experiences from her specific context. Moreover, even if her context changes—she may move from a leafy college campus to a dense urban area—she can be confident that the general relationship asserted by routine activities theory will still hold.

Building upon our discussion of routine activities theories of cybervictimization in the preceding chapter, we will introduce several additional theories used to explain crime and deviance in the digital world. For each theory, the main assumptions are introduced, basic concepts relevant to the theory are explained, and its applicability to cybercrime is discussed. These theories are listed next:

- Deterrence Theory
- Theories of Culture and Learning
  - Social Learning Theory
  - Labeling Theory

- Theories of Control
  - Social Bonding Theory
  - Self-Control Theory (A General Theory of Crime)
  - Techniques of Neutralization
- Strain Theory
- Theories of Anonymity—Deindividuation and Disinhibition

The list of theories is not exhaustive. There are many theoretical traditions not included in this chapter. Nor are the theories selected implying they are more important to explaining cybercrime than those not included. Although we believe that some of the more overarching "general" theories of crime such as strain theory and self-control theory will always be useful, it may be that as research on cybercrime continues to develop a few theories will be universally recognized as having the most explanatory value. That is not the case as of now. We chose these theories because, at the time of this writing, these are the theories that have been applied most often to cybercrime research.

Deterrence Theory

Deterrence theory argues that people will avoid criminal activity if the known punishments associated with the act outweigh any perceived benefit (Hua & Bapna, 2012; Shepherd & Mejias, 2016; Wrenn, 2012; Young & Zhang, 2007). This theory is grounded in the assumption that individuals are rational beings who weigh the costs and benefits of an action and then make logical choices accordingly. A logical choice is one that maximizes their gain or positive outcome in any given situation. In the context of crime and deviance, this means that an individual considering a deviant or criminal act will consider the likelihood of being caught and the penalties they would incur. For policy-makers and law enforcement personnel, the assumption of a rational actor also assumes that the criminal justice system can modify the punishments it administers to *deter* potential offenders—thus deterrence theory.

There are three components to deterrence: celerity, certainty, and severity. Celerity is the time it takes for a punishment to be administered. A punishment that is received closer to the violating act is theoretically more effective at deterring future acts. A punishment that takes longer to administer—say, a sentence of death carried out several years after a guilty verdict—is less associated with the crime. Certainty is the freedom from doubt that, given a crime, a punishment will be meted out. An offender who believes that they will certainly be caught once offending will rationally avoid committing the act. Severity is the level of punishment, regarding time spent in confinement, monetary fines, loss of privileges, or physical pain. Punishments that are more severe are theoretically more likely to deter crime.

There are two types of deterrence activities administered by states and other agents of authority—general and specific. **General deterrence** activities are undertaken to deter crime in the general population. A state levies a punishment on an offender to set an example, and the punishment is designed for public viewing. In ancient times, enemies of the state were killed, and their heads placed on pikes for others to see. This was done as a warning to others.

Public floggings were commonplace in Colonial Era New England in the United States. Modern societies are less violent and may use different methods of deterring criminal behavior. One example would be the "perp walk," where an offender must walk into a courthouse for the benefit of the media.

Because of the relative newness of cybercrime, states may make an example out of someone if there is public concern that the crime is a harbinger of things to come. Ross Ulbricht's punishment of life in prison with no possibility of parole, as discussed in Chapter 7 on Organized Cybercrime, may be an example of general deterrence. It is questionable whether a life sentence with no possibility of parole is justified for the owner of a site that traffics in narcotics.

Specific deterrence, on the other hand, is administered to prevent the individual from further criminal behavior. The "three strikes" laws, in which an individual will be given a life sentence if they commit three felonies, is designed to deter an offender from future offending. Specific deterrence may also be in the form of a tailored sentence, unique to that individual. For example, a person convicted of driving under the influence may be recommended to an alcohol recovery program. A famous example is that of Kevin Mitnick, who had committed so many hacking crimes he was sentenced to a psychological counseling program.[1]

Theories of Culture and Learning: Social Learning and Labeling

Another set of criminological theories focus on the learned values, beliefs, and practices of offenders. These theories have a core assumption that criminal behavior, as with most social actions, is learned. Sociologists have traditionally argued that there are four influences, or agents of socialization, that teach people their cultures, values, and beliefs. A person's significant others (family, close intimate friends) are the first and arguably the most important influence. A second influence is a person's peer group. For example, young people are influenced by their classmates and adults are influenced by their coworkers. A third influence is society's institutions (e.g. schools they attend, religious organizations, and social clubs). A fourth influence is the media. People learn culture from what they see on television and movies, or read online. The theories discussed below—social learning and labeling theory, and techniques of neutralization—begin with these core assumptions and then develop along different paths.

SOCIAL LEARNING THEORY

Social learning theory rests on the premise that behavior that is positively reinforced is learned, while behavior that is negatively reinforced is not learned (Akers, 1996, 2009; Morris & Higgins, 2010). Modern social learning theory is composed of two strands of thought. The first strand is Edwin Sutherland's theory of **differential association**, which asserts that individuals learn culture (values, beliefs, attitudes, norms) from the people they associate with (Friedrichs, Schoultz, & Jordanoska, 2018). Sutherland identified nine characteristics of differential association:

1. Criminal behavior is learned
2. Criminal behavior is learned through communicating with others
3. Learning occurs primarily in intimate personal groups
4. When criminal behavior is learned, the learning includes (a) techniques of committing the crime and (b) the specific direction of motives and drives, rationalizations, and attitudes
5. The specific direction of motives and drives is learned from definitions of the legal codes as favorable or unfavorable
6. A person becomes delinquent because they learn more definitions favorable to crime than definitions unfavorable to crime
7. Differential association may vary in frequency, duration, priority, and intensity
8. The process of learning criminal behavior by association involves all the mechanisms in other forms of learning
9. Although criminal behavior is an expression of general needs and values, it is not explained by those general needs and values, because noncriminal behavior is an expression of the same needs and values

One drawback of Sutherland's work is that the processes that link differential association to learning are not specified. In other words, *how* does a person learn new behavior? Ronald Akers applied ideas from behavioral psychology to illuminate these processes (see Table 10.1). Akers identifies four dimensions of social learning. Two of these are the aforementioned differential association and its definitions originally described by Sutherland. Akers adds **differential reinforcement** and **imitation**. These additions explain how a person comes to learn a new (criminal) behavior.

According to Aker's theory, a person experiencing associations that provide more definitions favorable to crime than definitions unfavorable to crime are only two components of the process. Those behaviors must be differentially reinforced—where they are given rewards for certain behaviors and punished for others. Consider a person who is learning the definitions associated with data theft—selling company secrets to competitors. If that person is in a company where many of her coworkers are also stealing data, she will not only avoid negative social sanctions but

Table 10.1 The Four Dimensions of Ronald Akers's Social Learning Theory

Differential Association	The process by which a person is exposed to definitions favorable or unfavorable to crime and deviance.
Definitions	Individuals learn the attitudes, beliefs, and justifications that underpin any given behavior.
Differential Reinforcement	When individuals are given rewards for behavior, they are more likely to continue that behavior. Conversely, if an individual is punished for behavior, they are more likely to stop that behavior.
Imitation	Individuals learn behaviors after observing others.

may also receive positive reinforcements. These positive reinforcements may be being invited out for drinks after work or having their mistakes at work overlooked because she is a part of the "club."

Akers also identifies imitation as another component of the social learning process. Individuals may not have direct communication with another person to begin adopting criminal behaviors. They can observe the behavior and then imitate.

The phenomenon of swatting—calling in a false report of an emergency (e.g. bomb threat, hostage taking, gunshot victim) with the intent of inciting an aggressive response from public safety agencies—serves to illustrate social learning theory. Swatting has become increasingly popular in recent years among subgroups within the online gaming community. Offenders learn the technique of swatting via other gamers who've either swatted or been swatted. Particularly important in facilitating the act is the knowledge gained concerning the technologies needed and the tactics necessary to successfully incite an emergency response without revealing one's identity or location.

Similarly, using the tools and techniques in online child pornography sharing rings is another example of social learning theory. To successfully commit the offense, an offender may need to be involved in an online community where he can learn the behaviors necessary to find images and share images while evading detection. In one of the largest formal crackdowns on child pornography, Operation Delego, offenders were identified and arrested via the child pornography online community called "Dreamboard." Members of Dreamboard had developed several techniques to evade law enforcement. These included:

- Using aliases and screen names to avoid detection
- Links posted on Dreamboard were required to be encrypted
- Members accessed the board through a proxy server to hide their IP addresses
- Members were also encouraged to use encryption programs on their computers to encrypt their data

These techniques are not likely to be randomly distributed throughout a user population. Rather, prospective members of Dreamboard would have had to learn these techniques from others connected to the online community, and success in evading detection (and thus, criminal prosecution) and accessing the pornographic material would have served as positive reinforcers.

LABELING THEORY

Labeling theory argues that deviance is socially constructed through the actions of an audience witnessing deviance, and not the individual who committed the act. Deviant behavior, according to proponents of the theory, does not exist until members in society define it as such. The location, the cultural context, and the characteristics of the offender and audience must be considered when trying to understand why some actions are defined as not deviant, mildly deviant, or worthy of severe negative sanctions.

Labeling theory is primarily understood as explaining deviance and crime at a micro level. By micro level, social scientists mean that the phenomena occur between individuals and in circumscribed, small group settings. **Micro-level phenomena** are contrasted with **macro-level phenomena**, which describe broad societal trends at the neighborhood or national level. For example, labeling theory may be used to explain why a group of kids in one setting smoking marijuana become seen as deviant, while in another setting the same behavior is ignored. It would not generally be used to describe the national increase in marijuana usage.

Labeling requires power. Some groups and individuals have more ability to label an action as deviant than others. Consider the example of a group of youths smoking marijuana. Suppose the group is smoking on the school grounds after hours. The group will not only be disciplined through the formally written measures of the school, but the teacher may also tell other teachers and administrators about the observed behavior. She may be so offended by what she saw that she describes the behavior in the worst possible terms. As a result, the group may become associated with deviance and bad behavior in the minds of the authority figures in the school. Words such as "weedheads" and "potheads" may be used in association with the group. Now imagine that the group gets caught by an unpopular student. The student may join in on the behavior in hopes of being accepted. In this case, the action is not even defined as deviant. Even if the student does not participate in the behavior, he or she will have less ability to influence how other students in the school think of the group. Her labeling has less weight in the minds of others.

Labeling theory asserts that the labels given to a person can cause further offending. The first acts of deviance are called **primary deviance**. Depending upon the context within which these first acts occur, a person may be labeled so severely and harshly that the label becomes a master status. A master status is a label that becomes the most important characteristic of the person. As a result of the label, the person may feel shame or embarrassment and commit further acts of deviance. Alternatively, they may embrace the label, which can also lead to committing further acts of deviance. This **secondary deviance** is progressively worse than the initial primary act. Labeling theorists argue that through the act of labeling early primary deviances, an individual may commit more serious secondary acts and embark on a career of deviance.

Importantly, the act of labeling is also an act of negotiation. It is not predetermined that an individual or group in power can describe an action as deviant and the offender accepts the definition. Again, returning to the marijuana example, some of the offending youths may have home environments or personal connections that allow that youth to resist the label. If the youth is also involved in other activities—let's say she is a star on the softball team—then her other extracurricular activities may become more important, and the label "pothead" is no longer associated with her.

As we described in Chapter 2 on cybertrespass, the meaning of hacking has changed greatly over the past three decades. Hacking in the 1960s and 1970s was primarily done by students and academics to learn more about technology (Levy, 1984). The hack was about making technology work better. As a result, the hacking label was not associated with deviance. Instead, the label connoted intelligence and ingenuity. However, as more human activity has migrated into the digital environment, especially economic activity, the meaning of hacking has become more negative. Groups in power began to associate the tinkering with computer technology with the disruption of business operations. The hacker label is now primarily associated with deviance and is linked to the creation and use of malware.

The negative connotations of hacking by journalists and people in law enforcement are resisted by hackers themselves. Turgeman-Goldschmidt (2008) interviewed a series of hackers in Israel, applying labeling theory to interpret their responses. Hackers, who were considered as "bad" hackers, described their hacking as a continuation of bad behaviors as children. In this sense, hacking is a type of secondary deviance. Moreover, these "bad" hackers rejected the labels they had been given, and used other terms or descriptions for themselves—preferring to see themselves as "wild" and "gifted" as opposed to immoral or criminal.

Control Theories: Social Bonding, Self-Control, and Techniques of Neutralization

Most of the theories discussed in this chapter focus on why people deviate from normative behavior. However, control theories ask a different question: Why don't we *all* commit crimes or act in deviant ways? Control theories begin with an assumption that people want to be deviant and require no special learning or motivation to do so. Moreover, this desire to break from normative behavior is consistent across individuals. The theories discussed now all assume that it is the controlling influences of society that prevent individuals from committing deviant acts.

SOCIAL BONDING THEORY

Social bonding theory asserts that crime and deviance result when an individual's bonds to conventional society are broken. There are, according to Hirschi (1969), four elements of the bond between the individual and society (see Table 10.2). Individuals vary along each dimension, but the less an individual is attached, involved, committed, and believes in normative or conventional aspects of society, the more likely they are to act in their self-interest.

Social bonding theory would predict higher rates of deviance among people who are loners, who are unemployed, single, or not members of a religious organization. People who lack these and other means of social integration are disconnected from normative goals and expectations. A person who is employed, for example, may become emotionally connected to her coworkers. She may care about how those coworkers view her and will embrace the norms shared by her co-workers.

The theory also explains the higher rates of offending among young people. Indeed, the theory originated as an explanation for juvenile delinquency. Young people, especially those who are not enrolled in high school or college, are often less integrated into society. They may not have started families. They are more transitory, especially males, and thus less likely to be integrated into a neighborhood. Moreover, they may experience unemployment or unstable employment.

Table 10.2 Hirschi's Elements of the Bond

Element	Explanation	Examples
Attachment	Emotional closeness to people	Friendships with schoolmates or workmates, favorable attitudes towards school and work, emotional bonds between children and parents, loving relationship with family
Involvement	The time invested in activities	Engaged in activities at work or school, attending religious services, participating as parent in child's school activities
Commitment	The willingness to conform to conventional behaviors	A desire to achieve or accomplish societal goals such as academic achievement, a desire to be seen in a positive light by one's peers
Belief	The ideas that support normative behaviors	An agreement with the laws that govern society, and a respect for authority figures such as police and teachers

Social bonding theory may explain how young men commit acts of domestic terrorism. On June 17, 2015 21-year-old Dylan Roof shot and killed 9 African-American worshippers and injured another at a church in Charleston, South Carolina. After a manhunt, Roof was arrested and is currently in prison. Dylan Roof appeared to lack social bonds. In the months after the shooting, the press asked about Roof to understand his motivations. Many people interviewed commented on his social isolation. A family member commented on Roof, "he was like 19 years old, he still didn't have a job, a driver's license or anything like that and he just stayed in his room a lot of the time."[2]

Social bonding theory can be applied to all types of cybercrime. However, one major application of the theory is in explaining extremist groups and the individuals who adopt extremist ideologies. Extremist groups use the digital environment to spread their message and recruit new members. A person who does not have strong social bonds in the physical environment to conventional norms may find the message of extremist groups in the digital environment appealing. In other words, they may become "radicalized" through content consumed online. Indeed, Roof was active on white supremacist websites the days and months before the shooting.[3]

SELF-CONTROL THEORY (A GENERAL THEORY OF CRIME)

Gottfredson and Hirschi (1990) argue that low self-control in individuals is a major predictor of crime and deviance. Individuals that lack self-control, according to Gottfredson and Hirschi:

- Prefer simple tasks
- Prefer physical activities rather than mental activities
- Are prone to emotional outbursts
- Are self-centered
- Prefer immediate gratifications

Gottfredson and Hirschi (1990) argue that children who receive inconsistent parenting are more likely to have low self-control as an adult. Inconsistent parenting includes not monitoring children, not recognizing behavior that is inappropriate given current social standards, and failure to discipline consistently.

Individuals with low self-control are attracted to crime because crime and other deviant behaviors offer immediate gratification, are exciting and risky, and most crimes do not require a high degree of intellectual investment. As an example, armed robbery is more attractive to a person who has low self-control because there is an immediate monetary reward possible. The long-term effects of jail time and emotional damage to a victim are ignored. Moreover, individuals with low self-control are also more likely to engage in deviant behaviors such as excessive drinking, smoking, and risky sexual behavior. Again, this is for the same reason of immediate gratification, excitement, and the disregard of long-term effects.

Self-control theory is meant to be a general theory of crime—meaning that it purports to explain all types of crime and deviance. But the wide range of cybercrimes presents an interesting challenge for self-control theory. On the one hand, many cybercrimes appear to require a person to have a high level of self-control. Learning the nuances of a coding language requires months to years of focused mental effort. The person who masters a coding language would not be the same type of person who prefers physical over mental activities. Similarly, a successful data breach may take months of planning and require several steps—from developing the exploit kit, to crafting a spear-phishing email, to successful exfiltration, to the monetizing of data stolen. The person involved in this type of activity is not the same as the person who prefers simple tasks and seeks immediate gratification. Even romance scams, which are not technically sophisticated, require months of grooming and a careful consideration of the words and symbols communicated to a victim. On the other hand, many types of cybercrimes appear to be readily explainable through self-control theory. Flaming, cyberbullying, and online shaming are all activities in which an individual can lash out immediately without regard for the emotions of those they hurt.

TECHNIQUES OF NEUTRALIZATION

Techniques of Neutralization stems from the delinquency research of Gresham Sykes and David Matza (1957). The theory assumes that individuals in society—including members of subcultures—generally adhere to conventional social norms. An individual, the theory asserts, will commit a deviant or criminal act if they can neutralize the guilt associated with violating those norms. For Sykes and Matza, the male juvenile delinquents they observed held honest and law-abiding people in high regard. To commit acts of deviance, they argued, the juvenile delinquents developed mental techniques to make violations of normative behavior acceptable. They write:

> Disapproval flowing from internalized norms and conforming to others in the social environment is neutralized, turned back, or deflected in advance. Social controls that serve to check or inhibit deviant motivational patterns are rendered inoperative, and the individual is freed to engage in delinquency without serious damage to his self-image.
>
> (1957, 666–667)

Using these techniques before participating in crime or deviance is an effort to neutralize guilt. These techniques can also be used after the crime is committed to *rationalize* the immoral behavior. For this reason, Sykes and Matza's theory has often been called techniques of neutralization and rationalization. It is also important to note that these techniques are used to excuse specific violations of social norms. They do not constitute wholesale rejections of a norm. For example, stealing is condemned by all groups in society. The techniques are used to excuse stealing under certain conditions.

Sykes and Matza identified five forms of neutralization (see Table 10.3). The theory and the neutralizations identified were initially identified and used to explain juvenile delinquency. However, the theory has been applied widely, including studies of cybercrime. We have listed these techniques in Figure 10.1 and given examples as they would relate to cybercrime.

The five listed above are the core neutralizations. However, scholars have developed other neutralizations for other crime types. Coleman (2006) identified techniques used by white-collar criminals. One technique is the claim of normalcy, where crime is justified by asserting that everyone else is doing it. Another technique is entitlement, where the white-collar criminal justifies theft by arguing that she deserves something for the hard work she has put in.

Techniques of Neutralization have been applied to cybercrime, mainly in studies of digital piracy (Ingram & Hinduja, 2008; Moore & McMullan, 2009). Smallridge and Roberts (2013) identified a new, digital piracy-specific neutralization called "DRM defiance." Digital rights management, or DRM, is the code embedded in digital content that manages how a person uses that content. For example, a company may limit the number of devices a movie can be downloaded to with DRM. Smallridge and Roberts found that computer users who had adopted the belief that DRM should be defied were more willing to illegally download digital content.

Table 10.3 Techniques of Neutralization and Cybercrime Examples

Technique	*Example*
Denial of responsibility—someone else or external factors are the reason the crime was committed	"I am not responsible for the drugs sold on my website."
Denial of injury—asserting that no one was hurt during the crime, or nothing was damaged	"That man is a billionaire. So what if I steal a couple hundred bucks worth of bitcoin from his account."
Denial of the victim—asserting that the victim was deserving	"Bank of America is a racist bank that denies loans to Hispanic people. They had that DOSS attack coming."
Condemnation of the condemners—alleging that those doing the policing or disciplining are being hypocritical	"The US government has been spying on people in my country for years. That is why I am developing spyware to use against them."
Appeal to higher loyalties—the crime had to be committed because of an association with a gang or family	"I had to hack into my company's systems and steal PII. I need to make money for my family."

STRAIN THEORY

Strain theory, most associated with Robert Agnew (1992), asserts that the presence of unwanted stimuli, called strains, produces negative emotions. The effort to cope with these negative emotions can lead to deviant or criminal behavior. Agnew posited three categories of strains:

1. *Strain as the actual or anticipated failure to achieve positively valued goals*—When there is a disjunction between what we want or expect and what we achieve, we experience negative emotions. An example of this would be a person who values athletic prowess but finds that she cannot compete at a certain level. This creates a degree of disappointment and stress. Another example would be someone who values social status and prestige but finds that they cannot get respect from others.
2. *Strain as the actual or anticipated removal of positively valued stimuli*—When something an individual likes or values is taken away or is threatened to be taken away, they will experience negative emotions. This could be the loss of income or a job, a child losing friends because of their parents' moving, or the death of a loved one. It could be a student learning that they may not graduate from college because they did not meet a certain requirement.
3. *Strain as the actual or anticipated presentation of negatively valued stimuli*—The presence or threatened presence of noxious and unwelcome phenomena can cause stress in one's life. Cyberbullying falls into this category, as insults and slights are unwelcome. Punishments, especially if they are perceived as unjustified, also fall into this category. Poor grades are also a negatively valued stimulus.

Strains often overlap. Consider the example above of a student in college who may not graduate. The student may value academic achievement and expects to graduate in a certain amount of time (failure to achieve positively valued goals), the student may not receive the degree (the removal of positively valued stimuli), and all this may be because of a failing grade in her cybercrime class (the presentation of negatively valued stimuli).

In a later article, Agnew further specified strain theory by describing the types of strain most likely to lead to crime and deviance (2001). These strains are perceived as unjust and high in magnitude, are associated with low social control from authorities, and create an incentive for coping through criminal means. Bullying, Agnew argues, is a type of strain that can lead to crime and deviance. It is likely to be perceived as unjust because young people will think they are being treated unfairly. It is likely to be perceived as high in magnitude because peers are central to the lives of young people. It occurs in spaces where there are few authority figures present—bullying happens on playgrounds or in moments when teachers and adults are not monitoring. Finally, students who bully are often engaged in other deviant acts, thereby modeling to the victim forms of criminal coping. For this reason, strain theory has been most commonly linked to cyberbullying—both victimization and perpetration (see Figure 10.1).

Several studies have explored the link between cyberbullying and strain. Hay, Meldrum, and Mann (2010) found that both physical bullying and cyberbullying are associated with delinquency. Both forms of bullying were positively associated with external acts of deviance towards

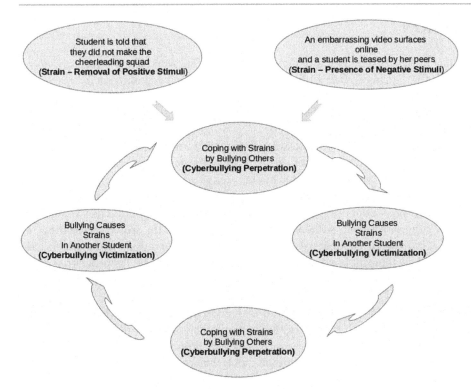

Figure 10.1 Links between strain, cyberbullying perpetration, and cyberbullying victimization.

others, and internal acts of self-harm. Jang, Song, and Kim (2014) link physical bullying to cyber-bullying, with the former acting as a strain and the latter being a response. Keith (2017) found that being bullied was positively associated with two coping mechanisms, avoidance behavior and bringing a weapon to school.

Deindividuation and Disinhibition Theories

The final two theories we will discuss in this chapter—deindividuation and disinhibition—attempt to explain the effects of anonymity online. Anonymity means that individuals can develop their identities and behaviors free from social sanctions derived in the conventional offline world—as they can explore and interact online using screen names. It has also meant, however, that people are freer to commit certain deviant or criminal acts because they can avoid detection and negative sanctions. Someone can be rude or hostile, attempt to defraud another person, or consume child pornography under the veil of online anonymity.

DEINDIVIDUATION

Deindividuation theory has its foundation in Gustav LeBon's 1895 work *The Crowd: A Study of the Popular Mind* (2001). During LeBon's life, France had undergone waves of social unrest. He had experienced the Paris Commune in 1871—a radical populist takeover of the French government—and other smaller protests during the 1890s. LeBon's study was an attempt to explain the violence and irrationality exhibited in crowds.

Two primary concepts in LeBon's work are submergence and contagion. **Submergence** refers to the process of losing one's sense of self and replacing it with an identification with the crowd. When this occurs, a person loses his/her sense of personal responsibility and becomes susceptible to subconscious instincts and desires. In this submerged state, a person is susceptible to **contagion**. A contagion, for LeBon, is an idea or emotion that passes through a crowd. A random suggestion from someone could lead to the entire crowd advocating for that idea. In this way, a crowd is capable of considerable variation in mood swings and is easily manipulated. One can imagine a situation where a crowd of people are protesting at an event and someone says "Let's smash windows," and all of a sudden a peaceful protest turns into a riot.

Researchers who use Social Identification and Deindividuation Effects (SIDE) theory are applying LeBon's core concepts. SIDE argues that communication in the digital environment minimizes social comparison and self-awareness. Anonymity reduces the ability to individualize oneself and others in a group setting (deindividuation), thus increasing the awareness of the similarities that all in the group share. Studies applying SIDE to the digital environment have shown that Internet users who become deindividuated adopt behaviors that are more like the general norms of the group online (Lee, 2005; Postmes, Spears, Sakhel, & De Groot, 2001). These behaviors can indeed be positive—for example, showing support for someone in an addiction forum. Unfortunately, these behaviors can be negative, as when a group of users insults and shame someone.

DISINHIBITION

A second theory that attempts to explain the effects of anonymity is the online disinhibition effect (Suler, 2004). According to Suler, six factors lead to a change of behavior online. These are:

1. Dissociative anonymity—Behavior is compartmentalized, such that an individual can dissociate themselves from their online behavior.
2. Invisibility—Individuals cannot see each other, giving people the courage to go places and do things they otherwise would not do.
3. Asynchronicity—Because people do not interact with each other in real time, the normative aspects of continuous communication are lost. People can send an email or post to a discussion board and not get immediate feedback.

4. Solipsistic Introjection—Because of a lack of context cues, individuals may "feel that their mind has merged with the mind of the online companion" (Suler, 2004, 323).

5. Dissociative Imagination—People may view their online experiences as not following the same rules and norms as their offline experiences—"they split or dissociate online fiction from offline fact" (Suler, 2004, 323).

6. Minimization of Status and Authority—In the physical environment, authority figures express their status and power in their dress, body language, and their environmental settings (e.g. an office space with a degree on the wall). This is missing in online environments.

Taken together, these six factors create the conditions for an individual to act in ways they normally would not. They feel liberated from the norms that govern offline behavior.

The disinhibition effect can foster two types of behaviors. Positive behaviors, called **benign disinhibition**, include reaching out to others to resolve interpersonal conflicts, exploring new avenues of one's identity, and efforts to improve self-understanding. Negative behaviors, called **toxic disinhibition**, include rude, racist, and misogynistic language, as well as the acting out of socially reprehensible behaviors including consuming and sharing child pornography.

These ideas may offer better explanations for trolling and harassment than traditional criminological theories. In online forums, where a person can detach their online identity from their physical identity, a user may be more likely to commit acts that can be categorized as toxic disinhibition. They may be more likely to bait, antagonize, or hurl racist and sexist language at another person online. They may also be more likely to exhibit behaviors that are not a part of their in-person persona. For example, the 4chan discussion board "Politically Incorrect" (http://boards.4chan.org/pol/) has a norm of posting off-color and controversial topics. A computer user, while conforming to normative attitudes and behaviors about race, class, and gender in the physical world, may be more likely to offer deviant contributions to this board.

Conclusion

In this chapter, we introduced theories to explain crime, deviance, and victimization. These theories come primarily from the discipline of criminology, with some contributions from sociology and psychology. We explored Deterrence Theory, Social Learning Theory, Labeling Theory, Social Bonding Theory, Self-Control Theory, Techniques of Neutralization, Strain Theory, Routine Activities Theory, and two theories of Anonymity—Deindividuation and Disinhibition. For each theory the main assumptions were introduced, concepts relevant to the theory were explained, and its applicability to cybercrime and digital deviance was discussed.

A common discussion in the cybercrime literature is whether cybercrime is old wine in new bottles. Meaning, are we looking at new types of crime that require new theories? In this chapter, we highlighted several pieces of research and presented numerous case studies demonstrating that traditional theories could be used to explain cybercrime. After all, the actors and the motivations are the same.

However, this does not imply that these theories cannot be improved or further specified. This is because although the actors and motivations remain constant, the environment in which they operate has changed. Traditional theories may need to be adapted to take the new environment into account. A prime example of this is the extensions to traditional Techniques of Neutralization by Smallridge and Roberts (2013) discussed previously. Theoretical developments may move in this direction, where traditional theories explaining broad crime and deviance processes are modified and extended to take into account the uniqueness of the digital environment.

Vocabulary

1. **Benign disinhibition**—Positive or harmless behaviors by individuals who are disinhibited online.
2. **Contagion**—An idea or emotion that passes through a crowd.
3. **Differential association**—The process by which an individual learns values, beliefs, attitudes, and norms from the people they associate with.
4. **Differential reinforcement**—The process by which an individual is rewarded for their behavior by the people they associate with.
5. **General deterrence**—A punishment against an individual that is meant to deter others within a population.
6. **Macro-level phenomena**—Observable behaviors or patterns that occur across a wide range of contexts or geographical settings.
7. **Micro-level phenomena**—Observable behaviors or patterns that occur in everyday settings in small contexts.
8. **Primary deviance**—An individual's initial act of deviance.
9. **Secondary deviance**—An individual's subsequent acts of deviance as a result of being labeled by others.
10. **Specific deterrence**—A punishment oriented towards the specific individual who committed the crime or violation.
11. **Submergence**—The process of losing one's sense of self and replacing it with an identification with the crowd.
12. **Toxic disinhibition**—Negative behaviors by individuals who are disinhibited online.

Study Questions

TRUE OR FALSE

1. According to deterrence theory, a punishment that is received further away from the violating act is theoretically more effective at deterring future acts.
   a. True
   b. False

2. One factor that can lead to changes of behavior online is that the traditional power of authority is reduced.
   a. True
   b. False
3. A disinhibited person online can exhibit both positive and negative behaviors.
   a. True
   b. False
4. Labeling theory is used to explain micro-level phenomena.
   a. True
   b. False
5. One type of technique of neutralization is to claim that the crime is commonplace and everyone is doing it.
   a. True
   b. False
6. The Techniques of Neutralization theory was initially developed by studying the motivations of hackers.
   a. True
   b. False

MULTIPLE CHOICE

7. According to strain theory, a bad grade would represent _____.
   a. the presence of negative stimuli
   b. the removal of positive stimuli
   c. both
   d. neither
8. Which of these crimes does self-control theory purport to explain?
   a. Hacking
   b. Romance scams
   c. Digital piracy
   d. All of the above
9. One way your text attempts to explain the mass shooting by Dylan Roof is through _____.
   a. self-control theory
   b. routine activities theory
   c. social bonding theory
   d. all of the above
10. One way your text attempts to explain the sharing of child pornography is through _____.
    a. social bonding theory
    b. social learning theory
    c. self-control theory
    d. routine activities theory

Match the assumption with the theory:

a) Deterrence theory
b) Social learning theory
c) Labeling theory
d) Self-control theory
e) Social bonding theory
f) Techniques of Neutralization
g) Strain theory

11. People will avoid criminal activity if the known punishments associated with the act outweigh any perceived benefit.
12. States may decide to make "an example" out of someone in order to prevent future crimes of the same type.
13. Focuses primarily on explaining crime and deviance in everyday situations.
14. Can be used to explain the negative adjectives used to describe hackers.
15. The willingness to conform to conventional behaviors is assumed to prevent crime and deviance.
16. Identifies the ways in which a person justifies their criminal or deviant behavior.
17. People who are self-centered are more likely to commit crime.
18. Assumes that differential association is a major predictor of crime and deviance.

Match the technique of neutralization with the example given.

a) Denial of responsibility
b) Denial of injury
c) Denial of the victim
d) Condemnation of the condemners
e) Appeal to higher loyalties

19. "It is not my fault that people flame and troll each other on my website."
20. "I had to hack into my company's systems and steal PII. I need to make money for my family."
21. "I don't think Drake is bothered by me making a copy of his new album."
22. "The US government has been spying on people in my country for years. That is why I am developing spyware to use against them."

ORDERING

Using strain theory as a guide, order the process below from beginning (A) to end (D).

23. Jose has enrolled in a dance class. He has always been a good dancer and expects to be one of the best students in the class.

24. Jose lashes out at his dance instructor by calling her names and disrespecting her.
25. Jose becomes frustrated and angry during his weekly dance lessons.
26. Jose has not had to learn formal dancing before and is not doing as well in the dance class as he expected.

NOTES

1 http://articles.latimes.com/1989-07-19/local/me-3886_1_hacker-kevin-mitnick
2 www.theguardian.com/world/2015/jun/18/dylann-roof-south-carolina-charleston-shooting-suspect
3 www.dailymail.co.uk/news/article-3136475/Dylann-Roof-active-white-supremacist-website-months-posting -comments-minorities-hate-filled-manifesto.html

REFERENCES

Agnew, R. (1992). Foundation for a general strain theory of crime and delinquency. *Criminology, 30*(1), 47–88.

Agnew, Robert. (2001). Building on the foundation of general strain theory: Specifying the types of strain most likely to lead to crime and delinquency. *Journal of Research in Crime and Delinquency, 38*(4), 319–391.

Akers, R. L. (1996). Is differential association/social learning cultural deviance theory? *Criminology, 34*(2), 229–247.

Akers, R. L. (2009). *Social learning and social structure: A general theory of crime and deviance.* New Brunswick, NJ: Transaction Publishers.

Coleman, J. W. (2006). *The criminal elite: Understanding white-collar crime* (6th ed.). New York: Worth Publishers.

Friedrichs, D. O., Schoultz, I., & Jordanoska, A. (2018). *Edwin H. Sutherland.* London; New York: Routledge/Taylor & Francis Group.

Gottfredson, M. R., & Hirschi, T. (1990). *A general theory of crime.* Stanford, CA: Stanford University Press.

Hay, C., Meldrum, R., & Mann, K. (2010). Traditional bullying, cyber bullying, and deviance: A general strain theory approach. *Journal of Contemporary Criminal Justice, 26*(2), 130–147. doi:10.1177/1043986209359557

Hirschi, T. (1969). *Causes of Delinquency.* Berkeley, CA: University of California Press.

Hua, J., & Bapna, S. (2012). How can we deter cyber terrorism? *Information Security Journal: A Global Perspective, 21*(2), 102–114. doi:10.1080/19393555.2011.647250

Ingram, J. R., & Hinduja, S. (2008). Neutralizing music piracy: An empirical examination. *Deviant Behavior, 29*(4), 334–366. doi:10.1080/01639620701588131

Jang, H., Song, J., & Kim, R. (2014). Does the offline bully-victimization influence cyberbullying behavior among youths? Application of general strain theory. *Computers in Human Behavior, 31*, 85–93. doi:10.1016/j.chb.2013.10.007

Keith, S. (2017). How do traditional bullying and cyberbullying victimization affect fear and coping among students? An application of general strain theory. *American Journal of Criminal Justice, 43*(2), 67–84. doi:10.1007/s12103-017-9411-9

Le Bon, G. (2001). *The crowd: A study of the popular mind.* Mineola, NY: Dover Publications.

Lee, H. (2005). Behavioral strategies for dealing with flaming in an online forum. *Sociological Quarterly, 46*(2), 385–403.

Levy, S. (1984). *Hackers: Heroes of the computer revolution* (1st ed.). Garden City, NY: Anchor Press/Doubleday.

Moore, R., & McMullan, E. C. (2009). Neutralizations and rationalizations of digital piracy: A qualitative analysis of university students. *International Journal of Cyber Criminology, 3*(1), 441–451.

Morris, R. G., & Higgins, G. E. (2010). Criminological theory in the digital age: The case of social learning theory and digital piracy. *Journal of Criminal Justice, 38*(4), 470–480. doi:10.1016/j.jcrimjus.2010.04.016

Postmes, T., Spears, R., Sakhel, K., & De Groot, D. (2001). Social influence in computer-mediated communication: The effects of anonymity on group behavior. *Personality and Social Psychology Bulletin, 27*(10), 1243–1254.

Shepherd, M. M., & Mejias, R. J. (2016). Nontechnical deterrence effects of mild and severe internet use policy reminders in reducing employee internet abuse. *International Journal of Human-Computer Interaction, 32*(7), 557–567. doi:10.1080/10447318.2016.1183862

Smallridge, J. L., & Roberts, J. R. (2013). Crime specific neutralizations: An empirical examination of four types of digital piracy. *International Journal of Cyber Criminology, 7*(2), 125–140.

Suler, J. (2004). The online disinhibition effect. *CyberPsychology & Behavior, 7*(3), 321–326. doi:10.1089/1094931041291295

Sykes, G. M., & Matza, D. (1957). Techniques of neutralization: A theory of delinquency. *American Sociological Review, 22*(6), 8. doi:10.2307/2089195

Turgeman-Goldschmidt, O. (2008). Meanings that hackers assign to their being a hacker. *International Journal of Cyber Criminology, 2*(2), 382.

Wrenn, C. F. (2012). *Strategic cyber deterrence.* Fletcher School of Law and Diplomacy (Tufts University). Retrieved from http://search.proquest.com/openview/2467c5b3016d7f027fc89d16acc6ffc1/1?pq-origsite=gscholar&cbl=18750&diss=y

Young, R., & Zhang, L. (2007). Illegal computer hacking: An assessment of factors that encourage and deter the behavior. *Journal of Information Privacy and Security, 3*(4), 33–52.

Index

Page numbers in **bold** refer to tables. Page numbers in *italics* refer to figures.

Keith, S. 207
Kelly, Kate 1, 3
keyloggers 28
Kickass Torrents (KAT) 123–4
Kilbride, Jeffrey 53
Kim, R. 207
Kingpin statute 143
Klaassen, M. J. E. 55
Klettke, B. 59
Korchmaros, J. D. 75
Kotlyak, Nathan 85

labeling theory 200–2
latent victims 182
Lauer, Matt 5
Lavorgna, A. 138
law enforcement: challenges for 126
law enforcement practices: changes in 4–5
laws: CFAA (Computer Fraud and Abuse Act)
    29–31; changing laws 3–4; cybertrespass 29;
    ECPA (Electronic Communications Privacy
    Act) 121–2; Racketeer Influenced and Corrupt
    Organizations (RICO) Act 142; revenge porn
    law 4
layered environment 13–17
layering systems 13–17
layers of digital environment **14**; and unauthorized
    access **28**
Leary, M. G. 63–4
LeBon, Gustav 208
legislating pornography 52–3
Leukfeldt, E. R. 141
Leukfeldt's typology 141
Levy, S. 32
Ley, D. 53
link layer 13
linking algorithms and Big Data 156–7
Little, Paul 53
Liverman, Justin Gray 34
loan scams **92**
logic of lulz 79
Loomis, Eric 163
low-tech hackers 33
Lyft 11
Lyon, David 163

macro viruses 36
macro-level phenomena 201
Madoff, Bernie 174
malware **92**
Maple, Jack 165–6
Massachusetts Institute of Technology (MIT) 31–2
Matza, David 204–5
Mayweather, Floyd 106

McComas, Grace 75
McDaniel, B. T. 59
McGuire, M. 139
McGuire's Organized Crime Typology 139–40
McMullan, E. C. 105
McNamara, L. 81–2
meaning-making 16
Meier, Megan 75
Mellor, D. J. 59
memory-resident viruses 36
Mendelsohn, Benjamin 181
Merdian, H. L. 58
metadata 121–2
#MeToo Movement 5, 17
micro-level phenomena 201
Milgram, Anne 162
Miller Test 52
Miller v. California 52
Milner, R. M. 79
minimization of status and authority:
    disinhibition 209
MIT (Massachusetts Institute of Technology) 31–2
Mitnick, Kevin 198
mobile driving services 11
money laundering: Organized Crime 136
money vs. information motivation **92**
Moore, R. 105, 174
moral panics 138
Morris, Robert Tappan 30
"Morris Worm" 30
Motion Picture Association of America
    (MPAA) 102
motivated offenders: cybervictimization 176–9
motivation for cyberdeception and theft 92–3
MPAA (Motion Picture Association of America) 102
myths: of cyberbullying 76–7; about Organized
    Crime 138–9

Nakamoto, Bitcoin 105
National Science Foundation (NSF) 9
negative behaviors: disinhibition 209
Netflix 51; digital piracy 102
network layer 13
networked computing 13
networks: Organized Crime 139–41
neutralization 204–5
New Jersey: algorithms to determine flight risk 162
Nick Sauer case 5
Nissenbaum, Helen 32
non-participating victims 181
non-rivalrous goods 103–4
non-sexters 59
Nosal, David 31
NSF (National Science Foundation) 9